TIWI WIVES

TIWI WIVES

A STUDY OF THE WOMEN OF MELVILLE ISLAND,

NORTH AUSTRALIA

Jane C. Goodale

WAVELAND
PRESS, INC.

Prospect Heights, Illinois

For information about this book, write or call:
Waveland Press, Inc.
P.O. Box 400
Prospect Heights, Illinois 60070
(708) 634-0081

ISBN 0-88133-784-6

Printed in the United States of America

7   6   5   4   3   2   1

TO THE TIWI
Without whose help
and friendship
this book would not
have been possible.

Acknowledgments

In the discussion of my field work and throughout the text, I mention many people by name, and some by reference, all of whom contributed in various ways to the pleasure and success of my research. To all of them I extend my hearty thanks. In particular I should like to take this opportunity to thank C. P. Mountford for inviting me to participate in his expedition, and both Ward Goodenough and Nancy Munn for their helpful comments and criticisms on this manuscript; and E. Hay for her preparation of the illustrations.

Contents

Illustrations

Figures

Tables

Preface, 1994

It is now forty years since I first set foot on the beach at Snake Bay (now known as Milikapiti Township), in 1954, and began what has become nearly a lifetime of friendship with the Tiwi residents there. As my own life has expanded and as I experienced many different events during the interim, so have my Tiwi friends who initially taught me their culture which forms the basis of this volume. I have decided, however, that this volume, in which I chronicle the life-course of Tiwi women and their relationships with men and women, should not be updated. I use instead the concept of the ethnographic present and describe what I learned of their lives in 1954 and in a brief visit in 1962. This volume should be read in the same way one would view a forty-year-old documentary film. The present tense used should not be misinterpreted as referring to life in the last decade of the twentieth century. It is, however, a detailed view of life before 1955 when the Australian government began a twenty-year period of intensive education for citizenship for the residents of the aboriginal reservations under their control. For readers who are curious, however, I summarize below the main events of this interim period.

Snake Bay Settlement, only a half-hour's flight from Darwin, became in 1955 one of the government's showcase aboriginal communities and received many official and unofficial visitors during this period. Two films—*Mourning for Mungatopi* and *Goodby Old Man*—were made at the request of the surviving families. A number of development schemes were tried. The only one surviving into the nineties was the Cyprus Pine Plantation and reforestation project. Many hectares of bush were leveled and planted with cyprus seedlings grown in a nursery at Pikataramor. It takes approximately eighty years for a seedling to mature into a harvestable tree, so eventually Caribbean Pine was substituted for Cyprus because it has a maturity period of only forty years. In 1986 the entire plantation was turned over to the Tiwi to manage and to eventually profit from.

One of the most significant changes to occur in this interim was a result of a Land Rights Bill for the Northern Territory passed in 1976, through which Melville and Bathurst Islands were returned to Tiwi ownership, and a Tiwi Land Council was created to administer the islands. But as the islands remain a part of the Australian commonwealth, the Tiwi are still governed by that nation's laws.

I returned to Melville Island briefly in 1962, in 1980-81 and 1986-87, and when I looked around the familiar landscape of the bush, sea and air, I found that while the setting appeared the same, the community was greatly changed. Today there is more permanent housing with two or three bedrooms, kitchen and bath. There is a greatly expanded school from preschool to the 6-year level. Further schooling is only available in Darwin or at the Mission on Bathurst. A clinic is managed by three local women highly trained to cope with all but major medical problems. A general store varies in its stock completeness but usually carries tinned and frozen food and, occasionally, fresh bread, vegetables and fruit. There are also clothes, videos, TVs, buckets, fishhooks, axes, etc. On the hill is the Milikapiti sports and social club with a football oval, where beer may be purchased in the evenings. Finally there is a township building from where the elected local council and town clerk organize labor to carry out the required tasks of township government. While there is a church and a residence for clergy, there is irregular attendance in both. The Church is still influential, however, at Bathurst and Garden Point.

My researches remain focused on the Snake Bay community. In the forty years since I began my research fieldwork, there are more than two new generations of descendants to attach to my genealogies. Many of my older friends are no longer alive. In deference, I should alter their names in this reprinting for it is discourteous to cause anyone to remember a deceased loved one. I have not done this, as I have chosen not to alter the original manuscript in any way. The Tiwi know of, and some have read, this book, and I think they would approve of my decision. But while I am not including data from this period here (it belongs in a volume to itself—yet to be written), I think the Tiwi would like readers to know that in addition to the above mentioned changes a few other aspects of their contemporary lives are different and some remain quite similar to that of earlier generations described here.

The *muringaleta* rituals of a girl's puberty are no longer held; however, some women are still married, or promised, to their mother's son-in-law. The *Kulama* ceremony is still being held by initiated men, few in number today and quite old. In 1987 a fifty-year-old male initiate was part of the Milikapiti ceremony. *Pukamani* rituals are having a revival from a period when they were discouraged by Church and government. Poles are being elaborately carved and painted, and young children are taught the appropriate dances. A slow death of the language however is ongoing. Without the language, ritual singing is affected, and as those who are knowledgeable in song performance die, fewer and fewer are there to replace them.

Hunting, fishing and collecting food are activities which are also having a revival after a period of deemphasis by government. Parents and grandparents say they must teach their children to know the bush and the food that it holds for them, for that is their survival no matter what the future brings. Changes in transportation have facilitated this revival—nearly every household has access to a private lorry and/or motorboat.

"We have grown old together," my older "sisters" now remind me. As the years march on, my position in the community has changed from that of a young outsider to someone who is almost, but not quite, a Tiwi *imaninga* (grandmother). With this change has come increasing responsibility toward my greater family. It is to this Milikapiti 'family' and the many I call:

> *nya imboka amantia nya imbunga,*
> my younger and older sister,
> *nya iwini amantia nya iwuni,*
> my younger and older brother,
> *nya ingnari amantia nya ilimani,*
> my mother and my mother's brother,
> *nya iringani amantia nya intinganinga,*
> my father and my father's sister.
> *nya maringa amantia nya morti; nya imerani amantia mya*
>   *imeraninga,*
> my daughter and my son; my brother's son and
>   daughter,
> *nya intamalinga amantia nya intamiliti,*
> my granddaughter and grandson,
> *amantia nya imbunei amantia mawana,*
> and my husband and his sister,

that I dedicate this republication. I shall not name them. They know who they are. To all of you and to your parents and grandparents, siblings and cousins who are no longer alive, I reaffirm my original dedication and say again "me sorry longa you" and "thank you" for the knowledge and the friendship you have given me in abundance over the years.

Bryn Mawr, Pennsylvania
1994

Introduction

The Field Work

Late in 1953 Charles P. Mountford of the South Australian Museum in Adelaide invited me to join him in an ethnographic study of the Tiwi of Melville Island, North Australia. I was an assistant to Carleton S. Coon in the Department of General Ethnology at the University Museum of the University of Pennsylvania, Philadelphia, as well as a graduate student in search of field work for a dissertation.

The National Geographic Society supported the expedition in the field and, in addition, provided me with a two-day crash course in photography. The University Museum initially paid my travel expenses and later supplied additional funds to support me in the field for three months after the other members of the expedition had completed their work.

I joined Mountford in Adelaide in February 1954, and during the next six weeks met many Australian anthropologists, both in Adelaide and in Canberra, who gave generously of their time in preparing me for the work among the aborigines.

On 16 April 1954, the National Geographic Expedition to Melville Island landed at Snake Bay Native Settlement on the north coast of the island. This area was selected mainly because of the presence and concurrent ethnographic investigation of Arnold R. Pilling at the much larger Sacred Heart Mission on Bathurst Island.

The Snake Bay Settlement in 1954 had a native population of approximately 180 to 200 and a white staff of six: the superintendent (F. H. Grimster), his wife, and four of their six children. During our stay a schoolteacher and an assistant superintendent joined the staff. Mountford's expedition varied in numbers and composition. In addition to Mountford and myself, George Joy and the late W. E. Harney remained throughout the six months. George Joy provided us with delicious and ingenious meals, while Bill Harney contributed uniquely and most valuably to every aspect of field work. A graduate student in geology, Brian Daily, was a fifth permanent member of the expedition. His primary purpose was to make an extensive geological survey of the island, but his intimate association with the Tiwi men who accompanied him yielded much ethnographic data that he passed on to Mountford and myself. David Parsons from the Yale Peabody Museum joined the expedition for a six-week period to make a collection of birds. On their way back from excavations in the Middle East, Dr. and Mrs. C. S. Coon stopped off at Snake Bay for a week's visit while they photographed and made anthropometric measurements of the native population.

Our expedition camp was located a mile from the main settlement on Banjo Beach, a lovely curving strip of sand named after a Tiwi "big man" of the recent past who was buried on the beach. Not being in continual close contact with the settlement presented some ethnographic difficulties, but at the same time it provided certain advantages in disassociation from the settlement life. We hired about a dozen Tiwi as permanent informants, hunters, fishermen, and household help. Although this primary group of informants was small, it represented a complete range of age groups, both male and female. We did not, of course, restrict ourselves to this group for observation and information.

During the six months I was at Banjo Beach, I accompanied various groups of Tiwi on trips into the bush, which lasted from several days to over a week. I therefore had the opportunity to observe closely the daily activities of a hunting-gathering group under the conditions that approximated the aboriginal way of life as opposed to the settlement way. However, much of my time was divided among interviewing informants, observing the settlement life, and attending—both as an observer and as a participant—the numerous funeral ceremonies held midway between the beach and the settlement.

In September, Mountford, Harney, and the others left, their investigations completed, while I obtained permission from R. K. MacCaffery and his successor H. D. Giese of the Department of Native Welfare to remain until December to complete my own investigations. Mr. and Mrs. Grimster generously invited me to share their quarters in the settlement, and in every way possible encouraged and aided me in my work. Here I was close to the main settlement where most of my work led me; but toward the end of my stay I again went for an extended period into the bush with a large group of Tiwi, who traveled by canoe to the headwaters of the Andranangoo River to hunt geese. This trip was memorable for several reasons. Bill Grimster, the superintendent's son, and some native men arrived one evening in the launch to go crocodile hunting, and they invited me to join them in what is surely one of the top big-game "sports" left for excitement and danger. It was also during this trip that one of my companions turned to me as I was chewing on a delicious roast wild-goose leg and said, "Jane, you no more like white fellow." I knew it was not my unwashed appearance she referred to but rather the invisibility of physical and cultural distinctions that comes with mutual respect and friendship.

I truly grew to admire, respect, and, in many cases, love the Tiwi of Snake Bay, who permitted me to share their life, their joys and sorrows, who fed and cared for me in the bush, and who patiently, willingly, and with genuine friendship instructed me in the intricacies of their ways and philosophy of life.

I left Melville Island in the middle of December 1954, with the full realization that I had only begun to understand the Tiwi. This is a common feeling among ethnographers, but several aspects of my field work contributed directly to the lack of essential data. While most of them were unavoidable, they need to be recorded here in order that my analysis can be correctly evaluated. Because this was my first field experience and because my academic preparation had not concerned itself with field methods (not unusual in 1954), much of my field procedure was learned by the time-wasting method of trial and error. This would have been far more serious had I been without Harney's and Mountford's advice. Certainly the inadequacy of the time spent in the actual field work—a total of eight months—will be apparent to any ethnographic field worker, but my full-time job at the University Museum, which was financing my studies, made it necessary for me to return. The third and perhaps the major inadequacy is that I did not attempt to learn the Tiwi language, other than a few common words. The majority of the Snake Bay Tiwi spoke the aboriginal brand of pidgin-English that I found quite adequate for the first six months but woefully inadequate for the type of information that I realized was essential only toward the end of my stay.

In working up the data I did obtain, I received invaluable advice from my two immediate supervisors, W. H. Goodenough and C. S. Coon. They advised me to treat my data independently, disregarding for the purpose of my dissertation the problems presented by correlation and comparison of my data with those of either Mountford or Pilling, both of whom published their findings before I had completed my analysis (Pilling 1957; Mountford 1958; Goodale 1959a). Shortly after completing my dissertation, I obtained a microfilm of Pilling's dissertation, and almost at the same time C. W. M. Hart's and Pilling's well-known "case study" on the Tiwi was published (Hart and Pilling 1960). Anyone who has read the two dissertations and the above-mentioned published studies will be aware of the apparent lack of agreement of the various analyses, primarily in the area of social structure. The publication of the Berndts' data, collected in 1953, has added to this lack of agreement (Berndt and Berndt 1964).

Knowing the inadequacies of my own data, I hesitated to prepare my dissertation for publication. I put the matter off with one excuse or another until I suddenly had a chance to gather some additional field data. In 1962 I received a grant from the National Institute of Mental Health to survey the possibilities for field research in New Britain, Territory of New Guinea. My plans to carry out this survey during July to September 1962 allowed time for a short return visit to the Tiwi in June before I traveled to New Britain. I obtained permission from Mr. Giese of the Department of Welfare, but was unable to arrange immediate transport to Melville Island. Thus, I spent only two weeks at Snake Bay in 1962.

During the week I awaited transport in Darwin, I copied the census records made available by Mr. Giese. These subsequently proved to be exceedingly valuable, for they have enlarged my sample data in such areas as descent, local group-affiliation, and distribution covering the entire Tiwi tribe, which is essential to my present explanation of the apparent discrepancies in Tiwi social structure.

The two weeks spent at Snake Bay, however brief, also provided many clues that aid the present analysis. I was extraordinarily lucky to find a superb informant, without whose help much would still remain in misty confusion. This informant was a young girl who I had known well in 1954, having made my first excursion into the bush with her and her parents. At the age of eleven, Happy had stood out as one of my chief informants of her age group, for she had a knowledge and objectivity about her traditional way of life that far surpassed that of all her contemporaries and many of the men and women. I found her attitude even more unusual in 1962 than I had in 1954, for during that time tremendous changes had been wrought at the Snake Bay Settlement through the establishment of a full-scale forestry project providing employment and training for most of the resident Tiwi as well as for a number of aborigines from other tribes.

During the intervening years Happy had completed the schooling offered at Snake Bay, had finished additional teachers' training in Darwin, had won a contest and received a trip to many of the capital cities of Australia, and was now in charge of preschool kindergarten training at the Snake Bay School. To my delight I found that this woman's objectivity about and knowledge of her traditional culture had been increased, rather than diminished, by her widened horizons. She explained her interest as growing from her experiences in the cities. In interviews for the press and radio she was asked about her tribal culture and realized then that it was important to represent her culture and her people in a "correct" way.

In two weeks of daily afternoon sessions, Happy and I cross-checked extensive basic and essential data. This sometimes tedious task was facilitated by Happy's acquired literacy and fluency in English. The sessions were never held in private; Happy's mother, stepfather, and often her promised husband, as well as others, sat in. Whenever Happy was uncertain and, indeed, often when she was certain, she turned to these older people for additional information or correction.

After 1962 other duties prevented me from reanalyzing my original data. When I finally began the task, I was dismayed to find that many apparent discrepancies still existed, that in fact new ones had been added to the already substantial number. Undoubtedly more research on the Tiwi would prove extremely rewarding, but it seems necessary to present an analysis of the available data now, giving a starting point for other students. This I have tried to do, and although my resolution of the apparent differences seems satisfactorily correct to me, I acknowledge that there may be other correct answers that are equally satisfying that differ from the ones I propose.

The Approach

In reading the available data on the Tiwi before my first visit, I became aware of a certain amount of confusion concerning the local organization and descent group principles of the Melville Islanders. Spencer wrote, "The descent of the totem is strictly in the mother's line (1914:210), while Davidson (1926:534) reported, "The peoples of Melville and Bathurst Islands . . . are characterized by reckoning of descent in the male line." In 1930 Hart (1930a) reported the existence of patrilocal and patrilineal hordes as well as matrilineal totemic groups that he considered not as important as the patrilineal descent groups. Elkin and the Berndts wrote (1950:258), "The basic form of social organization . . . was the grouping into matrilineal phratries which . . . [were] localized in the structure and mythology." Radcliffe-Brown had the final word in my pre-expedition reading. He wrote (1954:105-6), "Elkin's statement about Melville Island does not agree with earlier accounts. . . . They have normal organization into patrilineal hordes."

However conflicting these accounts were, they did seem to agree that, unlike many reported Australian societies, the Tiwi did not have a social organization characterized by "marriage classes." This prompted one of my professors, A. I. Hallowell, to remark, "Well, perhaps since you won't get bogged down in investigating complexities of marriage classes, you will be able to tell us something else about aboriginal life!"

Mountford suggested that I concentrate on the role of the women in the culture, since aside from the work of P. M. Kaberry (1939) and C. H. Berndt (1950a, 1950b), almost nothing was known about this aspect of aboriginal life. Most of the field work had been done by male investigators using male informants. In many of these cultures studied, the males played a dominant economic and ceremonial role, often to the exclusion of the women. Therefore, this approach was the most feasible and profitable, even if the resulting descriptions of the society and culture were incomplete in some respects. As Mountford's special interests were art, mythology, and ceremony, we expected that our investigations would complement each other.

Not long after our arrival we witnessed our first Tiwi ceremony, an abbreviated *kulama,* one of the two most important rituals in Tiwi culture. Although the women played special women's roles during the three-day event, they were not excluded entirely. Nor were they prevented from seeing all that was going on, even though this is the initiation ceremony for Tiwi males. Even more significantly, Tiwi women were also initiated by this same ceremony and at the same time as the males, according to my informants. Shortly after the *kulama,* a *pukamani* (funeral) ceremony gave me the opportunity to observe the important role that women played in this, the second of the two most important Tiwi ceremonies.

It was thus clear that women were directly and importantly involved in most Tiwi ceremonies. It also became apparent that Tiwi women played a dominant economic role. I therefore broadened my field work plans accordingly to include as complete an investigation of Tiwi culture as possible. Far from abandoning the women, I concentrated on using women informants. Much of my information was, however, checked by male informants.

For a short time I casually collected information on kinship

terms, descent, and local group structure, but my casual attitude was dispelled during that first *pukamani* ceremony. Whenever I asked the reasons for an individual's actions, the reply
almost invariably referred to his status in the formal aspects
of the social structure. During my field work, I observed funeral rituals, in whole or in part, for eleven individuals. As
these are lengthy ceremonies, consisting of many separate
parts, I estimate at least one-third of my active investigating
time was spent either in observing the events or in collecting
relevant information.

The funeral ceremony is a major rite of passage for all
Tiwi. The *kulama* also serves this function, but principally,
it seems, for the men. For the women, their puberty ceremony, the *muriŋaleta,* is the most significant. I learned about
the *muriŋaleta* when I introduced the subject of marriage
rules to a group of women. At first I thought they had not
understood my question, because they began by telling me
what happens when a girl has her first menses. Fortunately, I
let them continue, and it soon became apparent why they
had begun the subject of marriage in this way. It is during
this ceremony that the complex marriage system of the Tiwi
has its beginning and, I believe, its explanation in structural
terms.

Thus, the idea of using the life cycle of women as a framework for discussing Melville Island culture occurred to me
in the field, as a result of my growing realization that analyses
of the two most important rites of passage for the women—
the *muriŋaleta* and the *pukamani*—might provide clues for
clarifying the picture of the entire social organization. My
feelings about this have not changed since I presented my
original analyses in 1959, and thus this revised version is in
many respects similar to the first. Like the dissertation, it is
mainly descriptive: I have not attempted to relate the Tiwi
to other aboriginal cultures on the mainland. I have indicated
what information is the result of direct observation with specific questioning and what information was gathered from

interview reports alone. Using the life cycle as a framework has also allowed me to include data on many aspects of Tiwi culture other than social organization; however, some are touched on only in passing—principally art, mythology, and group conflict.

I have, however, expanded my original discussion of the social organization in order to incorporate not only the data of other anthropologists on the Tiwi and my own subsequent thinking on the subject, but also the data I collected in 1962. For these purposes the approach to the Tiwi culture through the life cycle of the women is equally satisfying and revealing.

Although my "ethnographic present" should be considered as being 1954, I have, to the extent that information is available, viewed Tiwi culture and social organization as a consistently fluid, flexible, and structurally changeable entity. For this reason I have used data from a time span of about fifty years, from 1914 to 1962. The device of using two diachronic lenses—the egocentric and the sociocentric—to view the Tiwi culture and society has revealed the clearest picture to me, and, I hope, to others as well. This approach presents certain organizational problems. I have selected the picture revealed through the egocentric lens as the major organizational device and have tried to incorporate the diachronic sociocentric analyses of various aspects of the culture in places where the "fit" seemed most appropriate.

J.C.G.

Bryn Mawr, Pennsylvania
June 1970

TIWI WIVES

A STUDY OF THE WOMEN OF MELVILLE ISLAND, NORTH AUSTRALIA

CHAPTER ONE

The Heritage

Pukwi made the country the first time. The sea was all fresh water. She made the land, sea and islands. She came out of the sky in daytime. She was as big as Karslake Island. Like an alligator she was and she was black.

First she camped at Urampuramum. She had paperbark and fire. Here she made the animals and trees. Then she started walking and as she walked, the waters bubbled up behind her. First she went to Darwin, then to Cape Don, then around Melville and Bathurst Islands counterclockwise. On her walks she made all the creeks. Then she went up Apsley Strait to Piper Head, Taiupu, and sat in a fresh-water billabong as a turtle. Two hunters, Iriti (jabiru) and Puruti (a fish), saw something move in the billabong. Didn't know what it was so they moved up and made ready to spear it. Puruti said, "Don't kill our mother." But Iriti went ahead and killed her. He struck her on the head. Her urine made the sea salty and her spirit went into the sky.

Now she travels by day from east to west and back along the

3

Milky Way at night. At midday she makes camp and builds a
big fire and causes great heat.

> Tiwi myth as related by a nine-year-old child.[1]

The Land

Melville and Bathurst Islands form both a geological and
cultural unit. They are located off the north coast of Australia
at a latitude of 11° 30′ south, and at a longitude of 131° 15′
east. The southernmost point of Melville Island, Cape Gam-
bia, is about thirty miles due north of Darwin. Together the
two islands contain approximately three thousand square
miles.

Generally speaking, the appearance of the land is flat and
monotonous. Running east to west across southern Melville
Island is a central ridge, with a maximum elevation of three
hundred feet, along which are the headwaters of nine rivers
that flow north to the Arafura Sea. Open marshlands can be
found near the headwaters of some of the rivers, but most of
them are lined with almost impenetrable jungle. In few places
does the solid ground of the true forest reach the banks of
the rivers.

Along the north coast of Melville Island and in some of the
deep bays there are long clean beaches and varicolored clay
cliffs; but these are more typical of the south coast, where
there are fewer mangrove-lined creeks and inlets. At various
places inland and jutting out as reefs from the cliffs are out-
crops of limonite or quartzitic sandstone, the underlying rock
formation.

Most of the land on both islands is heavily forested, mainly
with eucalyptus, ironwood, stringy-bark, woolly-butt, and
paperbark. These trees are fairly evenly distributed throughout the islands, with the paperbark clustering around and in
the freshwater swamps or billabongs and at the headwaters of
rivers and streams. Cyprus pine, tall cabbage palms, and

[1] Compare with Mountford's version (1958:24, 26).

kapok are less evenly distributed. Edible plants and trees, such as the cycad, fan, and cabbage palm, pandanus, wild plum, and apple, are also generally distributed.

The native land fauna of the island is, like that of the mainland itself, mainly marsupial. Wallaby, opossums, bandicoots, rats, and gliders are to be found everywhere. The reptiles are the next most numerous order. Snakes are well represented, and the majority are highly poisonous; only one, the carpet snake, is harmless. Lizards are also common: iguana, blanket, and blue-tongued. Of the insects, only a few bear mentioning. The stingless bee, or "sugarbag," is important economically. Although the mosquitoes and sandflies are significant nuisances, in 1954 malaria was absent on the islands. Ubiquitous termites, or white ants, chew their way through the vegetable kingdom and build large strongholds of secretion-hardened soil. Fruit bats or flying foxes, classed by the Tiwi as "birds," are also commonly found in the mangrove swamps.

There is a large variety of bird life: geese, ducks, cockatoos, secretary birds, jabirus, brolgas, parrots, parakeets, bower birds, jungle fowl, and hawks, to mention only a few of the most common species. In 1954, Parsons collected approximately seventy-five species of birds within only a few square miles (Mountford 1956:421).

Along the mangrove-lined rivers and shore reefs, oysters, snails, and cockles abound. Large crabs also inhabit this area. But by far the most important and dangerous wildlife of these rivers and coastal regions is the crocodile, which may range from the headwaters far out to sea. A significant number of Tiwi have lost their lives as a result of unprovoked attacks by these creatures. The green and hawksbill turtles are numerous, and turtle eggs are to be found in great numbers along unfrequented beaches. Of the many varieties of fish, the barramunda, rock cod, stingray, and shark are the most common. Occasionally a dugong may appear in these waters. Pearl shell and trepang, while unimportant economically to the Tiwi, have been found in the past, and their importance to others had significant results.

Of the introduced fauna, by far the most important is the dog. Dingos, the original introduced species, were presumably brought to the island by the first aboriginals. Today, very few, if any, of the hunting dogs are pure dingo; in fact, very few are pure anything except mongrel, with probably a good dose of dingo blood.

Buffalo, introduced in the nineteenth century, multiplied rapidly, but most were killed off at the turn of the century. It was estimated in 1954 that about a dozen were still roaming the forest. A few horses had been introduced some years before 1954, but they had been turned loose and were considered wild. In 1954 there was a small herd of domestic goats and one hen at Snake Bay.

The History

The location of Melville Island on the direct southerly sea route from Indonesia to the South Pacific via the Torres Straits indicates that contact with the outside world may go back a long way, although many records are now lacking. Before the seventeenth century contact probably consisted of accidental landings by Oriental seafarers blown off course. The Dutch sighted the Islands in the early part of the seventeenth century and named them Van Diemensland. Almost a century later M. van Delft surveyed and charted the west, east, and north coasts of Bathurst and Melville, but did not venture into Clarence Straits and thus failed to establish the insularity of the two islands. During the eighteenth century the Portuguese (Hart and Pilling 1960:97-98) may well have obtained slaves, presumably by force, from Melville and Bathurst Islands as well as elsewhere along the northern coasts of Australia.

In the nineteenth century Malays in search of trepang investigated nearly every inlet and bay along the northern coasts of Australia. They established camps for drying the trepang, and in this way made contact with the Aborigines. Undoubtedly Melville and Bathurst Islands did not escape this contact, but their trepang supply is not rich, so the contact was probably not as intensive or as early here as elsewhere on the northern coasts of the mainland. Moreover, if the Tiwi reception of these early strangers was like their documented reception of later visitors, whom they repelled with spears and well-developed techniques of ambush, the Malays probably avoided Melville and Bathurst Islands when they could. The Berndts (1954:76, 83) give reports of three Malay proas being wrecked on the northern shores of Melville Island, one in 1882 and two more in 1886. The Tiwi murdered one member of the first crew, and most of the two subsequent crews "escaped or were killed."

The beginning of the nineteenth century brought the first intensive contact with the Western world, with exploration by the French in 1802 (Hart and Pilling 1960:98) and occupation by the British. In 1818 Philip Parker King surveyed both the north and south coasts as well as the east and west, and although he did not actually circumnavigate the islands, he did establish their separateness. He renamed them for Viscount Henry Dundas Melville, first Lord of the Admiralty, and for His Majesty's Principal Secretary for the Colonies, the Right Honourable Earl Bathurst (King 1827:117). King had brief contact with the islanders, who appeared to mistrust him as much as he did them. However, in 1824 the British government, acting on King's accounts of the favorable location and anchorages, dispatched Captain Bremer with orders to "Take possession of Arnhem's Land upon the north coast of the continent, and to form an establishment upon the most eligible spot that could be found for a mercantile depot" (ibid.:233).

The spot where Bremer established Fort Dundas was on Melville Island opposite Harris Island in the northern part of Apsley Straits, which divides Bathurst from Melville. A

Lieutenant Roe, present during the construction of this fort, wrote a report to King, which I shall abstract here:

All disposable hands being employed on shore in clearing Point Barlow of wood and other impediments, we were speedily enabled to commence the erection of a fort, seventy-five yards in length by fifty wide . . . and surrounded by a ditch ten feet wide and deep. On the memorable twenty-first of October, our quarter-deck guns were landed and mounted, the colours were hoisted for the first time and the work was named Fort Dundas, under a royal salute from itself. . . .

Quarters were constructed within the walls of the fort . . . and about thirty huts of various kinds were erected . . . [outside].

The soil in the neighborhood . . . being exceedingly good, gardens were cleared and laid out, and soon produced all kinds of vegetables. In our stock we were rather unfortunate, for of six sheep . . . five died . . . pigs and ducks and fowls seemed however, in a fair way of doing well. . . .

The works were proceeding with such spirit and alacrity, that we were enabled to sail for Bombay on the thirteenth of November, without exposing the new settlement either to the jealousy of the Malays or the mischievous attack of the natives. No traces of the former people were observed at this place, nor any of the trepang that would be their sole inducement for visiting it. Not one native made his appeaarance before the early part of November, when as if by signal, a party of about eighteen on each shore [Melville and Bathurst] communicated with us on the same day, and were very friendly, although exceedingly suspicious and timid. . . . I was greatly astonished to see amongst them a young man . . . with perfect Malay features and like all the rest entirely naked. . . . It seems probably that he must have been kidnapped when very young, or found while astray in the woods.

These Indians made repeated signs for hatchets, which they called *paaco-paaco,* and although they had stolen two or three on their first appearance, it was considered desirable to gain their good will by giving them more, and three were accordingly presented to individuals among them who appeared to be in authority. They were of course much pleased, but the next day several axes, knives, and sickles were taken by force from men employed outside the settlement, . . . so that it was found necessary to protect our working parties in the woods by a guard; . . . The result of which was, that the natives threw their spears whenever resistance was offered, and the guard was obliged to fire upon the aggressors.

Open acts of hostility having now been committed, and the natives increasing daily in numbers to upwards of one hundred around the settlement, a good lookout was kept upon them; . . . Reports of musquetry were heard at our watering place and garden and proved to be in repelling an attack that about forty natives had made on our jolly boat watering and two men cutting grass. One of the natives was shot dead at about ten yards distance, while in the act of throwing his spear; and our people thought that several others were wounded, as they disappeared making the most strange noises and have not been near us since.[2] One of the spears thrown upon the last occasion had sixteen barbs to it, but in general they were merely scraped to a sharp point, without one barb, and were not thrown with anything like precision or good aim. . . .

Soon after this the *Tamar* left Fort Dundas for the India station. . . . The settlement was left in a very forward state, and consisted altogether of one hundred and twenty-six individuals, of whom there were three or four women and forty-five convicts, the remainder were composed of detachments of the third regiment and of the Marines. . . .

Such is the state of the settlement of Fort Dundas, which at some future time must become a place of considerable consequence in the eastern world. The soil and climate of Melville and Bathurst Islands are capable of growing all valuable productions of the East, particularly spices, and many other equally important articles of trade; it is conveniently placed for the protection of ships passing to our Indian possessions from Port Jackson, and admirably situated for the purposes of mercantile speculation [King 1827:237-43].

One wonders indeed what would have happened had not

---

[2] It is possible that the "strange noises" were the now famous Tiwi "mosquito call," a hair-raising vocalization. See p. 284.

disease and death been a constant companion in the fort; had
not the supply ships been lost, strayed, or delayed; had not the
termites eaten what few supplies were remaining, as well as
the food growing in the gardens; and had not the Tiwi been
ever-present to rob, annoy, and kill. Fort Dundas was abandoned in 1829, less than five years after its settlement. During
this time, however, the British had imported water buffaloes
from Timor, which they left behind to run wild when they
left the Islands to the Tiwi once more. The site of the gardens
of Fort Dundas was a Catholic mission for half-castes in 1954,
but the jungle has almost obliterated all traces of this fort that
was, in the words of Lieutenant Roe, to have been "of considerable consequence in the eastern world." Although the walls
have crumbled, the memory of the soldiers, their guns, and
their ships is kept alive in the traditions of the islanders. And
the legacy of the water buffaloes was the cause of the arrival
of Joe Cooper.

In 1894 two Australians, Joe Cooper and his brother, landed
on the southeast coast of Melville Island. The small party was
attacked, the brother killed, and Joe wounded. In 1900, however, Joe Cooper returned to stay for many years, bringing
with him a small group of mainland Iwaidja natives armed
with rifles. The rifles not only intimidated the Tiwi spear-
men, but they also were used to shoot buffalo, whose hides
had considerable commercial value. Cooper established his
main base at Boonali on the southeast coast of Melville Island,
and, although he encountered hostility from the Tiwi at first,
he gradually made friends with them by trading axes, knives,
tobacco, and cloth for peace.

Cooper's stabilizing influence brought visitors across the
straits from the mainland. In 1906, Herbert Basedow, the
Protector of Aborigines, visited briefly in his official capacity,
and in 1912 Baldwin Spencer stayed at Cooper's camp for a
short time. In 1910 Father Gsell, M.S.C., also visited Cooper,
and in 1911 he returned to establish the Bathurst Island Mission on a point of land just across the Apsley Straits from

Cooper's camp and within its sphere of influence. Father Gsell gradually won the Tiwi's confidence, becoming so fluent in their language that it is said the Tiwi once asked him to leave because they could no longer keep anything secret from him.[3] He established a school, which was a strong magnet, almost as strong as the flour, tea, sugar, axes, knives, and cloth. Father Gsell persuaded many men to trade their young (often prepubescent) wives to him in return for worldly goods, and thus the mission grew.

Around 1915 the buffalo were depleted to such an extent that trade in hides became less lucrative. During these fifteen years over eighteen thousand hides had been taken.[4] Cooper then turned to the stands of cyprus pine in the northern part of Melville Island. He set up sawmills at Danuru, Tuiu, and Ililiu, and began his timber exploitation, which brought many more Melville Islanders under his influence. Cooper's son Ruben, a half Iwaidja, married a Melville Island woman and was initiated in the *kulama* ceremony. Other Iwaidja lured Tiwi women away from their husbands, and eventually there was fighting in which several Tiwi lost their lives. Shortly afterward, when actual full-scale combat broke out, the government ordered Cooper and his Iwaidja to depart. About sixty people, including some Tiwi women and half-Tiwi children, departed for the mainland in seventeen canoes.

During the 1890s the Malay fishermen were replaced by Japanese pearlshell collectors. First on the south coast and later on the northeast coast of Melville Island, the Japanese established their form of trade with the Tiwi: flour, tea, sugar, and axes in exchange for temporary accommodation by the Tiwi women. Some of the Tiwi men were also recruited as crew members on their boats.

In 1937 the government established a settlement at Garden Point, close to the ruins of the ill-fated Fort Dundas, to counteract the pearlers' attractions for Tiwi women and the

[3] W. E. Harney (personal communication), 1954.
[4] Ibid.

Tiwi's attraction to Japanese goods. At this time Harney became acquainted with the Tiwi, for it was his task to distribute the government-supplied goods in quantities sufficient to draw the Tiwi away from the Japanese. This procedure was not entirely successful, and the Japanese continued, in their way, to influence the Tiwi until the outbreak of World War II (Harney 1957:73-74).

Early in World War II, the Snake Bay Settlement was established as an army-naval base, an airfield was built, and the bay was charted and marked with buoys. Melville Islanders went on patrols, rescuing distressed pilots and watching for stray mines. On Bathurst Island, American forces took over an emergency landing strip at Cape Forkroy. Many Tiwi also worked on the mainland before, during, and after the war.

The Snake Bay establishment was turned over to the Department of Native Welfare at the end of the war and became the Government Settlement. The Garden Point Settlement at this time was turned over to the mission for Catholic half-castes from all over the Northern Territory, while on Bathurst Island the large Sacred Heart Mission flourished.

When I arrived in 1954, the Snake Bay Settlement consisted of one white family, the superintendent's, and approximately 180 to 200 Tiwi. Many of these Tiwi had children at the Catholic Mission School, but preferred not to live there themselves. When the Snake Bay School officially opened in June, it was obvious from the attendance that literacy had become a prime goal. Parents not only urged their children to attend, but demanded and got an adult night school program.

Shortly after I left, late in 1954, the Department of Welfare began an intensive program on their native settlements. Snake Bay and Melville Island were selected as areas for maximum effort. There were two main reasons for this: (1) the Tiwi's positive attitude toward education and change, which they sincerely believe will regain for them the equality with the whites that they lost at the turn of the century, and (2) the commercial potential of the islands themselves, principally the termite-resistant cyprus pine.

The school continues to flourish, as do the cyprus pine plantations. The Department of Forests Cyprus Pine Development employs not only young Tiwi from Snake Bay and Bathurst Island but people from other tribes as well. The enlarged settlement itself employs most of the other able-bodied residents. In 1954 many of the Snake Bay Tiwi spent all the time they could in the bush, preferring the varied diet obtainable there to the erratic rice and corned-beef diet available at the settlement, but in 1962 there was almost no hunting. This was the only change about which I heard disparaging remarks, and it resulted principally from the necessity to ban the use of fire in hunting in order to protect the valuable young cyprus pine plantations.

The islands, their lands and waters and their history, are but parts of a Tiwi's inheritance. Every newborn Tiwi inherits land and membership in two or more major social groups beyond his immediate family. I must discuss two of these elements of the social heritage before introducing the individual female child whose life we shall be tracing. Into these social situations she is born; they are therefore part of her infant environment. What follows here are mere summaries. Fuller analyses will be made later as the finer points become essential to the understanding of the Tiwi woman's role in the social system.

The Countries

Every Tiwi man and woman is a landowner, inheriting rights to a segment of land through his father. The events of recent history, however, have inflicted greater change on the composition and function of the landholding groups than on any other island institution. Virtually every Tiwi, with few exceptions, now lives at the Snake Bay Settlement, the Bathurst Island Mission, or well within their spheres of influence, or in Darwin.

The Melville and Bathurst islanders are one cultural and linguistic group, but they have no name for themselves.[5] The Tiwi do have a name for the territorial divisions of the islands, and they use these names to identify themselves as members of an independent landowning group. There are two kinds of landowning groups, and an individual has membership in both. The smaller of the groups owns a section of land within the territory of the larger group. The Tiwi call the larger territory *tuŋarima,* which they translate as "country." I shall use the word "country" for this division, although the Tiwi may use "country" for the smaller division as well. The smaller divisions will be referred to as "subcountries."

There is another Tiwi term that applies to a geographical location, the word *tabuda.* The translation I received for this word was "camp." The word *tabuda* was, however, variously used to refer not only to a specific camping spot, but also at times to the area of the subcountry. I believe that the variable application of this term reflects the size and social composition of the specific group inhabiting the designated area, which varies considerably from group to group over time. I shall discuss this in greater detail later, as well as the variable rights that pertain to ownership and use of the different territorial divisions.

Each country, subcountry, and camp has a proper name that is usually, but not always, associated with a particular natural feature of the land, be it terrain or insect life. The Tiwi use these names to identify themselves as members of a geographical group.

Because only two groups of Tiwi are now living in the country that they own—the Wileraŋguwila of Melville Island

---

[5] The name Tiwi, first used by Hart (1930a:169-70), is the island word for "men." Readers are referred to Hart for further discussion of how and why he came to use this word as the tribal name. It has since been adopted by most of the anthropologists who have written on the islanders, but not by the islanders themselves.

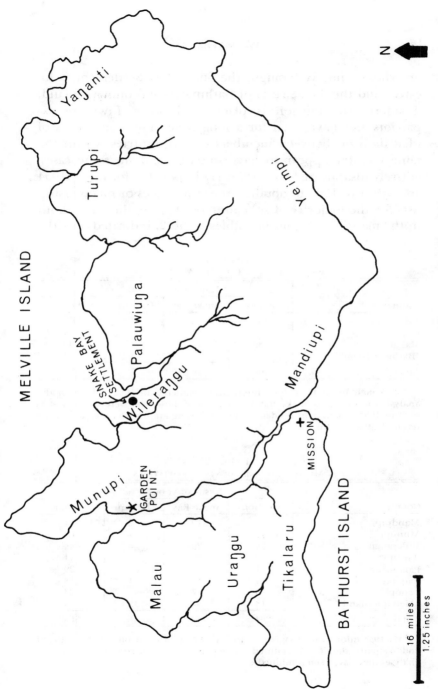

Fig. 1   The countries of Melville and Bathurst islands

on whose land, Wileraŋgu, the Snake Bay Settlement is located, and the Tikalaruila of Bathurst Island on whose land, Tikalaru, the mission is placed—all other Tiwi are expatriots and have been for a long time. The boundaries of identification between members of subcountries within the same country appear to have softened and, in some cases, entirely disappeared. It was nearly impossible for me in 1954 and again in 1962 to obtain either the names or membership lists for the majority of subcountries. I have, therefore, both in the map (Fig. 1) and in Tables 1 and 2, indicated only the

TABLE 1
BATHURST ISLAND COUNTRY AFFILIATIONS

Country	RESIDING AT OR NEAR*			
	Mission	Snake Bay	Darwin	Total
Tikalaru	168	2	3	173
Uraŋgu	143	3	—	146
Malau	89	11	1	101
"Bathurst Island"	6	—	3	9
Total	406	16	7	429

*Although my data include information gathered in 1962, I have in this analysis considered as Snake Bay residents only those who were considered as such in 1954. Changes in residence since that time are not considered, nor are recent deaths or births.

TABLE 2
MELVILLE ISLAND COUNTRY AFFILIATIONS

Country	RESIDING AT OR NEAR			
	Mission	Snake Bay	Darwin	Total
Mandiupi	59	19	3	81
Munupi	74	28	—	102
Wileraŋgu	24	20	—	44
Turupi*	8	33	—	41
Palauwiuŋa	1	28	—	29
Yaŋanti*	4	13	1	18
Yeimpi	16	7	—	23
"Melville Island"	18	—	12	30
Total	204	148	16	368

*My 1954 informants disagreed with my 1962 informants on whether Turupi and Yaŋanti should be counted as one or two countries. In subsequent analyses they have been combined.

TABLE 3
DISTRIBUTION OF TIWI POPULATION AT SETTLEMENTS

Location	Number	Percent
Bathurst Island Mission	610	76.5
Snake Bay Settlement	164	20.6
Darwin	23	2.9
Total	797	100.0

TABLE 4
DISTRIBUTION OF BATHURST ISLANDERS AT SETTLEMENTS

Location	Number	Percent
Bathurst Island Mission	406	94.6
Snake Bay Settlement	16	3.7
Darwin	7	1.6
Total	429	99.9

TABLE 5
DISTRIBUTION OF WEST MELVILLE ISLANDERS AT SETTLEMENTS*

Location	Number	Percent
Bathurst Island Mission	133	72.7
Snake Bay Settlement	47	25.7
Darwin	3	1.6
Total	183	100.0

*Two Melville Island countries, Mandiupi and Munupi, are quite close to Bathurst Island, resulting in a significantly longer period of contact with the mission than the other Melville Island countries. For purposes of analysis I have, therefore, divided Melville Island into west and east, with these two countries comprising West Melville Island.

TABLE 6
DISTRIBUTION OF EAST MELVILLE ISLANDERS AT SETTLEMENTS

Location	Number	Percent
Bathurst Island Mission	53	34.2
Snake Bay Settlement	101	65.2
Darwin	1	.6
Total	155	100.0

TABLE 7
COMPOSITION OF SETTLEMENT POPULATIONS

	Location	Number	Percent
Bathurst Island Mission	Bathurst Islanders	406	66.6
	West Melville Islanders	133	21.8
	East Melville Islanders	53	8.7
	? Melville Islanders	18	2.9
	Total	610	100.0
Snake Bay Settlement	Bathurst Islanders	16	9.7
	West Melville Islanders	47	28.7
	East Melville Islanders	101	61.6
	Total	164	100.0

countries. In the past these countries were fairly autonomous political and social units. Murder, feuds, and warfare were common among countries but were considered wrong among members of the same country. I was also told that before the white man came (to mess things up was implied) one was supposed to marry within the country. In the tables, I have indicated the present distribution of those Tiwi for whom I was able to get adequate information.

The Matrilineal Descent Groups

Every Tiwi is also born into a matrilineal descent group, which they call *pukwi,* or in pidgin, "skin." Earlier investigators called these groups "totemic groups," and some of the later writers call them "clans." Each group is identified by a proper name drawn from the animal, vegetable, and mineral environment of the islands, but as far as I could determine there was no attempt to trace one's line of descent to the namesake nor any ritual connection. I prefer to call these groups "sibs," after Murdock (1949), in order to avoid the confusion that has resulted from anthropologists' variable application of the word "clan."

The sibs acknowledge a common ancestry to the extent that they prohibit marriage between members of the same sib. The various sibs also align themselves with other sibs into *aramipi* or phratries,[6] which are considered to be exogamous. In the listing I have not indicated the phratry affiliations of the sibs, nor do I wish at this time to discuss even how many phratries there are or were at any given time, since the number and alignment appears to have been variable for the period for which I have information. This too will be discussed later (Chapter 4), as it pertains principally to the marriage system.

Information on the sibs contained in Table 8 is limited to what I obtained in 1954 and in 1962 from Tiwi informants at Snake Bay and from the census files in Darwin.[7] Snake Bay Tiwi gave the native names for their sibs, both to me and to the official census taker, while the Bathurst Island Mission Tiwi almost exclusively gave an English translation to the census taker. I have been able to correlate most of these directly, but for a few sibs that have no members residing at Snake Bay, my correlation is based on only one or two individuals whom my informants listed as members of a particular group but whose English translation does not agree with that given to me for the native term. My listing, therefore, is in both English and native terms, with the enumeration of members distributed at Snake Bay and mission according to the term in my records.

The present distribution of sib members in the two major

[6] There is some confusion in the literature, as well as in my own data, as to whether the phratries have proper names or not. My two sets of census data and the Darwin census data make it clear that some Tiwi have given the investigator the name of one of several sibs in a single phratry as the one to which they belong, but that more detailed questioning will often result in the naming of another sib within that phratry as the more "correct" designation of membership for the individual.

This tendency accounts for much of the confusion in the literature. Another reason is the informants' inconsistent statements concerning the affiliation of the sibs into exogamous phratries. I shall discuss this in greater detail as I take up the subject of marriage in Chapter 4.

[7] As the Darwin census included Snake Bay residents, I was able to cross-check the validity of this material. It proved 90 percent correct, and if we take into account the informants' tendency to give variable names of their matrilineal affiliation the data can be considered 99 percent correct, at least as they apply to the Snake Bay Tiwi, and presumably to the others as well.

TABLE 8
MATRILINEAL SIB CENSUS AND PRESENT DISTRIBUTION

Name Given by Informant	Total	Snake Bay	Mission
Crocodile, Alligator, Irikupe*		—	11
Mudaŋanila (Mudaŋgala)†	(15)	4	—
Ironwood		—	90
Kutaguni, Murtaŋapila	(95)	2	3
Mullet Fish		—	1
Purilawila (Purilaunila, Purilakala)	(13)	12	—
Parrot Fish		—	—
Wilintuwila (Wilintunila, Wilitiŋala)	(7)	7	—
Mosquito‡	(33)	—	33
Yellow Honey Eater (bird), Jidjini†		—	11
Tokombui (Tokombini, Tokombuŋa)	(34)	7	16
March Fly		—	24
Tapitabui (Tapitabini, Tapitabuŋa)	(35)	8	3
Bloodwood		—	6
Kurawi (Kurani, Kuraka)	(35)	25	4
Rain, Fresh Water		—	16
Andului (Andulina, Anduliŋa)	(21)	4	1
Stones		—	60
Arikuwila	(62)	1	1
Red Stones		—	—
Puŋaluŋwila	(3)	3	—
Pandanus		—	35
Miatui (Miati, Miatiŋa)	(47)	11	1
White Cockatoo		—	21
Milipuwila (Milipunila, Milipuŋala)	(21)	—	—
Flying Fox, Daniŋgini† (Bamboo)		—	37
Muraŋimbila (Muranila, Muraŋgala)	(50)	13	—
House Fly		—	—
Mandipalawi, Mandubowi	(0)	—	—
Wild Goose‡	(2)	—	2
Jabiru		—	98

TABLE 8 (cont.)
MATRILINEAL SIB CENSUS AND PRESENT DISTRIBUTION

Name Given by Informant	Total	Snake Bay	Mission
Tjilarui	(99)	1	—
Stingray		—	15
Yurantawi	(15)	—	—
Fire, Ikwani†		—	113
Uriubila		14	—
Kudalui (Kudalini, Kudaliŋa)	(152)	25	—
Red Ochre		—	11
Krutui, Utuŋa	(12)	—	1
Woollybutt tree flower		—	11
Arikortorrui	(11)	—	—
Yellow Ochre‡	(19)	—	19
Salt Water Mud		—	—
Paruliaŋapila	(0)	—	—

* Male or female member of the sib, given in parentheses.

† Native terms given on the same line as English are the common names for these animals sometimes given as alternates to the English.

‡ Correlations of sibs so indicated are based on less than adequate data.

settlements indicates a tendency for some sibs to group in one or the other settlement. At this time perhaps the most important point to make concerning the distribution of sibs and country-mates is that neither settlement provides a truly random sample of Tiwi, and that the significantly smaller number of Tiwi at the Snake Bay Settlement provides a skewed sample. This fact must be kept in mind, since what follows, except where specifically noted, is drawn from interviews and observation of the Snake Bay Tiwi exclusively. I have no doubt that much of my information also applies to Tiwi culture in general, but some of the specific details of behavior and social organization may be local or descent-group variations.

The Age Divisions

Sib, country, and camp are not the only means by which an

individual Tiwi woman is placed socially by her fellows. She is also classified according to degree of maturity, size, and number and sex of children. These somewhat dissimilar criteria all enter into the Melville Island system of age grading. But unlike sib, country, and camp, these grades do not correspond to social groups.

Since the Tiwi do not count years, the system of age grading closely parallels our own system when we refer to an individual as an infant, child, adolescent, mother, and so on. As in our own system, moreover, some of these periods are marked by a physiological or cultural event and some are not. Females have more marked physiological events than males, and the Tiwi have given more named periods of life to women than to men. Although I shall be dealing almost entirely with female age periods, I have listed both the male and the female terms.

Female		Male	
kitjiŋa	small girl	*kitjini*	small boy
aliŋa	young girl	*tajinati*	young boy
muriŋaleta	puberty		
murukubara	young woman	*malikanini*	youth
poperiŋanta[8]	pregnant		
pernamberdi[8]	mother of girl	*imbalinapa*[8]	father of girl
awri-awri[8]	mother of boy	*awri-apa*[8]	father of boy
badamoriŋa	barren woman		
parimariŋa	menopause	*arakulani*	big man
intula	old woman	*irula*	old man

These terms are given to the living. According to the Tiwi, individuals exist both before and after the above sequence. Unborn children are called *pitapitui,* and a person who has died becomes a *mobuditi*. In the life of any "typical" human being, physical horizons widen from birth to death, and social

[8] These are recurring conditions during a period in an individual's life; the period itself has no single term.

horizons also widen, shift, and change in content and importance. I shall therefore begin with the period called *kitjiŋa* and end with *mobudriŋa* (a female *mobuditi*). The category of unborn children, *pitapitui,* will be introduced at the appropriate time in the woman's life.

CHAPTER TWO

The *Kitjiŋa*

At the tender age of five days, the *kitjiŋa* is brought from her place of birth into the surroundings in which she will live during the remainder of this first period of her life. These surroundings include the natural features of her parents' camping grounds, as well as the group of people who share the physical places. Although total awareness of this environment comes gradually to the *kitjiŋa,* a brief description of the camp and its inhabitants will serve as a background for discussion.[1]

The best definition of a camp is a place where one sleeps overnight. An area large enough to accommodate the number of people who will sleep there is cleared, and fires are built in the cleared area—one fire to one or two adults is the usual ratio.

---

[1] This discussion of the *kitjiŋa* environment is for Tiwi in the presettlement period, and applies to the present only when they take to the bush on hunting trips.

Depending on the season and to some extent on the amount
of natural protection available, artificial shelters may be provided. During the rainy season from November to April, the
camp must have adequate shelter. These shelters are usually
made out of the bark of the stringy-bark tree, sheets of which
are supported on poles in a variety of architectural designs
(Fig. 2). In areas that are ideally suited for camp, close to a
permanent source of water or special resources, these shelters
are often left for use again. Otherwise, shelters are used only
for one continuous period.

Fig. 2   Shelter types

During the dry season shelter is necessary only to provide
shade, and then only if the camp is in an area not protected
by trees, such as in an extensive clearing or on a beach. These
dry-weather shades can be made from bark of the stringy-bark
or the paperbark tree, but more often they are constructed of
leafy branches set upright in an almost enclosed circle, with
more branches crisscrossing over the top to form a roof.

When settling in a new camp during the dry season, one of

the first acts is to burn off the grass surrounding the actual camping area as a protection against snakes. If one were to approach a dry weather camp during midday, when it is likely to be empty of people, the only indication of whether the camp was still inhabited or abandoned would be a few smoldering logs in the middle of a slightly burned and cleared area. If, however, one were to approach the camp at dusk, when the inhabitants had returned for the night, the picture would be entirely different.

For many reasons, the number of people camping together will vary from time to time. At a minimum there would be two, either two males out hunting together or a man and his wife. Only temporarily or abnormally would a person habitually camp alone. In describing the social environment of the *kitjiŋa* I shall consider a camp of a husband, his wives, and possible companions. The reasons for the inclusion and exclusion of certain people from this camp will have to be given at a later time, for there is considerable variation in the residence pattern. I selected the relatives who are most important to the *kitjiŋa* at this time, and chose a basic pattern.[2]

Sharing the light and warmth of two closely placed fires are the *kitjiŋa*, her mother, and perhaps her father. Close by, but sleeping near other fires, are the father's other wives and their small children. Older sons of the father sleep together at some distance from their mothers and younger siblings. Depending on the circumstances, the elderly parent(s) either of the father or of his wives may be members of the camp who sleep by their own fire. The camp may also include unmarried brothers of the father, who sleep with the bachelor sons, along with, perhaps, the husband of the newborn *kitjiŋa*. It is also possible that close by, around their own fire and separated from the

[2] Since I was unable to observe Tiwi camp organization as it would normally have existed, I am not able to describe or document with figures who makes up a "typical" camp nor how many people comprise an "average" camp. The information presented here is based on my observations of atypical camp groupings and on informants' statements about how it used to be.

first group by some bushes, will be the father's married brother(s) and his wife (wives) and children.

Basic to the personal and interpersonal activities, the responsibilities, and the education of the *kitjiŋa* are the inescapable facts of her growth and development as a human being. For this reason it is advisable to divide this period of her life into a number of subperiods based mainly on physical development and behavior. Briefly, the periods and their criteria are:

Kitjiŋa 1—continuously associated with her mother and completely dependent on her for food and transportation.

Kitjiŋa 2—semi-independent of her mother for food and transportation, and beginning to participate in play activities.

Kitjiŋa 3—weaned but still closely associated with her mother to a greater extent than with other children.

Kitjiŋa 4—entirely independent of her mother, closest associates are other children, extremely active and playful.

Kitjiŋa 5—still playful with other children, but assumes some social and economic responsibilities.

Kitjiŋa 1

When the mother brings the five-day-old *kitjiŋa* to her husband's fire, the father may not touch the child for the remainder of the first day, and he and his wife must sleep with a fire between them for a period of at least a week, sometimes a month. The baby is covered with charcoal, and the mother is painted with a red stripe down the center of her body, both front and back. The lower half of her face, from the bridge of her nose downward, is painted black, while the upper half is painted red.

During this first period of the *kitjiŋa*'s life, her activity consists of little more than eating, eliminating, sleeping, and vocalizing. She is kept constantly at her mother's side. She is nursed whenever she demands it. While sleeping during the warm day, she may be placed on soft paperbark, or, today, on lengths of calico, but her mother is never more than a few

feet away. During the night, the mother cradles the baby in
the curve of her body as she lies on her side by the fire.

Although the father may hold his daughter for brief periods after the first day home, he has no more contact with her
than do the other camp companions. Should the mother not
have enough milk to nourish her child, however, the baby
will be nursed by another woman, who is chosen principally
on the basis of availability. If there is a wet-nurse in the camp,
the woman is likely to stand in the same degree of relationship to the *kitjiŋa* as her real mother, that is, she may be a
sister of the real mother, another wife of the real father, or
wife of one of the father's brothers—a woman who the *kitjiŋa*
will call *iŋnari* (mother). If a wet-nurse is not available locally, one may be found in a neighboring camp, which will,
in all likelihood, be made up of father's brothers and their
wives, so that the woman will still be *iŋnari,* or "mother." If
a woman in this relationship is not available, however, expe-
diency dictates the choice. The *kitjiŋa,* when she begins to use
terms of reference, makes no change in the term she would
otherwise have used for this woman, but, naturally, close personal ties result from this intimacy.

During this first period of a *kitjiŋa's* life, her mother does
not participate in the daily routine of hunting or gathering,
unless the trip is to a location close by the camp and for the
purpose of collecting one particular item, requiring no extensive traveling other than to and from the locality. The *kitjiŋa*
is carried in her mother's arms either horizontally or with her
head resting on her mother's shoulder. Most of the time the
mother remains in the camp and receives her share of the food
obtained by others.

Starting almost from the first day of birth and continuing
for several years, the young *kitjiŋa* is encouraged to grow by
gentle pulling on her arms and legs. It is uncertain how often
she was bathed in the past, if at all, for there is a general fear
of water and the *maritji* (rainbow) spirits who dwell therein,
since they are particularly dangerous to very young children

and pregnant women. Older children and adults bathe regularly, sometimes twice a day during the warm weather. In any case, the very small infant is cleaned and dried for the first few weeks with a mixture of charcoal, dust, and milk.

Toward the end of this first infant period, the father must assume the grave responsibility of giving the child a first name. Of all the corporeal and incorporeal possessions belonging to a Melville Island woman or man during a lifetime, the names given them are the only ones of which they have sole and complete ownership. Personal names and the customs and traditions surrounding them are the subject of an article by Hart (1930b:280-90), who investigated them among the Tiwi in the late 1920s. From my own investigations it is evident that these customs and traditions have in no way changed during the intervening thirty years, except for the wider use of additional English names. In 1954 all these English names were (and had been) given to newborn infants by whites, and they did not fall into the traditional pattern of naming or use of names.

The most important aspect of a traditional name is that it must be unique. Hart made a careful study of thirty-three hundred names and found no two identical. For this reason alone the choice of a name for the child is no casual matter. The first name is always given by the mother's present husband (presumably, but not necessarily, the child's actual father). Before bestowing the name, he consults first with *his* mother and quite likely with other elderly people who are in a better position to know whether the name chosen is indeed unique. The name itself may be one of his own given names, which after he gives it to the child no longer belongs to him. But more likely it is one he has coined for the occasion. The subject matter of the name will be drawn from the total experience of the father both on this earth and in his dreams. As far as I could determine, this is the only factor determining the choice of subject matter for a name, there being no correlation with any of the other Tiwi systems of identification. For this reason it is difficult to generalize or to categorize names by subject, but some subjects or experiences are more frequently used for coining names than others.

One type of personal experience seems to be a "natural" for name coining: the activity or appearance of the child when the father "dreamed" her before she entered her mother's womb. (A full discussion of this belief will be deferred until our *kitjiŋa* herself becomes pregnant.) An example of this type of name is one that means "to spit in anger," given to a child who announced her presence in such a manner to her father while he slept. Another name means "inside a hole," for the unborn child was in a hole when her father "found her" in his dream.

Many names refer to objects seen by the father or peculiar to his country. Increased familiarity with Western material culture has opened up a new source of inspiration, and we find such names as "big teeth like the saw mill." These names are not as common, however, as those pertaining to the natural world. Names referring to crocodiles and sharks are extremely common. Demons and nonhuman inhabitants of the "other world" are frequently used, as are place names. Parts of the body as well as the physical prowess of the recipient are often referred to, more often for second names than for the first, however. Such names might be "She Runs After Anybody and Pretends to Fight," or "Think in Your Ears and No One Can Catch You." Examples could be given almost indefinitely, but there is one activity that comes up time and again in a list of names: murder. Murders are referred to as past events, as future prophecies, and as happenings in dreams; and both men and women are likely to have this subject for one of their names.

But there are not enough subjects to go around, and the result is a multiplicity of native names as well as multiple common words pertaining to the same subject. This situation reflects customs and beliefs associated with names. If, for example, a child is given the name *Komondao,* meaning crocodile tail, and either the owner or the bestower of the name dies, that name and word is dropped from the language and cannot be used for many years. Of the many words used to refer to crocodiles in everyday converstation today, none bears any relation to the name *komondao*. Its origin can only be guessed. Perhaps *komondao* as an everyday word had become taboo many years previously, but had been reintroduced as a personal name. Meanwhile the Tiwi had to find another word for crocodile tail. For a time the other word existed only in the memory of older people, who allowed it to be reintroduced again when enough time had elapsed to lift the taboo, in this case as a name, or in other cases as a substitute for the newer word, itself perhaps by then taboo. Many people were unable to give me translations of their names, the meanings having been lost over the years; however, the word or name goes on as a meaningless part of the native vocabulary. The tremendous influence the tradition of personal names has on the character and evolution of the Melville Island language, principally on vocabulary, should not be underestimated.

A given personal name is not frequently used as a term of reference or address, as the name is actually considered to be a possession of its owner. Indiscriminate use of anybody's personal possessions is not tolerated for long. There are particular times in a Tiwi's life when it is quite dangerous to the individual to mention his or her names. For example, if one's name is mentioned at night, the spirits will seek the owner out. Kinship terms and acquired English names are generally used for reference and address, or such descriptive terms as "that one from such a place." When the situation warrants it, the age-grade terms, initiation-grade terms, or special kinship terms denoting relationship to one recently deceased are used.

Once a father has thought of a name and had its uniqueness verified, he will wait for the appropriate time to give it to the infant. Informants differed as to what exactly they con-

sidered to be the appropriate time. Some fathers gave the first
name when the infant sat up by itself, and still others waited
until the day when the infant stood or even walked. In the
words of one informant, "If I name him before, he might
die and name no good." In view of the foregoing discussion
of personal names, this seems reason enough for waiting. Hart
believes that the waiting period was dictated by the need for
complete verification of a name's uniqueness, a process that
may indeed take time. Often this verification will take place,
as one man said, "When big mob gather, then anybody object,
he say so." Therefore the naming or renaming of individuals
is often associated with ceremonial gatherings.

Although the first name is given by the mother's husband,
an individual will be given many other names during her
lifetime. One woman of forty-five had at least eighteen names,
and was certain that she had forgotten several. Anybody
called *iriŋani* (father) considers it one of his duties to give a
name to a "daughter" or "son," a duty that he may or may not
fulfill depending on the closeness of the personal relationship.
Father's brothers will almost certainly bestow names on their
brother's children. So will mother's secondary husbands, all
of whom should be *iriŋani* to their new wife's previous children.[3] These additional names are not given all at one time,
but irregularly throughout the life of the individual. Additional names are most frequently given at ceremonial gatherings, when distant fathers are likely to be present. When any
father dies, the names they have given cannot be used by the
recipients; therefore, it is important to own as many names
from as many different fathers as possible.

Women can also give a child a name, but never the first
name, and as far as I could tell never a coined name but one
that they themselves had been given and owned. However,

---

[3] Hart and Pilling (1960:15) place a great emphasis on this renaming of
a widow's daughters by her new husband, stating that by doing so a man
acquires rights to control his stepdaughter's marriage. A father's rights in
relation to his daughter's marriages will be discussed fully in the next
chapter.

it is quite rare for a child to receive a name from a female relative. In the few cases I have recorded, the name was given by a father's sister. It might be imagined that certain names would show a tendency to be inherited from a paternal line, but this does not seem to be the case. Once a name has been taboo, it may be bestowed on any child of the tribe when the taboo is lifted.

When the *kitjiŋa* has been named, her mother takes her around the camp, and perhaps to neighboring camps as well, and announces, "Today my child has a (new) name."

Kitjiŋa 2

The *kitjiŋa* is now beginning to be semi-independent of her mother for food and transportation. Her milk teeth are appearing, and she is given an opossum bone to chew on to help the teething process. Soft yams are her first solid food. Later, when most of her milk teeth are in, she eats any food available. The women say that if they gave solid foods in any great amounts before all her teeth have erupted, "She greedy one all her life." She will still be nursed, however, upon demand.

Until the *kitjiŋa* becomes fairly proficient at walking, she is dependent on others for transportation. By this time her mother has resumed all of her economic responsibilities and spends the day in the bush either with the other women of the camp or with her husband. The child sits on her mother's or father's shoulders and clings to their hair, leaving her transport's hands free. Young children become so accustomed to traveling in this position that they frequently go sound asleep and still do not fall from their perch. When not traveling, a child sits or sleeps on the ground; I never saw a child crawling around the settlement or camps.

Although a child spends most of her time with her real mother and father, her other "mothers" and "fathers" in the camp spend considerable time playing with her, carrying her, and feeding her dainty tidbits. Strong personal attachments with her other mothers and fathers begin to develop at this early age, and it is hard to distinguish by behavior alone one nuclear family from another in the camp, except during the sleeping hours when each family retires to its own fire.

Once the *kitjiŋa* begins to walk, she spends part of her time in the company of the other young in the camp. All of the children in our "typical" camp are classified as sisters or brothers; either *imbuŋa* (older sister) and *iwuni* (older brother) or *iŋgalabuŋa* and *iŋgalabini* if they belong to a different sib.

Play activity can best be illustrated by actually describing the activity of two *kitjiŋa* aged about two and three who accompanied their mothers on a yam-digging expedition. On arrival at the yam site, the women dug a few yams and roasted them in the hot ashes of a small fire. They fed most of these to the children. Then the women returned to the digging. The two little girls spent about half an hour playing a game best called "Let's see how many yam holes we can fall into," which consisted of staggering around with eyes closed and arms upheld and tumbling into the holes, some of which were several feet deep. Tiring of this, they decided to build their own fire. They gathered a small heap of grass, collected a glowing stick from their mothers' fire, and carried it to their heap of grass. They held the glowing stick to the grass and then, lying on their stomachs, blew gently till a flame appeared. Then they scurried about trying to find enough small twigs to feed the fire, but it died out. They did not try again, but returned to their mothers' fire for the main meal of yams that were now roasting. Then, after nursing, they fell asleep. While they slept the women dug more yams, and all returned to camp a few hours later.

On opossum hunts baby opossums are often found in a female's pouch. These are rarely killed, for, as one man told me, "we feel too sorry long em." Rather the Tiwi take them back to camp and give them to the children. The two little

girls mentioned above each received a baby opossum when
they returned to camp, and they spent the rest of the evening
running about sticking the young, clinging, hairless animals
in everyone's hair, including their own, and laughing loudly
as their human victims tried to pry loose the small animals.
Such an animal might be old enough to survive the night,
"sleeping in the camp," in which case it would not be killed
and eaten, for it would now be considered a member of the
camp. The Tiwi children make pets of all young marsupials
and even young turtles found in newly hatched or almost
hatched eggs. The mortality rate is high, but pets are never
eaten. They may be given appropriate kinship terms, and
when they die the children bury them, often holding a funeral
ceremony.

Kitjiŋa 3

Transition into the *kitjiŋa* 3 stage is marked by weaning
the child. In order to accomplish this feat, her mother mixes
the "burned ear hole of the blanket lizard" with milk and
feeds it to the *kitjiŋa,* after which, it was emphatically stated,
"Baby no more drink titty." Weaning may take place either
before or after the birth of another child. Quite often a young
child will be allowed the comfort and security of her mother's
breast after her younger sibling has been fed, but eventually
she weans herself or gets the blanket lizard treatment.

Much of the *kitjiŋa*'s time is still spent accompanying her
parents into the bush in quest of food. She takes no active
part in the hunt, but merely observes the methods and eats
the products. She is carried when tired, more often than not
on her father's shoulders now that she is growing heavy. She
will also spend much of her time in the camp, playing with
the other young children under the supervision of the youngest or oldest "mother" or an old "grandmother."

Up to this time, she has been subjected to little parental
discipline, but as the *kitjiŋa* becomes more physically inde-

pendent of her parents her wishes may also become independent. We have seen that very young children are allowed literally to play with fire, and never once did I hear a parent telling their child, "Now be careful, dear." The maxim "experience is the best teacher" seems to be rigidly followed. Children have been burned, but every case I heard of happened when the child rolled over in her sleep into the night fire. Generally parents or other adults will only interfere in their child's activities when they become really dangerous to some other younger child who cannot fend for itself. I saw this illustrated one day while I was watching a group of Tiwi engaged in one of their favorite present-day pastimes, that of playing cards. Two young *kitjiŋa,* Althea and Dennis, and the latter's younger brother, Chrisy, were playing around the circle of adults. They repeatedly got into fights, but only when the wrangle became serious were they separated. The children received no words of reproach, nor was a hand laid on them, even when they eventually became "cheeky" and rolled about on their mothers' laps, kicking sand in the card-players' faces and grabbing cards. Then Dennis, a strong-willed *kitjiŋa,* "borrowed" a large hunting knife and began swinging it around jabbing at her much younger brother. One of the men took the knife away, whereupon Dennis went into a minor tantrum and the knife was given back to her. She then began to hit herself on the head with the knife and went into a long verbal tirade that sent the adults into roars of laughter. After quite some time the knife was again taken from her and thrown into some dense bushes where she was unable to find it. I asked the man who had taken the knife away why she was so mad. The reply was, "She say nothing. She only got maggots in her brain, that's why she hit it."

If a child gets really upset, every effort is made to divert her attention from her forbidden desire. Only once did I hear a young man threaten to use his belt on his sister's young daughter who was creating an uproar in the camp because she could not go crocodile hunting with her father in the middle of the night. Her uncle did not carry out his threat, for another "father" came up and carried her out of the camp long enough for the crocodile hunters to depart. When she was brought back to the camp she was again a cheerful, playful little girl. It is not considered good for the child, I was told, to let her cry herself to sleep, for "by and by she go crazy."

Although most of the rules and regulations governing adult social behavior are waived for young children, those concerned with death taboos are immediately enforced and quickly learned. No child can carry a light at night, for a *mobuditi* (spirit of one dead) can see her and carry her off. If she touches any belongings of a person recently deceased, she is firmly reprimanded. And she learns early to distinguish by paint and ornamentation the close relatives of one recently dead. These people must be fed by hand, for they cannot themselves handle the food they eat. But no child, no matter how close the relationship, will herself be placed under these and other rigid and personal death taboos.

Kitjiŋa 4 and 5

I shall make no descriptive differentiation between these two stages, for it is during this time that the *kitjiŋa* receives definite instruction in economic activities and begins to experiment on her own. During the first half of the period she receives more instruction in proportion to the amount of time spent in experimentation. The proportion is reversed in the second half, but it is more convenient to divide the discussion into instruction and experimentation. The play activities are the same for both, and indeed it is sometimes hard to distinguish play from experimentation.

Two important skills acquired early in this period are swimming and tree-climbing. I never saw anyone giving definite instruction in either skill, and it is probable that both are learned by imitation.

By now the *kitjiŋa* travels on her own two feet as she joins

her elders in the hunt for food. She is shown the signs that
indicate the presence or passage of an animal, and she is often
sent scrambling up a tree to test a hole suspected of sheltering
an opossum. When oysters, cockles, snails, cycad nuts, or other
gathered food are collected, she actively participates. Very
occasionally she is given a knife or ax and instructed in its
use, but most of the food she gathers requires nothing except
her hands or sticks and stones for tools. Her brothers, however, are instructed in the use of the fish spear at this age. Back
in the camp, the *kitjiŋa* helps in such tasks as filling the water
containers and gathering wood for the cooking and sleeping
fires. When she accompanies her parents in a canoe, she may
be given an undersized paddle to use when she feels like it.

As her hunting skills increase the *kitjiŋa* begins to join
other children of both sexes in independent expeditions.
The children wander about the bush in a gang, playing tag
and singing as they go. The boys may take pot shots at birds,
throwing stones high into the trees and making a contest of
it. The girls collect berries, small fruits, and birds' eggs. If
anything worthy of cooking is found and they are far from
camp, the gang will make a fire, cook, and carefully portion
out the food. I once saw one rather small fish divided among
eight hungry children. They are rarely successful enough to
bring anything back to camp to contribute to the family din-
ner. Should they have no gang with which to share their take,
they will bring home what they have not eaten.

Two seven or eight-year-old *kitjiŋa* one day built a "canoe,"
they called it, in the Banjo Beach billabong back of our expedition camp and invited me to go for an afternoon cruise
with them. The canoe turned out to be a paperbark raft, and
I first questioned its buoyancy. The girls went into a huddle,
emerged with shy giggles, and asked if I minded if they went
naked. When I shook my head, they stripped off their wrap-
around skirts *(nagas),* jumped into the shallow water, and
made their way to a large paperbark. Each carried a small
stick with which she struck the tree. If it gave a hollow sound,

they made a longitudinal cut in the bark, hacking away with the end of the stick to the limit of their reach. Then they peeled the bark off around the tree, sometimes with great care. They made no horizontal cuts, but ripped the soft bark at the top and bottom of the cut. When the sheets of bark were cut, they laid them on the raft, first carefully building up the sides and then laying them across the center. If the bark were very thick, they split it into two sheets.

Soon they announced that the "canoe" was ready. It measured about six feet by four feet, and must have been two feet thick. I boarded, finding it both stable and dry, and off we went. Rosemary pushed from the stern, and Yenna acted as pilot, minesweeper, and tug when we got stuck. Our progress was slow, for they frequently cut more paperbark to lay on top, while underwater snags and attempts to squeeze between two closely spaced paperbark trees brought us to complete stops, as did the egg collecting.

"Koraka! Koraka!" (eggs, eggs) one would shout, and off both would go splashing through the water. Reaching the tree, they would hug it with their arms and knees, and shinny up to the nest.[4] The birds' eggs were not to be eaten, for they said, "We will take them back and by and by they get big."

The billabong was full of large purple and white water lilies, which the girls collected for our expedition table. Yenna would break the flower off close to the bottom of the stalk and then, using her teeth, cut it to fit our tin-can vases. Both girls then munched on the remainder of celery-like stalk. Occasionally they plucked up the entire plant and saved the bulbs to take home to cook. If they found a small lily, they stripped the flower of all but the base, which they ate. Sometimes they used the stem as a straw for drinking the billabong water. Rosemary added a "whistle" to our ship's equipment by sucking on a blade of swamp grass.

[4] While girls and women use their knees against the tree, boys and men place the soles of their feet against the bark, to climb trees of small diameter. Other methods are used by both sexes to climb large trees, and they will be described later (see p. 162).

As the afternoon wore on, the evening chill descended and the two girls boarded the raft. The sticks they used as paddles were quite rotten from lying in the water, and they had to be replaced frequently, but we made slow progress. The girls used the sticks in the same variety of strokes as they used with real paddles in real canoes.

Many days later someone mentioned that large crocodiles are quite apt to sleep in the Banjo Beach billabong, and I marveled at the extent of the parents' belief in experience being the best teacher. I asked the girls if they had known about the crocodiles. "Oh, yes," they said, "that's why we get on canoe. When no more sun, can't see crocodile."

Many social situations are subjects for play-acting by the young children.[5] These include mock fights using pandanus fronds for spears, which cause realistic casualties, or various aspects of a ceremony. Once while waiting for a dance to begin, the children split into two groups. The group who was for this occasion arriving in a strange country for a funeral went into the bush. From the bush they sang out, "Oh, oh, oh," and an answering call was heard from the home group. Then the ones at home shouted out the name of the person who had died. Because the children used names of living members of the camp who were watching them, the adults were highly amused. The visiting group then slowly approached. When the two groups finally met, they fell on each others' shoulders and wailed loudly together for some time. Then the groups switched roles, and the wails abruptly changed to laughter as they reformed and repeated the performance, "killing" off another adult in the process.

Often children may be seen practicing dance steps, either singly or in groups. They also sing, often choosing love songs that they have picked up by listening to the camp's young women. Each of these songs belongs to the woman who composed it, and no other woman is supposed to sing it; however,

[5] See Goodale 1960a for fuller description of this, as well as some other aspects of Tiwi child life.

when the children sing these songs of legal and illegal love in their high-pitched and carrying voices, the response is amusement, not a reprimand.

A few of the children know string games, but aside from a brief period when I asked for them, I saw that form of play only once in eight months of investigation. The children said that everyone could do them: men, women, boys, and girls, but that girls could do them best. The string figures depicted myths and stories of lightning, moon, wallaby, fish, boat, canoe, crocodile, snake, spirits of the dead, and other forest spirits, to mention only a few. The myths that went with the figures were not always the same as those collected by Mountford and myself from the adults, but this is probably due to the natural distortion of children. It also appears that the stories are not being passed on to the children today as an important part of their education. Some children knew none of them, others only a few of the more important ones, and only one girl, Happy, was able to go on for several hours. The children also amuse themselves by making a variety of animal tracks in the sand with their fingers and hands.

The island children have absorbed all play items, forms, and songs from Western culture that they have been able to learn. In 1954 it was not an uncommon sight to see a gang of children coming down the road bouncing a soccer ball or skipping rope and singing, "The old gray mare he ain't what he usta be."

Participation in an important activity begins at this time. At intervals during their as yet short lives, the *kitjiŋa,* her brothers, and sisters have acted as observers at various ceremonies. As we have seen, they have acted out certain ceremonial roles in their play. Now they are encouraged to participate actively, particularly in the dancing. The *kitjiŋa* joins the dancing at a slightly earlier age than her brother, for she can join the women's chorus line where the steps are fairly simple and require less practice than do the other forms of dancing. Sometimes she is persuaded to do a solo. One of the most engaging sights I witnessed was a young *kitjiŋa* doing her first solo. She had to be persuaded for quite some time, but when she finally entered the ring, she executed the dance with precision and dignity, encouraged by clapping and singing from the entire adult group on the sidelines. When the dance was over with the final "Poop!" her dignity collapsed, and she rushed crying with embarrassment into her proud mother's arms.

CHAPTER THREE

Aliŋa and *Muriŋaleta*

The transition from *kitjiŋa* to *aliŋa* is not marked by any ceremony. There is no definite physiological change, nor any immediate change in social role. But at some time *during* this period the young prepubescent *aliŋa* makes an important change in interpersonal relationships. One night her father takes her to another fire in the camp and tells her, "You sleep here. This is your husband."

Thus, part of a marriage contract, arranged many years before at the time the young girl's mother herself reached puberty, is now carried out by the delivery of the *aliŋa* to her promised husband. Ever since the contract was made the young girl's husband has been fulfilling his half of the contract, and as this has involved his continual support of his mother-in-law, he has become either a permanent member of his father-in-law's camp or a frequent visitor. If the *aliŋa*'s husband has had other mother-in-law obligations elsewhere, he may defer his change of residence until his presently con-

43

sidered mother-in-law is in a position to carry out her half of
the contract. He must, however, be resident in his mother-
in-law's camp when he receives her daughter as an *aliŋa*-wife
and for many years afterward, ideally until his mother-in-law
dies.

The nature of this marriage contract—who it involves,
what it entails—need not concern us here, for it is a *fait
accompli* as far as the *aliŋa*-wife is concerned. Discussion of
marriage contracts will be deferred until our *aliŋa* herself
reaches puberty and becomes a *muriŋaleta* (pp. 44-57).

The young wife and her husband call each other *imbuneiŋa*
(wife) and *imbunei* (husband). They also use these terms to
refer to certain other people, who may or may not become
their actual marriage partners at a later date. However, there
are two statements that all my women informants used to
describe and distinguish their first husbands, the men to
whom they were married as an *aliŋa*. The statements, "He took
me like a daughter" and "He grew me up," are revealing of
the nature of the relationship of a prepubescent wife and her
husband, and we shall consider each statement in turn.

Although full discussion of relative ages of husbands and
wives is deferred until later (pp. 62-68), it is an inevitable
result of the contract that a girl's first husband is many years
older than she, certainly as old as her mother and quite likely
as old as her father as well. But it is not this age equivalence
of her husband and father alone that is implied in the statement, "He took me like a daughter," but rather a reflection
of the roles assumed by the young wife and elderly husband.

Essentially, the only real change in interpersonal relationships for the young girl-wife is that she now owes first alle-
giance to her husband and not to her parents. She accompanies him, or his other wives, in hunting and collecting
trips, and shares what food she obtains with them. She col-
lects water and firewood for his fires. Her economic education
continues, but her husband or his wives teach her, and not
her parents. If her husband has other wives, the *aliŋa* is under

the dominance of his first (and usually the oldest) wife, who is called *taramaguti* (a status term). The *taramaguti* can sit all day with her husband and send the other wives out to do the food collecting, I was told. She can relegate baby-sitting duties, and quite often this lot falls to the young *aliŋa*-wife. When the young wife has a child of her own, the *taramaguti* will tell her how to raise it. So while her husband assumes a "father's" role, at least initially, the *taramaguti,* the oldest co-wife, assumes a "mother's" role.

Because there is no change in camp residence, the young *aliŋa*-wife is still surrounded by those with whom she has always lived. Her adjustment to her husband and his treatment of her are under the eyes of her parents, and should any real difficulty arise her father has the *right* to take her away from her husband and give her to someone else, even though in fact her father had nothing to do with the initial contract. This right continues throughout her father's lifetime, and when he dies her brothers inherit the right—and indeed the duty—to look after their sister's marital welfare.

The second statement describing the relationship of a husband to an *aliŋa*-wife, "He grew me up," means not only that he took care of her while she grew up, but more significantly, "He made me a woman." Soon after the *aliŋa* moves to her husband's fire he begins her sexual instruction. From all accounts this appears to be a very gradual process. He begins by deflowering her with his finger, and perhaps only after a year does he have actual intercourse with her. Sexual intercourse is considered by the Tiwi to be the direct and only cause of breast formation, growth of pubic and axillary hair, menarche, and subsequent menstrual periods. Only the husband has the right to copulate with the young wife, and it is not common that a girl will form extramarital relationships before her puberty.

A husband could, if he wished, designate his young *aliŋa*-wife as a *niŋyka*-wife at the time he received her from her parents. A *niŋyka*-wife must never talk to any other man, or talk in a loud voice to anyone. She must not gather food alone or in the company of other women, but only with her husband. When out in the bush with her husband, she must walk behind him with her head cast downward and her hand on his shoulder for guidance. When she wishes to drink from a water hole, she must follow her husband into the water with her head bowed and wait until he drinks. She may not smoke, nor eat any food other than that given to her by her husband or her real parents. She must do what her husband tells her to do. She must sleep with her husband and (obviously) with no one else. If she does have intercourse with someone else, she is no longer a *niŋyka*.

The custom of making one wife a *niŋyka* (it is physically impossible to have two at the same time) is rather difficult to analyze today. All my Snake Bay female informants were emphatic in their denial that any of them were at that time or had ever been made a *niŋyka*, and they were positive that they would never have liked the life of a *niŋyka*. However, they admitted that some women might prefer this status, and they looked at all the young married and virtuous mission girls as being *niŋyka*-wives to their husbands. The men I consulted were, to a man, noncommital on the subject. There was one old couple in their seventies and eighties of whom, it was said, neither had ever had another spouse or lover. The woman was not a *niŋyka*, but as she had never looked at another man, she was, they said, "like *niŋyka*."

Unfortunately, I did not collect the mythological story for the beginning of this custom beyond the fact that it happened after Purakapali's death, an important date in the mythological past. The story of this death will come up again in another context, but it is interesting to note here that Purakapali killed himself after his wife left their son to die unattended in the hot sun while she had an affair in the bush with Tjapara, the moon. The problem of extramarital affairs has been with the Tiwi since almost the beginning of time, and the *niŋyka* custom may have begun and continued as an attempt to curb the extramarital affairs of at least one of an old man's wives. However, a husband cannot "punish" a roving wife by making her a *niŋyka,* for only an *aliŋa*-wife (a virgin) can be designated as a *niŋyka,* and the husband must do so when she is first received from her parents. The custom is perhaps connected with the prestige a man achieves when he receives an *aliŋa*-wife, who for many reasons is rarely if ever his first or only wife.

Muriŋaleta: Puberty

> I first married to Black Joe when I small girl. He grew me up. He made me woman with his finger. One day I think I'm woman. I little bit shamed. I go bush all alone. I sit down. Nanny Goat Jenny follow me up. Look about. Find me. She say, "You *muriŋaleta?*" I no say. Five times she say it. By and by I say "Yes." She cry, cry. Make me cry. She get pandanus and kill me on arms and back. She make tight rings on my arms, ala same *pukamani* (mourning). Can't touch food or drink. Might be by and by swell up. One week stay in bush. Someone tell Black Joe, "Rosie *muriŋaleta!*" Everyone happy. Paint up. Get girl-spear and hold it in front. Can't look at husband. He come up behind and kill me with *tokwiiŋa* (feather ball). Then I run. Kneel by tree. Husband grab me on shoulder. Tree marked over head. *Ambrinua* (son-in-law) get spear. Can't talk husband rest of day.

This week is perhaps the most important period in a woman's life. She has become a woman, and she has become a mother-in-law. The importance of these two events is marked by a series of customs involving a strict set of taboos and rituals. During this week she is also firmly established in her own marital interrelationships with not only her present husband but future husbands as well: she receives, ceremonially and ideally, marriage insurance to carry her through her lifetime.

From a theoretical point of view, this ceremony, particularly those aspects concerning her becoming a mother-in-law, explains much concerning the dynamics of Tiwi social organization. I shall describe this ceremony as it was described to me, for unfortunately I did not observe it, although it was still being held at Snake Bay in 1962. I shall also discuss the nature of the marriage contract that is made at this time and relate it to additional contracts that may succeed it, and in so doing I shall discuss the structural aspects of the marital relationship over the life span of an individual woman.

In the next chapter I depart from the central theme of the individual woman, in order to discuss fully the marriage system both analytically and quantitatively. Only after such a discussion can the question, "Who is selected as a first husband for an *aliŋa?*" and its corollary, "Who is selected as a *muriŋaleta*'s son-in-law?" be answered.

The Menstrual Taboos

During her first menstrual period the *muriŋaleta* is removed from the general camp and makes a new camp in the bush with a number of other women. Her companions usually include her mother, her co-wives, and any other senior women in her residential group. No men are allowed in this camp.

The *muriŋaleta* and her female companions remain in the bush camp for five to ten days. During this time the *muriŋaleta* cannot dig yams, or gather or cook any food. Nor may she touch any food with her hands, but must either use a stick or have someone place the food in her mouth, for if she did any of these things, she would "by and by swell up." She cannot touch any water, even in a container, but must wait for someone to lift the container to her lips, for otherwise she would fall ill. She cannot scratch herself with her fingers, but must use a stick, because later her arm might break. She cannot make a fire, for the flames might singe her arm and cause it to break at some future time. Breaking a stick in two is taboo, for it would cause her legs to break.

She cannot look at bodies of salt or fresh water, for the *maritji* might be angered and come and kill her. The *maritji* are spirit beings who have a body like a goanna or "quiet" crocodile. There are many of these spirits, men, women, and children, and they come in many colors. Their *imunka* (souls) are like rainbows. A big rainbow is likely to be the *imunka* of a woman and child *maritji*. The *maritji* are to be treated carefully, for they can kill a person or they can cause a great "sea" to rise up and destroy the land. They live in swamps at various localities throughout the two islands, and generally, if treated with respect and caution, will not harm the local inhabitants. Menstruating and pregnant women and new-born infants, however, are considered to be very vulnerable to the dangers of the *maritji,* and, therefore, must take extra precautions and completely avoid the homes of the *maritji.*

Lastly, the new *muriŋaleta* must not leave the bush camp, nor may she talk in a loud voice, but only in a whisper. If her husband accidentally saw her or heard her voice, he would fall ill. I was told that in the old days the *muriŋaleta*'s husband would die if he saw or heard his wife at this time; but perhaps it is harder to avoid such encounters today in the settlement pattern of residence.

These taboos apply only to the first period of menses. The next month she is taken only a short distance away from her husband, but not out of the camp proper, and she is subject to none of the foregoing restrictions. However, she may not renew sexual relations with her husband until after her fourth menstrual period. The third month she stays with her husband, but sleeps on the opposite side of the fire, as she will do every other menstrual period. If they slept together her husband's eyes would be weak in battle. After the fourth menstrual period she is no longer considered a *muriŋaleta.* Until she becomes pregnant she is a *murukubara.*

Although the strict taboos imposed during the first menstrual period no longer apply, a woman must observe several lesser precautions during her monthly periods. The *maritji* spirits are still something of a problem, and during these times the woman will not go near a small water hole or well, for it might dry up. However, it is all right to approach a large billabong or fresh-water creek. She must avoid a long canoe trip over wide expanses of salt water for fear that the *maritji* will be angry and cause a big wind to blow. She may not eat any food that a dog has caught or touched, because "next time a stick would lodge in her throat." If she happens to step over a turtle spear or rope, or over a bundle of throwing sticks, the spear or throwing sticks will not go straight. Fish spears were not mentioned, but the belief would probably also apply to them.

The *Muriŋaleta* Rituals

When a girl's menstrual flow has ceased, her female companions in the bush camp paint a red stripe down the front of her body, symbolizing, they said, a snake. The women then lead the *muriŋaleta* to a second bush camp where her father, her husband, and her husband's brothers are waiting for her. Waiting there too may be a man who has been selected by her father to become her son-in-law.

When she first arrives she "sleeps" for a little while under a blanket. As she lies on the ground her father takes an *arawunigiri,* an elaborately carved ceremonial spear with barbs on two sides,. and places it between his daughter's legs. He then presents it to the man whom he has selected to be his daughter's son-in-law. The son-in-law calls the spear "wife" and "hugs it just like a wife," I was told. If the son-in-law is not present at this time, the girl's father takes the spear to him sometime after the ensuing rituals. The young girl has by this particular ritual become a mother-in-law.

After the girl's father has presented the spear, he takes what my informants called a palm tree and sets it upright in the ground. The girl's husband and his brothers line up, with the youngest first in line and her husband last. One by one these men take their *tokwiiŋa* (feather balls) and strike the girl's shoulders. She stands there until it is her husband's turn, when she runs away. (My informants all said they had run slowly!) The husband pursues his wife, and everyone calls out to her, "Look behind you, him your husband." The girl looks back, and her husband catches her by one shoulder and takes her to the "palm" tree that her father had set upright, where he makes her sit down. Then he and his brothers take up spears and throw them at the tree, and while doing so they "pretend it is a boy or girl." I was told that none of the men hit the tree with their spears; whether they missed intentionally or whether, specifically in my informants' cases, their husbands and their brothers were poor shots, I do not know.

The husband and his brothers now dance around the sitting girl, and her father comes and lies down on the opposite side of the tree from his daughter. Her husband then marks the tree with a few strokes of an ax. The marked tree is thereafter known as *aplimeti* (translation unknown). The women bring water to wash the girl, and then they repaint her and place feathered pandanus arm ornaments on her. When her redecoration is complete, her father takes her back to the main camp, followed by all the ritual participants, and he once again hands her over to her husband at his campfire. The girl and her husband may not talk to each other upon their return, and that night she must sleep on the opposite side of the fire from him. The next morning the husband paints his young wife, and they may again talk to each other.

It is this final part of the *muriŋaleta* ceremonies that I have previously called a girl's ceremonial marriage insurance. It is significant that not only does her husband take part but also his younger brothers, for should the husband die, one of his brothers has first rights to take his widow (or widows) as wife with no further ceremony than washing off her mourning paint at the conclusion of her previous husband's funeral ceremony.

It is unfortunate that I did not observe a *muriŋaleta* ceremony because there is much in this ceremony in need of the kind of explanation that can only be obtained by questioning informants at the time of the event. This ceremony was still performed at Snake Bay in 1962, and my informants, both in 1954 and 1962, confirmed the essential sequence of events, and most importantly, who did what in relation to the girl as a wife, a potential wife, a mother-in-law, and a daughter.

The *Ambrinua* Relationship

The kinship term *ambrinua* is a reciprocal term of reference used by both a mother-in-law and son-in-law when speaking of each other. It is taboo for them to address each other directly.

Upon receiving the ceremonial spear from his mother-in-law's father at the time of her *muriŋaleta* (puberty) rituals, the new son-in-law and his young mother-in-law begin one of the most important and enduring social relationships that either may have. The spear, which the son-in-law calls "wife," is a visible symbol of the contract of marriage that now exists between the holder of the spear and his mother-in-law's future daughters, whom he will receive as each becomes an *aliŋa*. In return for this promise of future *aliŋa*-wives, the son-in-law accepts the responsibility of "feeding" his *ambrinua* from this time on until his or her death. The word "feeding" has been put in quotation marks, for it means much more than just supplying her with food. He must supply her with all she demands in service or goods, including today clothes, tobacco, money, and the like. If he is lucky to have a mother-in-law who gives him two or more wives, the payments do not increase, for the simple reason that there is initially no limit to what he must do for his *ambrinua* in return for only one daughter. He has initially and finally contracted for all of his *ambrinua*'s daughters, but his responsibilities do not end even when he has received all of her daughters; they end only with her death. It is therefore the *ambrinua* relationship that lies behind the ideal of a son-in-law's residence in his *ambrinua*'s camp, both before his wife's birth and for a considerable period after she has been delivered to him.

The *ambrinua* relationship also accounts for the significant

age difference between an *aliŋa*-wife and her first husband. The *ambrinua* relationship first entered into by a woman requires that the son-in-law not only must be alive when his *ambrinua* reaches puberty, but that he be of an age to assume his economic responsibilities to her. He is therefore a man not younger than his youthful mother-in-law and is in fact often ten or more years older. His mother-in-law may not fulfill her half of the contract for many years, but even if she should produce a daughter within one year or two of the start of the contract, he will be at least fifteen years older than his promised wife. At the other extreme, he may be dead before his wife is born if he was considerably older than his *ambrinua* when he entered into the contract.

In my previous analyses of Tiwi marriage contracts (Goodale 1959a, 1962), I have designated the contract initiated at the time of a mother-in-law's puberty ceremony as a Type A contract. Because every Tiwi woman's first marriage is arranged for by a Type A contract, and because it does not vary as to the principals of the contract (who has rights to make the contract, who may alter the contract, and under what conditions), I have considered it to be the basic contract underlying the entire Tiwi marriage system. It is also, not entirely incidentally, the most prestigious and preferred type of marriage contract a man can enter into. However, some men may never participate in a Type A contract, and it rarely results in any man's first marriage.

Hart and Pilling (1960) have discussed Tiwi marriage contracts from the point of view of the men, for whom acquisition of plural wives was (in the past) a dominant goal in their striving for prestige. And Hart (1930b:282) expressed the view that the significant age difference between husband and wife reflected the dominance of the old men in the marriage contract business. It is indeed the old men who control the distribution of women as wives, but it is evident that both Hart and Pilling, working in the Mission Settlement with male informants, missed the importance of the

Type A contract, which is even more fundamentally the
effective cause of the age discrepancy. Pilling (1957:195) says
that although some of the elderly informants talked about
promising their daughters, this practice had in fact died out
at the mission beginning around 1916. As I shall discuss
presently, the type of contract by which a father arranges the
marriage of his daughter (Type B), is considered by the Tiwi
to be a secondary contract that a father can make only if his
daughter's Type A contract has expired. The Snake Bay
situation appears to be quite different, for not only are some
men making Type B contracts for their daughters' secondary
marriages, but they are still making the Type A contracts for
their daughters' sons-in-law. More importantly, the intervening types of marriage contracts A2 and A3, derived from the
Type A, appear to be the most common contracts for a
woman's secondary marriage.

Types of Marriage Contracts

Before presenting the quantitative data relative to Tiwi
marriages and age discrepancy, I will summarize the various
types of contracts that may be entered into.

A Type A contract involves four principal individuals,
three of whom are alive when the contract is made—the
young mother-in-law, her father, and her son-in-law.[1] The
contract is arranged between a father and his daughter's son-
in-law, but the carrying out of the terms of the contract is the
duty of the two *ambrinua*. Except for death or barrenness of
the mother-in-law, or death or dereliction in duty of the son-
in-law, which will void the contract, a Type A contract will
result in a marriage of a prepubescent girl to a man considerably older than she. Because of this age difference, it is rare
for a woman to die before her first husband. If the bride has
gone through her puberty ceremony before her husband's
death, her husband's brothers, by participating in her puberty

---

[1] The identity of son-in-law in kinship terminology cannot be made clear
until the discussion of the contracts and social organization is complete.

ritual, have already entered into a marriage contract with their brother's widow, a contract that is merely a derivative of their brother's original Type A contract. No new contract is made; one of the brothers merely picks up where his brother left off, taking up the duty of feeding his new wife's mother with the expectation of receiving any other daughters his mother-in-law may produce. The age difference between a second husband and his brother's widow may be less than that found in her first marriage. I have called this type of secondary marriage Type A2, for with the exception of the husband/son-in-law, the other principals to the original contract remain the same.

Type A3 remarriage is also a derivative of the initial Type A contract. In this type of secondary marriage contract the four original principals remain involved, but the husband, having acquired a wife from his mother-in-law, gives his wife to another man. Here a new contract is involved, with the husband arranging the new husband-wife relationship as well as the new son-in-law–mother-in-law relationship. However, the original Type A contract remains in force in regard to future distribution of the *ambrinua*'s other daughters. This type of contract is common today at Snake Bay as an agreeable compromise solution to the present situation, where pressures against polygamy have increased and reasons for polygamy have decreased. I do not believe, however, that this is an entirely new type of contract, but that occasionally in the past a husband might distribute a wife or two to another man in this fashion. In some cases this may have been, in the past as it is today, to a man closer in age to the wife.

Hart and Pilling (1960:16) in their discussion of Tiwi marriage emphasize the role that the father of the bride plays in arranging his daughter's marriages, but they state that he "was seldom an entirely free agent . . . [as] . . . he was also caught in an intricate network of previous commitments, residual interests, and contingent promises made by other men who had some prior interest in the baby or the mother of

the baby." These commitments, promises, and residual interests are all contained in the Type A contract and its exten-
sions. But it does happen that a Type A contract can become
void in its entirety.

The elderly holder of a Type A contract may die before his
bride reaches puberty and therefore before his brothers have
ritually contracted the Type A2 contract. Or if the husband
does not serve his mother-in-law to her satisfaction, she may
void the contract. A girl's father does not have the right to
void such a contract, but should the girl's mother void the
contract he does have the right to make a new marriage
contract for his wife's daughter.[2] A father-arranged contract
for a daughter's marriage is always a secondary contract, and
because it does not necessarily relate to the original Type A
contract, I have called it a Type B contract. This type of
marriage contract may vary considerably from the accepted
principles of marriage exchange, as I shall discuss later
(pp. 125-26).

Once a woman's mother has died, she no longer has any
"fathers" to arrange succeeding marriage contracts should she
find herself a widow. In this case there are several possible
solutions, which may give rise to considerable debate among
the males involved. Her Type B husband may have "given"
his wives to a younger brother before he died (a Type B2
contract), or her own brothers, inheriting from their father
the duty to look after their sister's marital welfare, may
arrange the next contract, a Type C contract.

And finally, if a woman should outlive her brothers and
become a widow again, her sons have inherited the duty to
look after her welfare and nominally have the right to arrange
their mother's remarriage. Although I have no cases of this
Type D contract, I suspect, and Hart and Pilling (1960:53)
seem to agree, that it was the mother who did the actual

---

[2] A father always has the right to take a daughter away from any of her
husbands (including a Type A husband) if she is mistreated. He then has
the right and duty to arrange a new marriage for her.

arranging. Since all contracts involve an exchange, the arranger getting a wife in return, mothers anxious for their sons' advance might agree to exchange sons!

The last type of marriage, Type E, is one arranged by the bride and groom themselves, who defy custom and contract and elope! This happened occasionally in the past, but rarely had any great effect on the ultimate marriage exchange system, for the elopers were usually pursued by the offended contract makers, who often killed the groom or even both parties. Today, at Snake Bay many girls marry boys of their own choice, but the majority of these marriages are of the Type A3, in which the first husband actually gives his wife willingly to a groom of her choice. I do not know what the current situation is at the mission, but if as I suspect the girl's puberty ceremony is no longer being held, the marriages are most likely to be Type B, father "consented," or Type E, arranged by the young couple themselves. In spite of this fact, it is interesting to note the high degree of adherence to the exchange pattern of marriage between kin and local groups that is still evident in the mission census data (see pp. 104-6).

Quantitative Analysis of Plural and Serial Marriages and the Age Difference Between Husbands and Wives

Although plural marriages have lost much of their prestige value for Tiwi men, a number of men at Snake Bay and some affiliated with the Bathurst Mission have more than one wife living with them today. Tiwi men have, however, always evaluated their wife-wealth in terms of how many contracts they have made for wives rather than the number of living, delivered, coresident wives. In the table of marriage rates of Tiwi males (Table 9), I have followed this custom by counting unborn and deceased wives as well as living ex-wives along with the coresident wives. True, this may inflate the incidence of polygamy among the Tiwi, as it is usually regarded by recorders, but it does no damage to the Tiwi concept of polygamy, and thus I believe presents a more meaning-

TABLE 9

NUMBER OF MARRIAGE CONTRACTS FOR TIWI MALES

Men's Age Group	B†/S†	No. of Men	Un-Married	Percent	Number of Wives							No. Polygamous	Percent	Married Men	No. of Wives	Avg. No. of Wives per Man
					1	Percent	2	3	4	5	10					
1-9 years	B	26	26	100.0												
	S	3	3	100.0												
Subtotal		29	29	100.0												
10-19	B	56	49	87.5	7	12.5								7	7	1.00
	S	12	10	83.3	1*	8.3	1*					1	8.3	2	4	2.00
Subtotal		68	59	86.8	8	11.7	1					1	1.4	9	11	1.22
20-29	B	62	10	16.1	50*	81.6	2					2	3.2	52	54	1.04
	S	6			4	66.6	2*					2	33.3	6	8	1.33
Subtotal		68	10	16.1	54	79.7	4					4	5.9	58	62	1.07
30-39	B	68	10	16.1	56*	82.4	1	1				2	3.0	58	61	1.05
	S	15	2	13.3	8*	53.3	3*	1*	1*			5	33.3	13	21	1.61
Subtotal		83	12	14.4	64	78.3	4	2	1			7	8.4	71	82	1.15
40-49	B	51	3	5.9	43	84.3	3	1	1			5	9.8	48	56	1.17
	S	13			1	7.7	6*	3*	1*			10	77.0	13	24	1.85
Subtotal		64	3	5.9	44	65.0	9	4	2			15	23.4	61	80	1.31
50-59	B	35	3	8.6	23*	65.7	8		1			9	25.7	32	43	1.38
	S	15	1	6.6	7	46.6	2*	3*	1	1*		7	46.6	14	29	2.07
Subtotal		50	4	8.0	30	60.0	10	3	2	1		16	32.0	46	72	1.56
60-69	B	27	3	11.1	10	37.0	7	3*	1		1	14	51.9	24	57	2.38
	S	8	2	25.0	2	25.0	3*		1	2		4	50.0	6	12	2.00
Subtotal		35	5	14.3	12	34.2	10	3	2	2	1	18	51.4	30	69	2.30
70-79	B	3			1	33.3	2	1				2	66.6	3	5	1.66
	S	6			2	33.3	2*	1	1			4	66.6	6	13	2.18
Subtotal		9			3	33.3	4	1	1			6	66.6	9	18	2.00
Total		404	122	30.0	215	53.0	42	13	8	3	1	67	19.2	284	394	1.38

* Undelivered wife (wives).
† B = Pathurst; S = Snake Bay.

ful picture of marriage patterns. My information concerning contracts of marriage among Snake Bay men is reasonably accurate; but that for the mission population is derived from the census record alone. Although I was able to add some information by cross-checking for men and women who have children in common but who are not now officially married to each other, I am well aware that, at best, my Bathurst figures are probably only one-half to two-thirds accurate. I have therefore presented the data from the two settlements separately in the tables.

Estimating the ages of adult Tiwi is a difficult task, particularly when one does not have the complete genealogies. In Table 9, I have, therefore, grouped individuals by the decade of estimated date of birth; and in Tables 10-13 I have taken a date midway in this decade for calculating the average age of those born within the decade. In certain of the Snake Bay cases, I have altered the official census to conform to my genealogical data and additional information. However, all the age information and analysis should be considered a rough approximation of the truth, at best.

As might be expected, the Snake Bay males of all age groups are involved in more contracts per man than the Bathurst group, but the mean number of wives per man exceeds the 2.00 figure only after a man has passed the age of fifty at Snake Bay and after the age of sixty among the mission affiliated men. We must keep in mind that the Catholic Mission of Bathurst was founded when these sixty-year-old men were ten to twenty years old, and it is only among this age group that we can reasonably expect to see evidence of a significant number of plural marriage contracts. I have indicated the incidence of Type A (promised but undelivered wives), and it will be noted that some of these are to Bathurst men. All of these wives are, or presumably will be when they are born, Snake Bay women, promised to Bathurst men by Snake Bay men.

The one incidence of "excessive polygamy" is a man with

ten recorded contracts who lives today midway between the two settlements, but is carried on the Bathurst Island census roles. His country affiliation is Uraŋgu on Bathurst Island, and he is acknowledged by my Snake Bay informants (and I believe also by Pilling's Bathurst informants) as the only living representative of the old-fashioned "big-man," a man who had "a hundred wives." Although ten is hardly a hundred, I

TABLE 10
SERIAL MARRIAGES—SNAKE BAY

Wives Age Group	"Promised"	HUSBANDS				No. of Women	No. of Husbands	Avg. No. Husbands per Woman	Widowed
		1st	2nd	3rd	4th				
Unborn M*	8					8	8	1.00	
1960 P*	1					1	1	1.00	
Subtotal						9	9	1.00	
0-9 M	2					2	2	1.00	
1950 P	4					4	4	1.00	
Subtotal						6	6	1.00	
10-19 M	2	1	2			5	7	1.40	
1940 P	4	3				7	7	1.00	
Subtotal						12	14	1.17	
20-29 M		3	5	3		11	22	2.00	
1930 P		6	2	2		10	16	1.60	1
Subtotal						21	38	1.81	
30-39 M		2	3	1	1	7	15	2.14	
1920 P		4	3	1		10	19	1.90	
Subtotal						17	34	2.00	
40-49 M		2	5	1		6	15	2.50	
1910 P		1	4	1		6	12	2.00	
Subtotal						12	27	2.25	
50-59 M			4	1		5	11	2.20	
1900 P		1	3			4	7	1.77	1
Subtotal						9	18	2.00	
60-69 M									3
1890 P			3			3	6	2.00	
Subtotal						3	6	2.00	
70-79 M		1				1	1	1.00	3
1880 P	1	1				2	3	1.50	
Subtotal						3	4	1.33	
Total	21	25	35	10	1	92	156	1.70	8

* M = monogamous marriage; P = polygamous marriage.

am quite sure he has been involved in more contracts than I have been able to trace.[3] All the information I can gather both from earlier observers and from my informants indicates that in the past some men might contract for twenty to thirty wives over their life span, but it is unlikely that at any one time this number actually coresided with him. Some were probably deceased, while others were yet unborn, some may have been subcontracted (and given away), and others may have eloped, been stolen, or remained undelivered, but the "big man" still counted them among his assets.

As a final comment on the data presented in Table 9, it will be noted that some men in the over-fifty age range are recorded as unmarried single men. Three of the Snake Bay men in this unusual state never entered into any contract for marriage (why, I do not know), and were considered by my informants to be definite exceptions to the norm.

Whereas most Tiwi men are normally involved in more than one contract of marriage, Tiwi women also normally expect to be involved as wives in a number of different types of marriage contracts because of the age discrepancy between them and their first husbands. While a woman's multiple marriages are serial rather than simultaneous, the figures in Table 10 are quite revealing.[4] Perhaps most interesting is that the mean number of husbands per woman in all age groups exceeds the mean number of wives per man in all age groups: women on the average have 1.70 husbands, while men have on the average 1.38 wives.

I have for the record divided the first marriages into two groups, those promised and those delivered, although conceptually they belong in a single group. I have also divided the figures in each age group according to whether the woman is

[3] This man is Summit, who figures in Hart and Pilling's account. He managed to acquire six wives at the age of thirty-six in 1928-29 (Hart and Pilling 1960:63).

[4] Because this type of information requires more exact knowledge of a woman's marital history than can be found in the official records, I have considered only Snake Bay women in this table.

married to a monogamous or polygamous husband, and it will be seen that those in the monogamous group tend to have more husbands than those married to polygamous husbands. I believe this reflects the attitude of the two groups of men. Polygamous men tend to hold onto their wives more than the present-day monogamous men, some of whom have a rather rapid turnover of wives.

While the figure 2.00 for mean number of wives per man is not reached until the seventh decade of a man's life, thirty to forty is the critical decade in a woman's life, when the mean number of husbands per woman reaches 2.00.

This pattern of plural marriages for men coupled with serial marriages for women has an important influence on the dynamics of Tiwi social organization, and is definitely related to the nature of the various marriage contracts. I have previously discussed the inevitable age discrepancy between a wife and her husband under a Type A contract, and suggested that under successive contracts of any type, the relative ages of wives and husbands may well become less with each successive marriage. Tables showing the relative ages of wives and husbands demonstrate this both quantitatively and diagrammatically.

In Table 11 I consider the relative ages of husbands according to the age group of their wives. I have separated the Snake Bay women from the Bathurst women, but have not considered whether the contract was a primary one or a secondary one for the woman. The average difference is found to be 9.0 years. However, the greatest age difference occurs in the first two decades, the 1960s and 1950s, with the unborn and undelivered wives in Type A contracts that are all from Snake Bay. It is far more meaningful to consider Snake Bay women alone and to separate the primary from the secondary marriages. This I have done in Tables 12 and 13.

It must be noted that I have not considered what type of contract resulted in these primary and secondary marriages. My available criteria are only that a woman has or has not had

TABLE 11
SNAKE BAY AND BATHURST, ALL MARRIAGES

Wives' Age Group	No.	1950	1940	1930	1920	1910	1900	1890	1880	1870	Average Age Husbands	Average Age Difference
0 S* B*	11		2	3	2	1	2	1				
Subtotal	11		2	3	2	1	2	1			35.3	+35.3
0-9 S B	5				2	1	1	1				
Subtotal	5				2	1	1	1			46.5	+42.0
10-19 S B	13 19		3 4	2 11	3 2	3 1	 1	2				
Subtotal	32		7	13	5	4	1	2			29.7	+15.2
27 B	4 49		10	7 4	4 15	1 6	1 3		1			
Subtotal	76			28	25	13	7	1	2		35.9	+11.4
30-39 S B	21 76			4	3 36	6 33	12 3					
Subtotal	97			4	39	39	12	3			41.9	+7.4
40-49 S B	16 33			1	4 1	5 11	5 9	1 9	3			
Subtotal	49			1	5	16	14	10	3		52.5	+8.0
50-59 S B	13 23				1 1	3 1	5 8	1 13	3			
Subtotal	26				2	4	13	14	3		58.3	+3.8
60-69 S B	4 9				1		1 3	1 5	1 1			
Subtotal	13				1		4	6	2		59.9	−4.6
70-79 S B	2 4			1		1		1	1 1	1		
Subtotal	6			1		1		1	2	1	61.0	−13.5
80-89 S B	2								1	1		
Subtotal	2								1	1	79.5	−5.5
Total	327		9	50	81	79	54	39	13	2		+9.0
Avg. Age Husbands		10-19	20-29	30-39	40-49	50-59	60-69	70-79	80-89			
Avg. Age Wives		11.0	22.5	30.0	33.0	40.8	47.2	54.4	79.5			
Avg. Age Diff.		−3.5	−2.0	−4.5	−11.5	−13.7	−17.3	−20.1	−5.0			

* S = Snake Bay;   B = Bathurst.

a previous husband. A woman who has had a previous husband is tabulated separately for each husband for whom I have information. If anything, my data are weighted on the "primary" side, for I did not include anyone in the "secondary" category for whom I did not have direct information. For instance, I am quite sure that the single representative in the eighty-to-ninety-year age group, who is shown married to a man ten years her junior in a primary marriage, must in fact be in a secondary marriage, but I have no record of a previous marriage.

Even by depressing the age difference between husbands and their unborn wives to the difference that now exists,

TABLE 12
SNAKE BAY PRIMARY MARRIAGES

Wives	No.	HUSBANDS									Average Age Husbands	Average Age Difference
		1950	1940	1930	1920	1910	1900	1890	1880	1870		
1960 Unborn	44		1	1	1		1				32.0	+32+
Infants	7		1	2	1	1	1	1			37.3	+37.3
1950 1-9 years.	5				2	1	1		1		48.5	+44.0
1940 10-19	11		2	1	3	3		2			38.1	+23.7
1930 20-29	11				3	4	3	1			46.3	+21.8
1920 30-39	9					2	7				52.2	+17.7
1910 40-49	5					2	2	1			52.3	+8.2
1900 50-59	2						1		1		64.5	+10.0
1890 60-69												
1880 70-79	2								1	1	79.5	+5.0
1870 80-89	1								1			−10.0
Total	55		4	3	10	13	16	5	4	1		+23.6

and by including in the primary group women fifty years or more (whom I suspect are really in a secondary marriage), the average age difference of wives and their primary husbands at 23.6 years is significantly above the average age difference of only 3.9 years for women in known secondary marriages.

Perhaps a more revealing way to show the relative ages of husbands as women grow older is by means of a diagram. In this diagram (Fig. 3) we can clearly see that while women are assigned to husbands before they are born, a man will not receive a contract for a wife of any type until he reaches the age of ten to twenty. At this age he may receive a wife who has been previously married, and he may also enter into a Type A contract, but his Type A wife is rarely given to him until he

TABLE 13
SNAKE BAY SECONDARY MARRIAGES

Wives	No.	Husbands									Average Age Husbands	Average Age Difference
		1950	1940	1930	1920	1910	1900	1890	1880	1870		
1950 0-9 years												
1940 10-19	2		1	1							19.5	+5.0
1930 20-29	17			4	7	4	1		1		39.2	+14.7
1920 30-39	12				3	4	5				46.2	+11.7
1910 40-49	11			1	4	3	3				41.7	−3.0
1900 50-59	11				1	3	4	1	2		54.4	−0.1
1890 60-69	4				1		1	1	1		57.0	−7.5
1880 70-79	1							1			64.5	−10.0
1870 80-89												
Total	58		1	6	16	14	14	3	4			+3.9

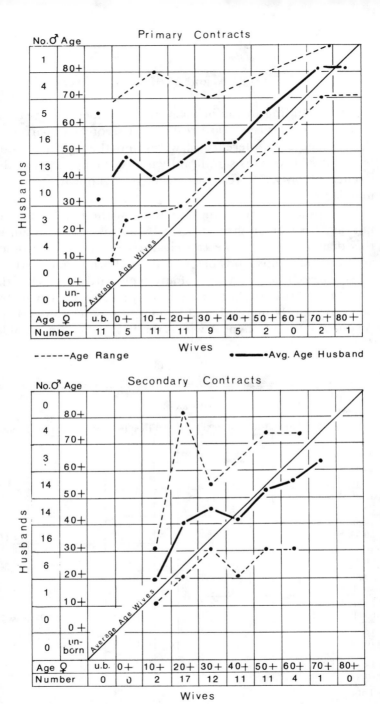

Fig. 3 Relative age of husbands as wives age

is in his thirties or forties. A man generally acquires actual wives during the period from his thirties through his fifties. This is the time when he is most apt to acquire both secondary and primary wives. It is interesting to note that my figures do not show any significant change in regard to a man's marital expectations at given ages from that determined by Hart for Tiwi men in 1928-29 (Hart and Pilling 1960:54).

The consistency of the lower range of secondary husbands below the wife's age level indicates the probability that a man's first wife will be older than he; however, the *average* age of secondary husbands does not drop below the wife's age until both husband and wife reach the age group of forty to fifty. I believe that the average age of secondary husbands reflects the prevalence of Type A2 marriage contracts in the early part of a woman's marital life.

The drop of the average age difference for primary marriages to less than twenty years difference and the drop of the lower range of primary marriages to below zero difference, when a woman reaches the age group of thirty to forty, I believe reflects only my conservative handling of the data and not any significant change in Tiwi marriage patterns. It may reflect the Type A2 or A3 contracts which, because they derive from the initial Type A, my informants were less likely to distinguish from primary marriage unless questioned specifically and directly.

In my analyses of data obtained in 1954 (Goodale 1959a, 1962), I calculated an average age difference between wives and their first husbands as being 18.9 years. The increase to 23.6 years is due to the presence of many of these women's previous husbands in my more extensive collection of genealogies in 1962. The age difference of approximately twenty years, resulting from a Type A contract, was the basis of my previous analyses of Tiwi marriage contracts, in which I suggested that this inevitable age difference was the effective cause for selecting a girl's patrilateral cross-cousin as her first husband, a choice that was preferred as well as inevitable. I reasoned that since women may be expected to have children twenty years before a man (legitimately), a "father's sister" would be expected to have a son before a "mother's brother," and thus when the Type A contract was arranged a "father's sister's son" would be the only available cross-cousin in the correct age group. With my increased census and genealogical data obtained in 1962, I find that the situation, while basically correct, is quite a bit more complicated. In the next chapter I will discuss the various factors that are taken into consideration when a husband is chosen for a Tiwi woman in Type A and succeeding contracts.

CHAPTER FOUR

Tiwi Social Structure and Marriage

The criteria by which social anthropologists separate the aggregates of individuals that they consider significant units of social structure from those they do not consider significant have been variously enumerated and endlessly discussed. My desire in this discussion is to describe the organization of Tiwi society in such a way that both the structure and the dynamics of the society may be appreciated by all who may read my description, including members of the described society. Although I will make no comparisons with other societies, I have attempted to be precise in description and in choice and definition of terminology, so that valid comparisons are possible.

My emphasis shall be on the cultural principles by which I feel Tiwi sort themselves into significant social groups. There are a number of different cultural principles that the Tiwi recognize as primary bases for the formation of social groups— for example, descent, residence, ownership of property, and so forth. Some units, however, are based on a combination of two different cultural principles, such as the domestic unit. In the discussion, I have called social units that are based on a single or double cultural principle a *type* of social unit, each type further distinguished by reference to the underlying common cultural principle—matrilineal units, patrilineal units, landowning units, domestic units, and the like.

Some *types* of Tiwi social units are actually aggregates of subunits, each with a distinguishing refinement of the common basic cultural principle by which the Tiwi identify themselves and others according to the *kind* of subunit membership or affiliation they wish to recognize in a given activity. For example, within the matrilineal *type* of social unit, each matrilineal unit is subdivided into four and possibly five *kinds* of subunits. An individual with membership in a matrilineal unit will identify himself as a member of all of the kinds of subunits. The four or five kinds of subunits are ranked by degree of exclusiveness of membership determined by the degree of refinement of the common matrilineal principle.

The rights, duties, privileges, and obligations that accrue to the members of Tiwi society are culturally defined according to both the *type* unit and *kind* of subunit, so that for any given individual there is a rough *scale of preference* with regard to both type and kind of unit within which he should operate for any given activity. I shall examine the various types and kinds of Tiwi social units, with particular attention to their relative importance in providing their members with options and limitations of choice, and with preferential guidelines in the exchange of women for the purpose of contractual marriage. Their importance in other activities will be discussed in succeeding chapters.

The Matrilineal Type

Every Tiwi is automatically assigned to his or her mother's matrilineal descent group at birth. Actually, the Tiwi belief system assigns individuals *before* birth to a particular matrilineal descent group to which the infant's mother also belongs, but discussion of this belief and its relation to the social organization is best considered in detail later (see pp. 139-43). The greatest number of kinds of subunits may be distinguished within these matrilineal groups. I shall begin my discussion with the kind of subunit that is the most exclusive because it applies the most restrictive refinement of the matrilineal principle.

The Matrilineal Sibling Set

The matrilineal sibling set is a social unit composed of siblings. It does not, however, include all individuals who may use the sibling terminology in reference to each other, but is restricted to those siblings who, as the Tiwi phrase it, are "one-granny" siblings. In Tiwi pidgin "granny" refers to one's maternal grandmother, called *imaniŋa* in the kinship vernacular. The exclusiveness of the sibling set depends on the unit member's extension of the term *imaniŋa* to siblings of one's mother's mother. The data that I was able to collect on this extension are fragmentary, but most of the sibling sets of which I had detailed knowledge restricted this term to a single woman, their real mother's real mother. However, I was told that some sibling groups shared the same "granny's mother" (MMM), and called all of this woman's daughters *imaniŋa* (MM), and by this extension formed a sibling set that is less exclusive genealogically but is conceptually the same as "one-granny" sibling sets.

The Tiwi language contains no term for the matrilineal sibling set (unlike the patrilineal sibling set to be discussed later), nor are the sets known by proper names. However, reference to this kind of matrilineal subunit was made time and again as I probed into reasons for certain attitudes and behavior patterns among siblings as well as when my informants attempted to explain genealogical connections among two or more individuals. Siblings within this group were sometimes referred to as "true" siblings, "proper" siblings, or "close" siblings, but as these pidgin adjectives were also applied to siblings in another type (patrilineal) of sibling unit, they did not always discriminate satisfactorily. The two most obvious occasions that necessitated discrimination of matrilineal "one-granny" siblings were when the application of taboos between siblings of opposite sex were enforced or necessary, and when the finest distinctions in genealogical relationship between two individuals was required.

Taboos restricting certain behavior between siblings of opposite sex apply only to "one-granny" siblings and take effect for each individual shortly before puberty. Such siblings may not touch each other, nor may they talk to each other directly, but only through a third person.

Collecting accurate genealogies of the Tiwi was perhaps the most frustrating task I faced in the field. In 1954 I attributed much of my failure to get usable or useful genealogical data to the taboo on using names of deceased persons, which tended to terminate rather quickly any interview dealing with this subject, for it was considered improper even to remind someone of a deceased person. My young informant in 1962 eliminated this problem by her complete disregard of the traditional taboo. However, her inability to conceptualize "one-granny" siblings as anything but a single person presented its own difficulties to one trying to trace exact lines of descent and kinship. My informant was able to distinguish children of one mother from those of another mother within the sibling sets with which she herself was most closely affiliated or whose births she personally knew about. She would make these discriminations only when hard-pressed by her questioner, and perhaps in the next sentence would neglect the discrimination in referring to the unit in relation to another individual. Typical of the outsiders' conceptual unity of these sibling sets was the common reference to all individuals of the same sex in the set with the same kind and degree of attitude proper to the kin-type they represented. For example, when my informant said, "My mother fed me when I was small until my brother was born, but often my mother beat me so hard I ran away. But Polly, that's my mother, would come after me and bring me back," I found it unwise and invalid to assume that my informant was referring to any specific number of "mothers" within a single "one-granny" sibling set. Even in cases where my informant knew that I knew the exact genealogical relationship between her and her real mother and her mother's "one-granny" sisters, she rarely made discrimination unless I demanded it. In the specific instance quoted above, I found that she was referring to three "mothers," only one of whom was named "Polly."

The further away from one of these sibling sets the informant is genealogically, the less he or she is able to discriminate within it even on demand. I am fairly certain that it is completely unnecessary for Tiwi to make such discrimination, which is one that they not only do not, but also cannot, ordinarily conceptualize. They do, however, discriminate *between* sibling sets containing similar kin-types when such discrimination is considered necessary to the consideration or explanation of interpersonal behavior.

The reality of this "one-granny" sibling set as the most exclusive and therefore the most consciously loyal and cohesive of all kinds of matrilineal subunits can be brought into focus by relating it to the type of domestic unit that I shall consider typical and into which members of a matrilineal sibling set are born. We need only to reconsider the relationship *(ambrinua)* between mother-in-law and son-in-law, and the influence that this relationship has on the composition of a typical domestic unit. Such a group is diagrammed in Figure 4, which shows a domestic group at a point in time when the mother-in-law has produced a number of daughters, all of whom have been handed over to her coresident son-in-law, and who themselves have given birth to a number of children. We have at the base of the pyramid a group of individuals who grow up in close proximity to each other in the same camp and whose mothers are all married to the same man at any given time. The mothers of the basal sibling set are themselves members of another "one-granny" sibling set, and as a set usually (preferentially) move as a unit of co-wives into the domestic group of their successive and common husbands. The exceptional cohesiveness of sibling-set sisters is enforced by the intensity of their lifelong economic and social cooperation.

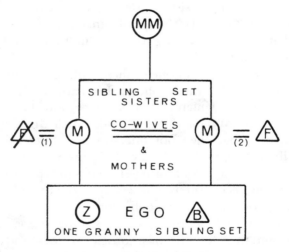

Fig. 4   Basic elements of a domestic unit

Let us now consider the domestic group of a man who has received wives from two mothers-in-law (Fig. 5). The location of this domestic group will depend on the weighting of preference given by the common son-in-law if both mothers-in-law are alive and not themselves localized as members of the same sibling set. But regardless of whether one or both mothers-in-law are resident members of the domestic group, the children of the group will belong to multiple "one-granny" sibling sets. Some of these multiple sibling sets, domiciled

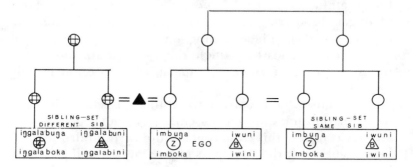

Fig. 5   Domestic unit and sibling terminology

together with a common "father," will be members of the same kind of less exclusive matrilineal subunit, the sib or phratry, but some may belong to different matrilineal groups altogether. Children of the domestic group with a common matrilineal affiliation but belonging to different "one-granny" sibling sets refer to each other with the same kin terminology they use for members of their own sibling set: *iwuni* (older brother), *iwini* (younger brother), *imbuṇa* (older sister), *imboka* (younger sister). They will not, however, observe the restrictive taboos between the sexes, and they will often make qualifying distinctions in reference to these siblings, expressing the separateness of their relationship according to the matrilineal principle. Their relationship is, however, considered a close one, according to the patrilineal concept to be discussed later. Likewise, the sibling set diagrammed in Fig. 5, who are affiliated with a different matrilineal group altogether, are comembers with the two other sibling sets in a common patrilineal sibling group and are therefore considered by the members in the two other sets as fairly close siblings. The restrictive taboos between the sexes are not observed across the sibling-set lines, and, furthermore, special

sibling terminology is used among these siblings who, although they share the same "father" and are members of the
same natal domestic group, are members of different matrilineal affiliations: *iŋgalabuni* (older brother), *iŋgalabini*
(younger brother), *iŋgalabuŋa* (older sister), *iŋgalaboka*
(younger sister). These sibling terms are never extended
beyond the bounds of a single domestic group, unlike the
terms *iwuni, iwini, imbuŋa, imboka,* which are indefinitely
extended.

All members of a matrilineal sibling set remain in close
daily relationship only during childhood, but segments of a
set may continue this close contact into their adult life. As I
have mentioned, the daughters of one mother will generally
be co-wives of the same successive men throughout their lives.
A man may contract for the daughters of two mothers who are
themselves in the same sibling set, and thus, more of a
woman's "granny" sisters will remain in the same domestic
unit as co-wives. Brothers in a matrilineal sibling set will, as
the occasion demands, be resident in different localities from
their "one-granny" siblings, but the attitudes of respect,
sibling affection, mutual responsibility, and close social
cooperation result in much interaction among sibling-set
brothers and sisters throughout their adult life.

The Matrilineal Sib[1]

The second kind of matrilineal subunit, the matrilineal
sib, is recognized by the Tiwi as the next most exclusive, after
the sibling set, in which the matrilineal principle applies.
Members of a matrilineal sib assume a common line of descent
through women of the sib. They do not and cannot trace their
exact relationship to an ancestress, and, in fact, it does not
appear to be important even to acknowledge a common
ancestress; rather, the importance lies in the assumed close
relation traced through females that members of a sib

---

[1] Hart and Pilling (1960) have designated this kind of matrilineal subunit
as a matrilineal clan.

acknowledge. A sib is also an aggregate of "one-granny" sibling sets. Loyalty, cooperation, and mutual aid may be invoked by members of a sib on either the sib or sibling-set level, depending on the circumstances. Since the feeling of group identity and loyalty is less on the sib level than on the "one-granny" level, an individual will turn to the most available kind of subunit. Because of the assumed closeness of the relationship of all members of the sib, marriage within the sib is considered incestuous and is prohibited.

Sib members are expected to help each other to the extent that they are called upon to do so, by giving food, military aid, and shelter. These obligations are particularly important when a member is geographically far removed from his other types and kinds of social units or when the occasion may call for the combined help of a number of people. In daily life other types and kinds of social units are more important to an individual than is his sib, and individuals actively conceive of themselves as a member of a sib only intermittently: when involved in marriage exchanges, when traveling through or taking up residence in a strange locality, or when a fellow sib member has died.

The ideology of kinship descent and concomitant attitude of loyalty within a sib appears to be tenuous, a result, perhaps, of the lack of regulated interaction of the entire membership at specified intervals. The operation of various exogamous marriage rules works to scatter sib members unequally throughout the two islands, but one marriage rule—that of direct exchange of women between two sibs—has a counteracting effect on sib distribution and results in the continued resupplying of a particular locality with groups of spouses of the same two sibs. These localized segments of sibs are in turn often made up of closely related "one-granny" sibling sets, but it is their more continuous interactivity as sib mates that strengthens their local sib attitudes of loyalty and cohesiveness. There are occasions of record when a local sib segment has felt it necessary to act as a unit in opposition to

the sib as a whole, and has seceded and declared itself a
separate identity as a sib in its own right. The dissident segment often assumes a new name for itself, and for a time it
will remain geographically restricted. Examples of such secession, drawn largely from Pilling (1957), will be given shortly
(pp. 91-93), but I wish to mention here in connection with
the concept of matrilineal descent that in most documented
cases secession has been instigated by the male members of
the sib, usually "one-granny" brothers, who with their sibling-
set sisters provide the nucleus of the new unit. However,
Pilling cites one case (1957:347) where members of a dance
group. composed of individuals who inherited from their
fathers the right to perform a certain dance, forsook membership in their several sibs and declared that they were now a
new matrilineal sib, the *ilitui*.

The Matrilineal Super-sibs

The third kind of subunit in which membership is derived
through the cultural principle of matrilineal descent is the
matrilineal super-sib. This unit is made up of a group of
affiliated sibs who consider themselves closely related and, for
the purposes of marriage exchange, as an exogamous unit.
Pilling (1957:62) has called this kind of unit a super-clan. In
his analysis of group conflict among the Tiwi, Pilling found
that individuals often allied themselves for purposes of
mutual support with individuals from certain sibs other than
their own. These alliances, however, never appeared to involve the total membership of the several sibs, but only certain
local segments. I found that unity of the super-sib, however,
is usually recognized by all its scattered members in connection with marriage exchange; and one sib within a super-sib
alliance may fulfill another member sib's obligation to provide
an exchange woman when that sib is unable to do so. Super-
sibs may well be formed through the process of sib segmentation, the two new-formed sibs remaining united in a different kind of unit organization which requires less in the

way of loyalty and cooperation among its members. However, some super-sib alliances appear to have been formed by two previously unrelated matrilineal sib units for purely political reasons involving either mutual defense or marriage exchange opportunities. However, once allied, they assume a common matrilineal affiliation. Whatever the causal factor leading to sib-unit affiliation, these super-sibs appear to be fairly stable, in that the alliance is usually, but not always, acknowledged by all members of the sibs involved, rather than only by those in the particular locality where the affiliation had its beginning as a unit.

The Matrilineal Phratry

The fourth kind of matrilineal subunit, like the third, is made up of affiliated sibs, or when they exist super-sibs, but the degree of unity and cohesiveness as a social group is far less than that found in the super-sib affiliations. The Tiwi call these subunit organizations *aramipi;* in the literature they have been termed phratries.

The *aramipi* maintain a fiction of common matrilineal descent as a reason for stating preference for exogamous marriage exchanges with members of other *aramipi*. It is evident from the data that continued nonobservance of the exogamous ideal does not unduly trouble the existence of *aramipi*. Individual members of the intermarrying sibs of one phratry may acknowledge the peculiarity of their relationship by qualifying their joint membership in a single unit, using the term "half-*aramipi*" in referring to each other. Over a period of time this ambiguous situation may endure, but eventually it will readjust either by resolving the factors leading to separation or by admitting "full-*aramipi*" status of each. However, a history of disunity within a phratry may lead to the formation of phratry segments, a kind of matrilineal unit structurally indistinguishable from the super-sib, which is conceptually the same in the minds of its members. Among the Tiwi one phratry does not seem to have developed semi-independent segments other than the sib kind of unit. Other phratries exhibit two, or in one case three, such super-sibs or phratry segments in their structure, which reflect variable events in the history of their development as distinctive social units.

Although I have called the *aramipi* a kind of unit formed through the application of matrilineal descent concepts, the fictional quality of the Tiwi concept of descent should be emphasized. There is evidence that some of these *aramipi* have extended membership to segments of other *aramipi,* who for one reason or another desired complete separation from their parent unit and affiliation with a new group of sibs.

The Matrilineal Moieties

The fifth and final kind of matrilineal subunit is the exogamous moiety mentioned by the Berndts (1964) and Pilling (1957), both of whom questioned mission-affiliated informants primarily if not exclusively. My Snake Bay informants did not indicate to me by word or behavior that they recognized this kind of matrilineal organization. However, when I arranged my data on marriage exchange between matrilineal units according to the proposed moiety affiliations, a patterning did appear to be present to a degree that suggested that moieties do exist at least as analytically significant social units.[2]

[2] Pilling expresses, both in his dissertation and in subsequent conversations with me, his firm belief that *his* informants did recognize the moieties as matrilineal units within which competition for wives and resulting fights and feuds should take place, although they did not always in fact do so (1957:70). One could speculate that the moieties, as an analytical feature as I found it at Snake Bay, may represent the remnants of a formerly recognized dual division, or one could explain the recognition of such a dual division by the mission informants as an example of a latent structural feature, becoming recognized under proper stimulus, whatever it may be. As a third alternative one could explain the difference in data as a result of the lack of appropriate data collection among the Snake Bay Tiwi. However, I would prefer to suggest that the dual patterning of exogamous exchanges evident today results from multiple but regular dual exchange patterns regulated by other kinds of matrilineal units, the sibs and super-sibs, and leave the question of the recognition or nonrecognition of moieties and their historical position for further investigation and clarification.

Let me now briefly summarize the five kinds of matrilineal units of social organization. In order of degree of exclusiveness in membership and sentiments of group identity, loyalty, and amount of cooperative behavior, they are:

1. The unnamed matrilineal sibling sets, or "one-granny" sets, which are too numerous to count and are the most exclusive and cohesive of the matrilineal units.

2. The named matrilineal sibs, which numbered approximately twenty-four in 1962.[3]

3. The matrilineal super-sibs or phratry segments are unnamed and are not found in all matrilineal group affiliations. I have determined seven of these units distributed in three of the four phratries.

4. The matrilineal phratries are also unnamed, but there is a relevant term *(aramipi)* in the vernacular to distinguish this kind of matrilineal unit. The number of phratries appears to vary in time and space.

5. The two matrilineal moieties are unnamed and unrecognized by the Snake Bay Tiwi, but appear to be recognized by the Bathurst Island Mission Tiwi.

The Structural Dynamics of the Matrilineal Descent Units: The Data

One of my primary goals in this book is to try to explain the variations in the published and unpublished listings of matrilineal sibs and their affiliations as phratries, moieties, or both. In Table 14 I have arranged the various listings chronologically by date of data collection. Within each listing I have assigned arbitrary letters to the phratries so that they will be designated uniformly throughout, but I have kept the various affiliations consistent with that originally presented by the various investigators. I believe that in the majority of

---

[3] I consider the number of sibs approximate, for at least one sib appears to have no members and yet is listed by my informants, and because there were about six individuals in the official census who gave English translation of their sib names which I was unable to correlate with an equivalent vernacular term. I do not believe that the number of sibs is variable to a greater degree than perhaps plus or minus two.

TABLE 14
Matrilineal Sibs and Phratries

Snake Bay 1962 Goodale	Snake Bay 1954 Goodale (1959)	Bathurst 1953-54 Pilling (1957)	Bathurst 1948? Berndt (1964)	Bathurst 1938-47 Harney & Elkin (1942)	Bathurst 1928-29 Hart (1930)	1912 Spencer (1914)
A Mudaŋabila crocodile	A Mudaŋanila crocodile	A Murtaŋapila	A Mudaŋinila wild pumpkin		D Mutunibila fish	(C) Urduŋui crocodile
A Murtaŋapila ironwood	B Mutanjintika ironwood					
A Kutaguni ironwood						
A Takariŋui mullet	A Walaka	C Walakuwula	A Ariwudi		D Ariwudi mullet	Arriwidiwi
						Takariŋa mullet
A Purilawila mullet	A Purilakala mullet	A Purilawula			B Walakuwila stars	
A Wilintuwila parrot fish	A Wilintunala parrot fish		A Wuluntuwilŋila earth mother			

TABLE 14 (cont.)

	Col 1	Col 2	Col 3	Col 4	Col 5	Col 6	Col 7	Col 8
B1	Miatui pandanus	B Miarti pandanus	A Wyajupila / B Miyartuwi	B Miadini pandanus	B Miatui pandanus	B Mierdui pandanus	Ind.	Mierti pandanus
B1	Milipuwila white cockatoo	B Milipura white cockatoo	B Milipuruwila			B Milubruwila cockatoo	Ind. (cf. D)	Jabijabui white cockatoo
B2	Muranjimbila flying fox	B Muranimbila flying fox/bamboo	B Tarnikuwi / B Murupunjama	B Murubuluwinila flying fox skin	B Murukpunjama flying fox	B Tarnikui flying fox		
B2	Mandubowi house fly	B Mandubani house fly	B Mantupawi	B Mandubani little fly	B Mandupowi fly	B Mandubowi fly		
B2	Tjilarui jabiru	Tjilarui	Tjilarui	Dilarni jabiru	Tjilati jabiru	B Tjilarui jabiru		
C1	Yurantawi stingray	C Urantawi stingray	C Warantawi (Punkkawarinui)	C Wureindani stingray	C Pinkwarui stingray	C Orandjowi stingray		
C1	Krutui red ochre	C Krutui red ochre	C Krurututuwi	C Jerinjabinila red ochre	C Yarinapila red ochre	C Yarinabila red ochre		
C1	yellow ochre							
C1	Utuna "same as Krutui"	A Utuna "same as crocodile"		A Wudunjanila earth mother		B Udunui crocodile	A Udunjui crocodile	
C1	Arikortorrui woolly-butt	C Arikortui woolly-butt/honey	C Arikatoruwi	C Aragidurini woolly-butt flower		Timiririnjui woolly-butt tree	C Timarerinja wood	

TABLE 14 (cont.)

	C Parulianjapila salt-water mud	C Parulianpila salt-water mud	C Paroliyanjapila	C Ilidini	C Ilitui	C Paroliunjibila mud	C Namunjarau wild dog
fire	C2 Uriubila fire	C Uriubila fire	C Ilituwi	C Wuribinila morning star	C Woriapila	C Ilitui	
fire	C2 Kudalui fire	C Kudalui fire	C Wuripula		C Kudjarli fire		
			D Taparui			D Taparui moon	
	D1 Tokombuwi yellow honey eater bird	D Tokombini yellow honey eater bird	D Tjitjiyuwi (alt. name)	D(1) Dogambini small birds	D Tukambini martin	D Tokwombui a bird	Jabijabui white cockatoo
	D1 Tapitabui march fly	D Tapitabini march fly	D Tapitapuwi	D(1) Djabidjabini march fly	D Tapitapini march fly	D Djabijabui march fly	Ind. (cf.B1)
	D2 Arikuwila stones	D Arikunala stones	D Arinkuwula		D Aringuwila stone	D Aringuwila stones	
	D2 Punjalunjwila red stones	D Punaluwala red stones	D Punjarluwula	D(1) Bunjaliwinila	D Bunjaluwila stone	D Pinaluwila wood	
	D3 Kurawi bloodwood	E Kurawi bloodwood	D Korawi	D(2) Gwurani bloodwood		D Wirinigitui bloodwood/fish	Wanninjetti bloodwood Ind.
	D3 Andului rain/fresh water	E Andului fresh water	D Antuluwi	D(2) Andjuluni rain	B Andolui spring	C Andjului rain/turtle	D Andjului rain/turtle

cases I have matched the sibs correctly by native name or by English translation, or a combination of the two.

Some of the sibs changed their names over the period of time for which we have information. Pilling (1957) gives a number of cases where this has occurred at the time of segmentation.

Also no one listing contains all the sibs mentioned in either preceding or succeeding listings. The difference between the earliest and latest listings can be partially explained by the process of segmentation, but the difference between the listings gathered at roughly the same time can only be explained by the differential local situation in regard to the distribution of sibs. All the listings with the exception of my own were, as far as I know, gathered in the vicinity of the Bathurst Island Mission and, I believe, from informants who were affiliated either with a Bathurst Island country or with one of the two "west" Melville Island countries, Mandiupi or Munupi. My informants on sib and phratry organization in 1954 came chiefly from Mandiupi, one of the "west" Melville countries, but in 1962 I used informants from Turupi, a country located at the far northeastern section of Melville Island. The present distribution of sibs by country affiliation (Table 16, p. 107) reflects local variation in both segmentation and marriage exchange patterns.

The number of phratries appears to have increased from three to four between the time Hart collected his data (1928-29) and the more recent collections by the Berndts, Pilling, and myself in 1962. It will be noted that my listing for 1954 contains five phratries, for at that time my Mandiupi informants insisted that one of the phratries had split into two "half-phratries" in order to facilitate marriage exchange. However, my Turupi informants in 1962, having apparently never acknowledged this split, insisted that it did not exist. Unfortunately, I did not check the situation with a Mandiupi informant in 1962.

A number of sibs appear on one or more of the listings that

do not appear in the analyses of marriage exchange, and one
sib (yellow ochre) technically should not appear on my 1962
Snake Bay list. For those that do not appear in the analyses,
the explanation is simple: no representatives of these sibs
appear either in the official census or in my own Snake Bay
census, and I presume they are extinct but not forgotten.
The yellow ochre sib turns up only in the official 1960 census
and appears to be a post-1954 segmentation occurring among
the red ochre sib localized at Bathurst. Pilling knew members
of the yellow ochre sib to be former members of the red
ochre sib. Recently Pilling has confirmed my suspicions by
recalling a certain amount of conflict among his red ochre
Bathurst friends at the time of his study, which has evidently
resulted in the formation of a new sib after the time of his
investigation.

Marriage Exchange by Matrilineal Units

Members of all kinds of matrilineal units express their
affiliation by recognizing the principle of common descent
through females, and marriage within a matrilineal descent
group is considered incestuous. I have analyzed marriage
exchanges among several of the less obviously cohesive kinds
of matrilineal units—the moiety, the phratry, and the phratry
segment or super-sib—in order to test the conceptual and
analytical validity of these units in Tiwi social structure.

Because of the local variation in matrilineal sib distribution, I have considered Bathurst Island separately from Melville Island. Because, as I show later, marriage exchanges are
also directed by a preference for local endogamy, separating
the two island populations for the purpose of matrilineal unit
analysis will present a more reliable picture than combining
them into one population.

The marriage exchanges indicated in Figure 6 are, in
theory, and often in practice, direct exchanges between more
exclusive units than the super-sibs used in this analysis. The
rule states that "One should marry someone in one's father's

sib." However, a diagram showing exchange patterns among twenty-two sibs would be excessively complex.

A circular diagram is the clearest way to show the pattern of marriage exchanges both quantitatively and qualitatively, for it is only by considering both the kind and the amount of *exchange* that the quality of the matrilineal affiliations can be expressed.

The Diagrams: Placement and Distribution (Fig. 6)

According to the Berndts (1964), the phratries that I am calling here A and B are grouped into one exogamous moiety, while C and D form the other moiety. I found it necessary to diagram the AB moiety in three *inner* circles, with the CD moiety forming the outer circle.

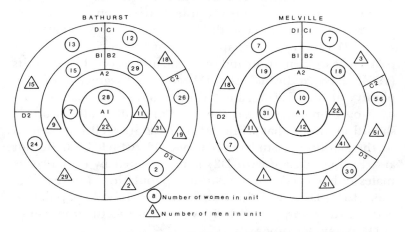

Fig. 6   Distribution of super-sibs

Phratry A is diagramed in the two inner circles and shows a separation of one sib (*kutaguni* ironwood, A1) from the other four sibs (A2). This is the only super-sib separation that I am doubtful of, for I do not have any evidence that the A1 and A2 super-sibs are *recognized* as such by Tiwi. However, the distribution of these two "segments" of the A phratry varies significantly between the two island populations, and I believe this distribution has an important effect on the exchange patterns. The A1 and A2 super-sibs should probably be regarded as being significant units of organization only from a structural standpoint.

Phratry B consists of two super-sibs, B1 and B2. Pilling (1957) confirms the recognition of these super-sib affiliations in time of conflict. With some minor variation, the B1 and B2 super-sibs appear to be equally represented in the two island populations.

Phratry C segmentation and formation of super-sibs C1 and C2 is confirmed by Pilling's conflict data. But while C2 is well represented in both island populations (with concentration on Melville Island), C1 is decidedly a minority super-sib on Melville Island, while it appears codominant with C2 on Bathurst. This variable distribution must be considered when we discuss the marriage exchange patterns.

The D phratry is perhaps the most interesting one in its pattern of segmentation and super-sib affiliation. The Berndts (1964) have indicated the D1 and D2 segments of this phratry in their listing, and Pilling (1957) confirms this dual division of phratry D on the basis of conflict affiliation. It should be noted that while D1 and D2 are well represented in the Bathurst Island population, D3 (which both Berndt and Pilling affiliate with D2) is represented by only two females and two males in the Bathurst population. The distribution of D1, D2, and D3 members in the Melville population is quite different, particularly with regard to the dominance of D3 as a major super-sib.

In the discussion of marriage exchange patterns between the super-sibs, I shall present the available historical data that pertain to the matrilineal units.

The Diagrams: Marriage Exchange (Fig. 7)

I have mentioned that Tiwi marriage contracts ideally involve direct exchange of women between two matrilineal groups, and that, once initiated, these exchanges are expected

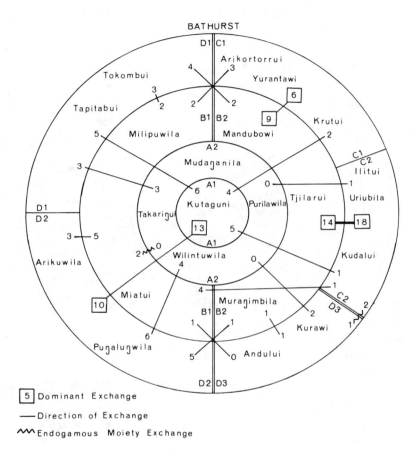

Fig 7a.   Marriage exchanges between super-sibs

to continue in succeeding generations. In these diagrams the lines indicate the direction of exchange, while the numbers at either end of the connecting lines are the number of women members of the super-sib involved in the exchange over the period of time covered in my census data. The straight lines show moiety exogamy in exchange, and wavy lines indicate endogamous moiety exchange. Even a casual glance will suffice to show the strong support that the marriage exchange data

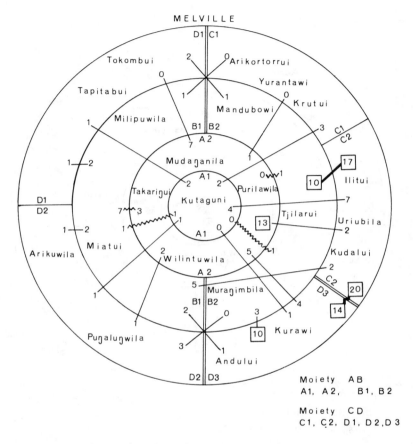

Fig. 7b.   Marriage exchanges between super-sibs

give to the structural validity of exogamous moieties; however, one can also see some significant exceptions to moiety
exogamy.

We now turn to a detailed description of the exchange
patterns of each phratry or phratry segment.

PHRATRY A: BATHURST

All its phratry women have been sent to men in the CD

moiety. The A1 segment, which is dominant, appears to have set up a major exchange pattern with the D2 segment, receiving ten D2 women in exchange for thirteen A1 women. Exchanges with D1 (six A1 for five D1 women) and to a lesser extent with C1 (four A1 for two C1 women) complete the regular exchange patterns of A1. The A2 segment shows a similar pattern of exchange with D2 and D1, but even though it has received a wife from C2, it has given no women to C1 or C2 men. A2 has also received two wives from the B2 segment of its own moiety, but has evidently refused to sanction this "incest" by reciprocating.

PHRATRY A: MELVILLE

This group appears to have had a rather difficult time arranging marriage exchanges. For instance, the A2 segment, which is dominant, sent seven women to D1 and got none in return. It sent thirteen women to C2 and got only two women in return. Its most successful exchanges were made with D3 and B1. The latter exchange is a fairly regular one *within* the AB moiety. A similar exchange of one woman each was made between B1 and A1, but no such endogamous moiety exchange was made with the B2 segment (in spite of the fact that both A1 and A2 received one wife each from B2).

Moiety endogamy by the A phratry appears to have occurred primarily on Melville Island and with the B1 segment of the B phratry rather than with the more numerous B2 segment. A possible explanation for this is the historically close affiliation of at least one of the B2 sibs, the *tjilarui* (jabiru), with the A phratry. According to Pilling's informants, this sib was formed by certain members of the crocodile sib of the A phratry around 1893, during a series of intersib and intercountry attacks and counterattacks. A local head of the crocodile sib declared that he was no longer a member of the crocodile, but rather of a new sib, the jabiru (Pilling 1957:312-17). He further separated his new local sib from its past affiliation by removing it from the A phratry altogether and affiliating with the housefly and flying fox sibs of the phratry B2 segment.

PHRATRY B: BATHURST

The majority of B1 women have been exchanged with the D1 and D2 segments of the CD moiety. Almost as many women have been sent to the C1 and C2 segments but with less success in reciprocity. The dominant exchanges for B2 women have been with C1 and C2.

PHRATRY B: MELVILLE

The exchange pattern of the Melville Island B phratry is similar to that of Bathurst Island, with the exception that there are no exchanges with the C1 segment of the C phratry. The C1 segment is poorly represented in the Melville Island population, which may explain this variation in pattern. The majority of the endogamous AB moiety marriages have been arranged for Melville Island B1 women, eight out of nineteen women having been given to A phratry men.

PHRATRY C: BATHURST

This group exchanges the majority of its women in both C1 and C2 with the B2 segment, with only minor exchanges with the other segments of the AB moiety. I have already mentioned the recent segmentation of the red ochre sib and the formation of the yellow ochre sib among the Bathurst population after 1954.

PHRATRY C: MELVILLE

Composed primarily of the C2 segment, this phratry segment exchanges an almost equal number of women with B2 and D3, an *intramoiety* exchange discussed below. Although I have no historical information, it appears from the census that the split of the fire sib into the *uriubila* and *kudalui* sibs occurred in and is confined to Melville Island, with the *kudalui* being the younger of the two.

PHRATRY D: BATHURST

D1 section shows a fairly equal exchange pattern with all the segments in the AB moiety, whereas D2, the predominant D phratry segment, shows a distinct preference for exchange with A1; there is lesser exchange with A2 and B1, and unequal exchange with B2. The Bathurst D3 exchanges reflect the marriage patterns of this segment in the Melville Island population, where the great majority of D3 members are located.

PHRATRY D: MELVILLE

The D1 segment on Melville Island has more than twice as many men as women, an unfortunate situation that is reflected in its unequal patterns with A2 and its endogamous CD moiety contract with C1. The unequal distribution of sexes is reversed in the D2 segment, which has only one man and seven women.

According to Pilling (1957:334, 347) D1 and D2 were originally one sib. Sometime before 1880 the first split occurred, and the yellow honeyeater (a bird) and the stone sibs were formed. Each of these subsequently split, forming the four sibs presently grouped into two segments.

We now come to the interesting problem of the D3 segment located primarily in Melville Island countries. This segment is made up of the bloodwood sib and the rain/turtle/fresh-water sib. Table 14 (pp. 82-84), indicates that, of all the sibs, the rain/turtle/fresh-water has been the most variably affiliated. In 1954 my Mandiupi informants, who belonged to the two D3 sibs, agreed that they did form a closely affiliated unit, but they added that they were a new fifth phratry *(aramipi),* having recently separated from a previous affiliation with the B2 segment of the opposite moiety. They considered members of the B phratry (both B1 and B2) to be "half *aramipi,*" in that whereas exchange of wives between the two ex-phratry groups was possible, it was still considered "a little bit wrong." The D3 group has sent ten women to B2 and received three

in return, and has sent one woman to B1, getting two in
return. Most of these D3-B marriages have occurred among
Mandiupi members of the sibs in question. In 1962 my Turupi informants said that bloodwood and fresh-water (D3) sibs
were now *and had always been* affiliated with the other sibs in
the D phratry, and in this they agreed with Pilling's and the
Berndts' informants. The marriage exchange pattern of the
D3 segment appears to reflect its variable affiliation. It is the
only D phratry segment that consistently exchanges women
with the C2 segment, an *endogamous* CD moiety exchange
that numerically exceeds *any* other exchange pattern of two
segments. If D3 is derived from B2 as my Mandiupi informants claim, their excessive amount of endogamous moiety
exchanges with C2 continues a previous dominant exchange
pattern of B2 and C2 women found in both island populations. Its contrasting minimal exchange with B1 can also be
explained by a continuing pattern of phratry exogamy.

SUMMARY

The analyses do support the conception that the various
kinds of matrilineal affiliation, with the possible exception
of the moiety, are cohesive social units of recognized importance in consideration of marriage exchange. The most important kinds of matrilineal organization, however, appear
to be the phratry segment or super-sib, and the lower levels
of affiliation, the sib, the local sib segments, and ultimately
the "one-granny" sibling sets.[4]

The Patrilineal Type

In the process of organizing this discussion of Tiwi social

[4] After many hours of frustration, I decided that the analyses of marriage
exchange between local sib segments would take either ten thousand man
hours or a computer, neither available to me at this time. I am, however,
quite convinced that more refined analyses would prove valuable in enabling
me to discuss the particular history of each locality with more precision, but it
would not add anything significantly to the discussion of major patterns of
exchange that I can show on the super-sib level of organization and the
variations evident in the two island populations.

structure, I have shifted the position of the patrilineally organized units many times. While I can demonstrate their
existence in various capacities, today their real significance to
the Tiwi is most apparent in the organization of funeral
rites. Part of the difficulty lies in the close conceptual identity
of the patrilineal units with the landowning or land-using
types of social units. The nature of this relationship as it
existed in the past is now obscured through the relocation of
the population in new settlement patterns and concomitant
changes in the patterns of activity involving cooperation and
competition of many of the Tiwi social units.

The Patrilineal Sibling Set

Hart in 1930 discussed a social unit consisting of individuals
who recognize common descent from the same father's father.
The kinship term for father's father is *amini,* and Hart
reported, "the members of this group will frequently refer to
one another as *nia yirt'amini* (my one grandfather) in preference to *ni'iwuni* (my brother)" (1930:173-74). Members
of this unit, said Hart, maintained exclusive rights to a
geographic area validated by the presence of the grave of the
common ancestor (father's father) in the area. Hart goes on to
say that not every Tiwi belongs to such a group, but essentially
only those individuals who were descended from "important" grandfathers—men who had enough wives to produce
enough grandchildren to enforce their claim and demonstrate
their separate existence as a localized social group (*ibid.:*
175).

Pilling discusses this social unit under the term *aminiyati*
(grandfather one), but in defining the criteria for membership in the group, he removes it from the unilineal classification of descent groups. Pilling writes, "The term *amini* is
applied by a male or female to his/her father's father, his/her
mother's father, and his/her father's mother's brother. All
individuals who call the same person *amini* by reason of *any*

one [emphasis mine] of these genealogical ties call each other by the term *aminiyati"* (Pilling 1957:46).

In 1954 my Snake Bay informants made no reference to a patrilineally organized sibling group in either speech or behavior, although I was aware of Hart's discussion of the *yirt'amini.* The first time I heard the term *aminiyati* was in 1962. My informant referred to a *muriŋaleta's* husband's brothers, who participated in the young wife's puberty rituals, as the husband's *aminiyati,* defining these as the husband's full brothers, half brothers, and one-grandfather brothers. Later on during the collection of genealogies, my informant used such phrases as "one-father brother" and "one-grandfather brother" to define relationships to me.

Although my evidence for the existence of this patrilineal sibling set is in some ways more tenuous than that for the "one-granny" matrilineal sibling set, in other respects it appears as a more clearly defined unit because of the existence of a technical term in the vernacular, *aminiyati,* used in reference to the unit and among members of the set, a characteristic lacking in the "one-granny" matrilineal sibling set. This is one case where the explanation for the apparent difference in emphasis of one type of sibling set over the other in the literature may be entirely due to a conceptual difference in relative importance of the two types of groups given by male and female Tiwi. I do think both types of sibling sets (the matrilineal and patrilineal) are recognized social units in Tiwi life, and that both figure importantly in contracting marriage exchanges as well as in defining roles among kinsmen. For these reasons, I am unwilling to think of the *aminiyati* (the patrilineal sibling set) as a nonuniversal Tiwi social group, existing only when one's father's father was a famous "big man."

The problem, I think, involves determining the basic cultural principle underlying the formation of this group. Both Hart and Pilling imply that the basic principle was exclusive occupancy, defense, and use of land by descendants of a common father's father. Thus, when a man died and was buried in a territory claimed by others than himself or when he had been unsuccessful in acquiring multiple marriage contracts and thus had few children, his descendants could not form an *aminiyati*. However, I disagree with Hart and Pilling on the matter of what is the basic cultural principle underlying this group. I do not believe that it is ownership, occupancy, or defense of land, but rather a principle of patrilineal descent. Thus, whereas in the past some of these *aminiyati* units were indeed large, cohesive, and localized groups, other similar types and kinds of groups with smaller memberships were dispersed and geographically intermingled with members of other *aminiyati* units. Hart says that dispersed female members of a localized *aminiyati* were still considered to be members even when they resided in an outside geographical area, but male members who chose to reside outside their area would relinquish their original *aminiyati* membership and affiliate with the groups in their area of residence (Hart 1930a:176). I have recorded a few adoptions into both *aminiyati* and local groups, but those are overshadowed by the many cases of men retaining their original *aminiyati* affiliations when residing outside their geographical area. This, plus the weak but continued existence of this unit in the present-day situation of delocalization, makes me believe that the *aminiyati* is fundamentally a unit formed by a principle of patrilineal descent rather than one based on residence.

If I am correct in assuming that the *aminiyati* sibling set is conceptually parallel to the matrilineal sibling set so that members of such a set are considered as being "one person" by kinsmen outside the set, the paradox presented by Pilling's nonunilineal definition of the *aminiyati* may be resolved. As we shall see later, because of the preferred exchange pattern of marriage, one's father's father, one's mother's father, and one's father's mother's brother *could* be members of a single *aminiyati* sibling set, and this situation would violate no rules of exogamy. Thus, a single ego could, in such cases, trace his relationship in all three ways to a sibling unit containing three different kintypes, but conceived as a single identity. Whether this is ever actually the case, I cannot say.

The Patrilineage

In 1954 I isolated a patrilineal group that appeared to function significantly in the organization and performance of the funeral ceremonies for its members. This group has the structure of a limited (minimal) patrilineage, with members tracing descent through males to a known patrilineal ancestor two or three generations removed at the most. Unlike the *aminiyati* sibling set, the patrilineage is composed of individuals on several generation levels. Some members of a single patrilineage may make up a large proportion of a geographically localized population, but its separate existence as an exogamous lineage can be demonstrated.

Summary

Both the *aminiyati* sibling set and the patrilineal lineage are limited in a way that is overshadowed by the matrilineal system of affiliation into larger and larger units, maintaining the fiction of common descent. Although the patrilineal units do affiliate into larger groupings, this results not from applying the concept of common patrilineal descent but rather from recognizing larger territorial unity for purposes of economic cooperation, mutual defense, and preferred marriage *endogamy*.

Because previously these patrilineal units had close functional and structural relationship with geographically determined social groups, what we see of them now is but a faint reflection of their past significance. However, both Pilling (1962) and I have noticed a tendency for localization of these patrilineal units *within* the mission and Snake Bay settlements when choice is allowed.

Residential Types

The traditional residential groups have been altered significantly by the mission and government settlements. Older patterns can be reconstructed only by analyzing what our informants say used to be the principles of local group affiliation, as well as the demographic situation as it exists today. The margin of error in such analysis is large, but this should not invalidate its usefulness, for the results may contain clues for interpreting Tiwi social organization.

We must distinguish between the group of people who reside in a given locality at a given time, called here a *residential group,* and the group of people who are co-owners of the locality, a *landholding group.*

Membership in a *residential group* is determined by an individual's active residence with other members of the group for periods of time consistent with being considered a resident member rather than a visiting individual. All residents share (1) equal rights to the *use* of the resources of the locality, (2) patterns of economic cooperation consistent with the size of the unit and the nature of the endeavor, (3) under certain conditions the responsibility to act as a member of the group in relation to other residential units (for example, warfare), and (4) the responsibility to act as a member of the group in regard to certain situations concerning individual members of their own residential unit (for example, death).[5]

The membership of a *landholding group* is composed of individuals who collectively own, or consider that they own, the same bounded locality. Only owners of a locality may allocate use of the natural products of the area to those residents who are not owners and to visitors. Individuals are members of the same landholding group as were their fathers. In most cases one's father lived, died, and was buried in a locality where he was also an owner. Should one's father

[5] See Chapter 9 for full discussion of these activities.

reside in, die in, and be buried in a locality of which he was
not also an owner, his patrilineal descendants could claim
landholding group affiliation with the rights of co-ownership
with members of the group owning the locality in which
their father was buried. As I shall discuss later, the ghost of
a deceased Tiwi remains near the site of its grave. The exact
relationship of the living to the dead is complex, but I believe
that it is this relationship that underlies such corporate
claims. Whether such claims were actually exercised in cases
where a change in landholding group membership was possible
appears to have been determined by many factors affecting
the advantages of one choice over another.

Let me now return to the local residential unit in order to
discuss the considerations that determine both the individual
choice of residence and the group's acceptance of the individual as a resident member. The rules governing the residence of a Tiwi woman are quite simply stated. She resides
with her "father" (her mother's husband) until handed over
to her first husband before puberty. After this she lives with
her husband(s) wherever he happens to be residing until she
dies. The only exception to this latter rule is if her husband
mistreats her to an excessive degree so that her father, brothers, or sons rescue her. In this instance she will reside with her
rescuers until remarried. The Tiwi women told me that in
the past if a husband left his wife for a temporary visit elsewhere, his wife should properly reside with her "father" until
her husband returned. This pattern is still followed to a certain degree when Tiwi husbands maintain temporary residence in Darwin without their wives. But another custom,
which the Tiwi claim is a "mainland" one, of a husband's
brother caring for the wife while the husband is away, is gaining popularity. This is due in large part to the Tiwi "custom"
of young unmarried men forming "lover" relationships with
their "older brother's" wives, which I will discuss later. In the
past these love affairs were never sanctioned, but probably
were tolerated only up to a certain point. Today, however,

these "affairs" are often sanctioned and, in a way, are similar to the Type A3 contract where a husband gives his wife to another man.

For the Tiwi man the rules of residence are more variable and complex. There are three basic kin relationships by which a male justifies his rights to membership in a residential group: (1) his father or mother or both are residents in the locality; (2) his mother-in-law is resident in the locality; and (3) he is a co-owner of the locality. Custom dictates which of these relationships holds precedence over the others. Until a young man becomes a son-in-law through any type of marriage contract, he preferentially lives with the residential group of his mother and father. If his first wife is a woman whose mother has died (so that he has no mother-in-law), he may continue to live with his wife in his parent's residential group. When a man acquires a mother-in-law through any type of contract, he should become a member of his mother-in-law's residential group, his wives residing with him. If a man acquires two mothers-in-law through additional marriage contracts, he must weigh the advantages of residing with one or the other, unless both mothers-in-law are themselves members of the same residential group. If his mothers-in-law die before he does, he should reside in the group in which his *mother* (and mother's husband) are residing. If he should survive his own mother and all his mothers-in-law, he may reside in the locality of which he is also an owner, if he wishes.

Much of this complexity can be reduced by following the marriage rules for landholding group exchange. The first preference is to marry someone in one's own landholding group. However, if one's father married a woman (ego's mother) from a different corporate group, ego should marry a woman belonging to his mother's landholding group. If the first preferential rule were followed consistently for a number of generations, all women a man would marry and all women he should reside with would be members of the same landholding and residential group as he. While he may change domestic groups from time to time, no great geographic distance separates him from those he is obliged to reside with. In the second instance one is expected to marry a woman from one's mother's landholding group. Since ego's father is obliged to reside with his wife's residential group, ego is born in his mother's country; his own mothers-in-law reside in his mother's country, and so must he until his mother and mothers-in-law die, when he can, if he wishes, return to his father's landholdings. However, if his father has been buried in his mother's country, he may exercise his rights to corporate ownership of the locality in which his father lies buried, and thus remain in the locality where he has been a lifelong resident. Eventually he may be buried in his adopted country, and if he does his descendants may exercise their rights to corporate ownership in this country.

In this discussion I have used the terms "domestic group," "residential group," and "landholding group" without defining their relationships to geographically bounded localities. In the past all these groups occupied or owned sections of land whose boundaries were at any one time fixed and known. In Chapter 1 I discussed the nature of Tiwi local organization, as it concerned what the Tiwi call "countries" *(tuŋa-rima)*, "subcountries," and camps *(tabuda)*.

The named countries *(tuŋarima)* are the largest geographically bounded residential localities, whose boundaries set the limits of land ownership of a specific *affiliation* of landholding groups. At any given time the named subcountries with recognized boundaries were occupied by a discrete residential group and owned either by a single patrilineal descent unit *(aminiyati* or patrilineage), or by a group of affiliated patrilineal descent units. Owners used either the name of their owned subcountry or that of their country to identify themselves as members of a landholding group. Nonowner residents did not use the name of the locality in which they resided for purposes of group identification.

Owners of subcountries might defend their exclusive ownership of their subcountry's assets against other members of their own country, but how restrictive or widespread this was is difficult to ascertain today. Certainly boundary infractions by members of different subcountries within one country were not treated as seriously as infractions by members of a different country.

It appears that the nature of the subcountry community was always variable and dependent on its specific composition at any given time. If its component parts were, as Hart said (of the *yurt'amini*), able to proclaim and defend their exclusiveness in relation to the larger country of which they were a part, they probably did so. In time, if their members increased numerically, they expanded their boundaries, or became recognized by other local units as an independent country, or perhaps did both. The life history of a subcountry as a distinct social and geographic entity is only as stable as its owning group. Because this group is more exclusive than the country social and geographic unit with which it is affiliated, the country as a unit of social organization appears to introduce a necessary amount of stability in the total social organization. Over the period of time for which we have information, countries also had fluctuating boundaries according to the size and importance of the relevant owning groups. However, the total number of such country units does not appear to have changed over this time period. Stability in the country unit organization is also shown in the present situation.

I have used the term "domestic group" to designate the group of coresidents in one camp *(tabuda)*. Membership in a domestic group fluctuates according to individual obligations and desires, but resident members of all domestic groups within a subcountry locality have rights to use all the resources of that subcountry, and individuals may affiliate with various resident domestic groups from time to time.

The relocation of the Tiwi population has had an interesting effect on the composition of what are now known as residential groups and on what remains of the function of the local corporate groups. Today there are essentially two major residential groups, the mission "mob" and the Snake Bay "mob," as the Tiwi refer to them. In funeral ceremonies these new residential groups function in the same way as the former country units. To the extent that local residents are not restricted by official regulations, all residents have rights to use the local resources, rights presumably given them by the owners of the localities. For purposes of corporate group identification, Tiwi today use almost exclusively the name of their country rather than their subcountry affiliation. These corporate groups still figure significantly in allocation of use rights of land and resources, and in marriage exchange; and within the two settlements, the corporate groups show a marked tendency to reside in close pseudo-domestic group proximity.

In Table 15 I have presented the pattern of local landholding group marriage exchange according to the census data obtained in 1962. Although the percentage of country endogamy reflected in today's marriage contracts is in all cases less than 50 percent, the percentage of island endogamy is in all cases above 60 percent, and for one country, Palauwiuŋa, there is 100 percent island endogamy.

The landholding (country) group is the largest permanent unit of organization recognized by the Tiwi, but geographic proximity of landholding groups appears to be an important consideration in arranging marriages that are exceptions to the preferred country endogamy. The percentage of island endogamy shown in the analysis should be considered only as an expression of the statistical effect of various intercountry exchanges that have been maintained over a period of time and not as an expression of Tiwi group identity as Bathurst or Melville islanders.

It is true, however, that the mission settlement on Bathurst and the Snake Bay Settlement on Melville draw their populations to a great extent from those countries making up the

TABLE 15
MARRIAGE EXCHANGE BY LANDHOLDING GROUPS

Land-holding Group	Tikalaru	Uraŋgu	Malau	Total Bathurst	Mandiupi	Munupi	Wileraŋgu	Palau-wiuŋa	Turupi & Yaŋanti	Yeimpi	Total Melville	Percent Country Endogamy	Percent Island Endogamy
	BATHURST				WEST MELVILLE		EAST MELVILLE						
Tikalaru													
64 women	23	15	9	(47)	6	4	1		3	3	(17)	35.6	76.6
69 men	23	21	12	(56)	4	5	2		2		(13)	33.3	81.0
Uraŋgu													
57 women	21	12	12	(45)	4	5	1			2	(12)	21.0	78.1
50 men	15	12	16	(43)	3	4					(7)	24.0	86.0
Malau													
63 women	12	16	13	(41)	1	11	5		4	1	(22)	20.6	65.1
45 men	9	12	13	(34)	3	7	1				(11)	28.8	75.5
Mandiupi													
35 women	4	3	3	(10)	6	3	6	1	4	5	(25)	17.3	72.9
48 men	6	4	1	(11)	6	4	1	5	15	6	(37)	12.5	77.1
Munupi													
63 women	5	4	7	(16)	4	21	15	2	3	2	(47)	33.3	74.6
58 men	4	5	11	(20)	3	21	6	1	4	3	(38)	36.2	65.5
Wileraŋgu													
15 women	2		1	(3)	1	6	2		1	2	(12)	13.3	80.0
41 men	1	1	5	(7)	6	15	2	1	8	2	(34)	4.9	82.9
Palauwiuŋa													
35 women				(0)	5	1	1	12	12	4	(35)	34.3	100.0
18 men				(0)	1	2		12	2	1	(18)	66.6	100.0
Turupi & Yaŋanti													
58 women	2			(2)	15	4	8	2	25	2	(56)	43.1	96.5
53 men	3		4	(7)	4	3	1	12	25	1	(46)	47.1	86.8
Yeimpi													
15 women				(0)	6	3	2	1	1	2	(15)	13.3	100.0
23 men	3	2	1	(5)	5	2	2	4	2	2	(17)	18.6	73.9

island on which the respective settlement is located. Since the census figures used in the analysis represent for the most part marriages set up in postsettlement days, we cannot disregard the possible effect that the settlements themselves may have had on the percentage of island endogamy. Nor may we disregard, however, the effect that preferred country endogamy, attitudes of country identity and loyalty, and established inter-country marriage exchanges have had in *creating* the present skewed distribution of landholding groups in the two modern residential units. It is obvious that there are multiple forces working today that both promote and restrict continuation of the old system of landholding unit exchange, which make it impossible to analyze the data with more precision than presented here.

There is one final analysis I wish to make concerning landholding and the two descent groups, matrilineal and patrilineal. This is, however, a subject more for speculation than for demonstration. If the Tiwi consistently followed the two major rules of marriage exchange—(1) marry someone in one's father's matrilineal sib who is also (2) a co-owner of one's own country, or if possible one's subcountry—the structural result should be the localization of two matrilineal units in each country or subcountry, and the units formed by a cultural principle of patrilineality would be unnecessary for identity discrimination or group behavior patterning.

The Tiwi do not now or did they ever, I believe, practice either of these two rules exclusively. Therefore, the concept of patrilineal descent appears necessary to account for the allocation of membership in the important landholding groups but not for membership in local residential groups. Because of the preference of marriage exchange among both matrilineal units and landholding groups, we should find greater concentrations of certain matrilineal groups in certain countries. We would expect that within localized segments of a matrilineal group there would be a degree of loyalty and feeling of distinctiveness not found among members of the larger, dispersed matrilineal group as a whole.

Table 16 shows the tabulated figures for the distribution of the matrilineal sibs according to landholding group affiliation. Although sib members are widely scattered among the countries, concentrations in one or a few localities should also be noted. The localization (by country affiliation) of matrilineal

TABLE 16
DISTRIBUTION OF MATRILINEAL SIBS BY COUNTRIES

| | BATHURST | | | WEST MELVILLE | | EAST MELVILLE | | | | |
	Tikalaru	Uraŋgu	Malau	Mandiupi	Munupi	Wileraŋgu	Palauwiuŋa	Turupi & Yaŋanti	Yeimpi	Total
Population	181	148	101	80	99	44	29	60	22	
Sib										
(A1) Kutaguni	8	42	13	3	18	2	1	1	3	91
A2 Mudaŋabila	1		1	5	2	2		1		12
A2 (Mosquito)	2	8	14	1	5	3				33
A2 Takariŋui		1		4	4		3	4		16
A2 Purilawila		1		2			9			12
A2 Wilintuwila			2		2	2		1		7
B1 Milipuwila	10		6	1	4					21
B1 Miatui	10	3	14	7	5	1	1	5		46
B2 Tjilarui	53	14	6	4	1			1		79
B2 Muraŋimbila	12	10	4	6	8	7		1		48
B2 Mandubowi			1	4	4	1	6	3		19
C1 Arikortorrui	5	9	1	1	3					11
C1 Yurantawi	2	6	4	2		1				14
C1 Krutui	3	3			5	1				12
C1 Yellow Ochre	5	9	1	1	3					19
C2 (Fire)	33	10	6	18	14	8		4	8	101
C2 Uriubila				1	1	2	5	3	2	14
C2 Kudalui				1	2	7	1	13	1	25
D1 Tokombuwi	9	9	2	3	5	3	1	2		34
D1 Tapitabui	18	5	5	1	9	1	1	1		41
D2 Arikuwila	9	24	16	3	6				2	60
D2 Puŋaluŋwila			3							3
D3 Kurawi			2	7	1	1		17	2	30
D3 Andului	1			4		1	1	3	5	15

sibs is an important concept in Tiwi beliefs about conception (see Chapter 5). Briefly, a Tiwi cannot be born without having been "dreamed" by his or her father. A father, they say, cannot dream a child when he is geographically outside his own country (his landholding group's locality). *Unborn* Tiwi children belong to their mother's matrilineal sib. This whole concept seems to depend on marriage exchange between two localized matrilineal sibs and on country endogamy. The localization of matrilineal sibs is also mythologically supported (Mountford 1958:35-37), although in many cases it is impossible to correlate with present matrilineal descent units.

We can only speculate about the origin of the units of Tiwi social organization. However, before leaving the subject of social organization and marriage, I must make one final remark regarding the continuing debate on the relative importance of the local group and the patrilineal and matrilineal descent groups. The most recent debaters, Berndt (1960) and Pilling (1962), seem to me to be arguing at cross-purposes. Berndt maintains that the matrilineal descent units "are and were the basic social units"; Pilling agrees that the matrilineal descent groups are now an important social group, but in the past, he said, the landholding group played the most important role in group conflict. Berndt has interpreted this to mean that Pilling (and Hart) believe that the Tiwi have changed from a patrilineal to a matrilineal orientation. In the above discussion I have presented my speculation concerning the *relationship* of the matrilineal and patrilineal descent groups to both the local residential and landholding groups. My contribution is to propose that the next round of the debate take as its subject this: Resolved; In the past the two basic and most conceptually important social groups to the Tiwi were the localized segments of matrilineal units and the local landholding group, membership in the latter being determined patrilineally—and, further, both of these social groups are of equal importance today.

Tiwi Kinship and Marriage Contracts

In the Tiwi system of kinship nomenclature, with few exceptions, the kin terms are indefinitely extendable to include every member of the Tiwi tribe. By these terms individuals are differentiated on the basis of sex, generation, and relative age, criteria that imply certain definable behavior correlations when interaction between two or more individuals occurs. I present here only that part of the Tiwi kinship terminological system that is basic to an understanding of the fundamentals that guide behavior, and specifically the behavior of kinsmen who are involved in marriage contracts.

Basic to the Tiwi is a division of "kin" on the basis of genealogical and geographic distance, the two criteria that the Tiwi conceive as one when they use the phrases "close kin" and "long-way kin." Genealogical distance refers to the relative positions of ego and alter ego in the matrilineal and patrilineal descent group system, while geographical distance refers to the relative positions of ego and alter ego in both the landholding group and the residential group system. The "closeness" of the relationship is directly correlated with the assumed relationship of the units to which both ego and alter ego may belong.

I have already presented the case for considering the matrilineal "one-granny" sibling set as conceptually the most exclusive and cohesive unit in the matrilineal system: siblings within one of these sets consider each other not only as "close" siblings but as the "closest" of all those they call sibling.

Another important group from the point of view of intensity of cohesiveness is the local residential group composed of individuals with whom one cooperates on a regular, if not always a daily, basis. This local group includes some members of one's matrilineal sib and some members of one's father's matrilineal sib. If all marriages that have occurred within the local residential group have conformed to the ideal of exchange between two matrilineal sibs and of local landholding endogamy, ego needs only to consider the closeness of his relationship to others in the two matrilineal units and one landholding group. This determines the closeness of his relationship to everyone in the society, should this ever be necessary. But the emphasis that Tiwi males place on multiple marriage contracts as a major element in their individual achievement ideology precludes the possibility that the ideal of marriage exchange between two jointly localized matrilineal sibs could satisfy the demand of some individuals for increased prestige through marriage contracts. Much of the Tiwi system of social organization above and beyond the localized matrilineal units appears to me to be the result of compromises between the ideal of marriage exchange and the reality of the marriage system. As we shall see, the kinship terminology appears to reflect the compromise situation rather than the ideal.

The local patrilineal descent group (the limited patrilineage) and the "one-grandfather" sibling set (the *aminiyati*) serve to incorporate into one's "close kin" group individuals who are not members of one's own "one-granny" group or one's own local matrilineal sib segment (or one's father's localized matrilineal sib unit), but who are members of one's domestic or residential group. This would be particularly important to the functioning of a cohesive local residential group of any size whose members had multiple matrilineal sib affiliations.

We therefore find classed as "close kin" those who (1) share the same mother's mother, (2) share the same father's father, or (3) belong to the same local corporate landholding group, the limited patrilineage, or any combination of these. Within the limits of the "close kin" group, individuals are differentiated by terms that express rather precisely the genealogical relationship of each member and the sex. Most but not all of these terms are also extended to "long-way kin." This extension is without regard to genealogical relationship, but depends on the generation or relative age, on sex, and on whether the individual is considered to be a "maternal" or "paternal" relative, reckoning through assumed genealogical ties.

Figure 8 diagrams the basic principles of kinship classification. Within ego's "close kin" there is no alternation of terms throughout the five generations represented; furthermore, the only terms that are not extended to "long-way kin" are those for ego's close maternal kin of the second ascending and second descending generation. Thus, the terminology reflects the importance of genealogical relationship within the "close kin" group of "one-granny" siblings. The restriction of *iŋgalabini* and *iŋgalaboka* to "close" siblings who share the same father's father but whose matrilineal sib affiliation differs from ego's terminologically expresses the unity of the patrilineal "one-grandfather" sibling set under circumstances where the "one-granny" sibling set does not suffice to differentiate "close kin" from "long-way kin." These terms are not extended beyond the *aminiyati* ("one-grand-father" sibling group).

Ego's maternal "long-way kin" are differentiated from his paternal "long-way kin." If only two matrilineal descent groups were represented in reality, ego's maternal kin would represent those in ego's own matrilineal group and its affiliates, while those classified as paternal kin would all be members of ego's father's matrilineal group and its affiliates. Actually, however, since these terms are indefinitely extendable, sib and matrilineal group affiliations are subordinated to assumed genealogical relationship, and the terms are applied according to recognized bounds of incest prohibition.

Three statements suffice to cover the Tiwi definition of incest: (1) marriage between "maternal" kinsmen of any degree, (2) marriage within the "close kin" group, and (3) marriage between individuals in adjoining generations. Thus we find the "long-way kin" terminologically differentiated between those ego can marry and those ego cannot marry, on two dimensions. One dimension involves "descent" (genealogical), the other generation. All "long-way kin" are thus in

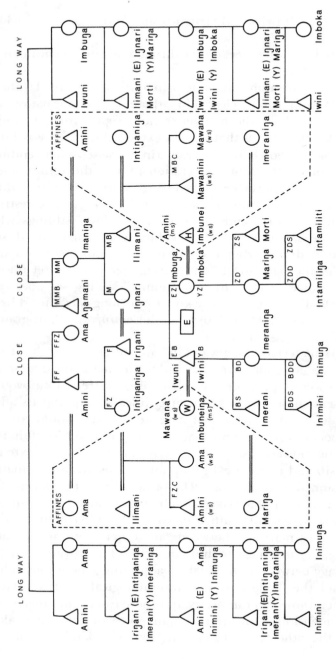

Fig. 8 Principles of kinship classification

one of four categories from the point of view of each individual ego. In Category 1 are ego's "brothers and sisters" who are long-way maternal kinsmen in ego's own generation, or in the second ascending or second descending generation. These "long-way" brothers and sisters are further distinguished by sex and relative age. Older brothers are called *iwuni,* younger brothers, *iwini,* older sisters, *imbuŋa,* and younger sisters, *imboka.* Actual generation is subordinated to relative age when close contact requires more precision in behavior regulation.

Category 2 includes ego's "long-way maternal" kinsmen of the first ascending and first descending generations. Here again the terms are differentiated by sex, and if necessary relative age takes precedence over actual generation in deciding which term to apply. Older males are called *ilimani* (mother's brother), while younger males are called *morti* (sister's son). Older females are called *iŋnari* (mother), while younger females are called *mariŋa* (sister's daughter).

Category 3 includes "long-way paternal" kinsmen in ego's own generation and in the second ascending and second descending generations. Males are called *amini* (father's father's brother) if older than ego, and *inimini* (brother's daughter's son) if younger than ego, while older females are called *ama* (father's father's sister) and younger females called *inimuŋa* (brother's daughter's daughter). Ego can marry any individual of the opposite sex in Category 3 of his "long-way kinsmen" without violating incest taboos.

Category 4 includes ego's paternal "long-way kinsmen" of the first ascending and first descending generations. Older males are called *iriŋani* (father), younger males, *imerani* (brother's son), while older females are called *intiŋaniŋa* (father's sister), and younger females, *imeraniŋa* (brother's daughter).

Although this terminological classification of "long-way" kin conforms to the stuctural ideal of a "four-class" system, I believe that it is functionally misleading to emphasize this sociocentric picture for the Tiwi as a society. Actually, the four classes of "long-way" relatives are discrete as groups only to individual egos and their "close" siblings.

One final comment on the inclusion of certain selected affinal kinsmen in Figure 8. Their placement between ego's "close" and "long-way" kin is not without meaning, for these *particular* spouses of ego's close kin are conceptually "half-close" relatives of ego. However, ego's own particular spouses and spouses' siblings, called *imbuneiŋa* (wife) or *imbunei* (husband) by ego, are, of course, long-way kinsmen.

The ambiguous placement of ego's first-degree cross-cousins reflects a preferential asymmetrical first cross-cousin marriage that is, however, secondary in preference to marriage between certain long-way kin. Female egos consider their matrilateral first cross-cousins *mawanini* (mother's brother's son) to be "too close kin" to marry, while male egos consider their patrilateral first cross-cousins *mawana* (father's sister's daughter) to be "too close kin" for marriage. However, under certain conditions both male and female egos will marry their first cross-cousins (a boy his matrilateral and a girl her patrilateral cousin), as these are considered to be acceptable alternatives to the preferred marriage of a female ego to someone she calls *amini* (FFB) or *inimini* (BDS) and that of a male ego to some he calls *ama* (FFS) or *inimuŋa* (BDD).

Marriage Contracts and Kinship

Although all types of marriage contracts should conform to the basic rules of matrilineal descent group and local corporate group exchange and/or endogamy, what I have called the Type A contract that results in every woman's primary marriage (and the most prestigious contract for men to make) is more likely to conform to the rules than are contracts that lead to a woman's secondary marriages. However, in every type of contract one primary factor will influence the ultimate choice of a woman's husband: that of being assured or hopeful that a reciprocal contract can and will be made. Although a few of the exchange contracts may be delayed ones, contracts are usually made in pairs, with two men agreeing to supply a contract to each other.

First let us examine the Type A contract, in which the man selects a son-in-law for his daughter at the time of her puberty ceremony. The selected son-in-law is expected to provide a marriage contract for his mother-in-law's father, preferably a Type A contract. Although any two men who call each other "brother" are in the appropriate descent and generation groups to exchange correct Type A contracts, the superior value of this type of contract appears to result in its being arranged between two close kin "brothers": "one-granny" brothers, "one grandfather" brothers *(aminiyati),* or same-father-different-matri-sib brothers *(iŋgalabini).*

The structural results of a Type A marriage contract exchange between two close kin brothers (who are in the same generation, as definition of being close brothers) is partially shown in Figure 9.

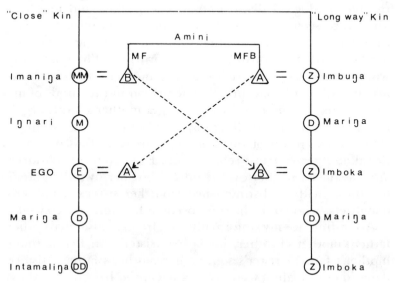

Fig. 9   Exchange of Type A contracts

Ego and her "one-mother" sisters are promised wives of "A," their mother's father's close-kin brother, a man actually two generations above ego. At the same time ego's mother's father (B) receives from A, the future husband of ego, a promise of wives, who are his brother's daughter's daughters. Ego's first husband might conceivably live long enough to continue with another Type A marriage contract with the same brother, exchanging this time the promise of their daughter's daughters, four generations removed from the contract arrangers and their respective husbands to be. It is, however, unlikely that any man would live long enough actually to receive his promised wife from the fourth descending generation. If ego's first husband should die before ego's daughter reaches puberty, ego's second husband will arrange a Type A marriage contract for ego's daughter with a close brother, resulting in an exchange of daughters as mothers-in-law.

It is only in relation to this type of marriage contract that the terminological distinctions between close and long-way kin can be seen to have real functional significance. A female can marry any mother's father *(amini)*, including her "real" mother's father, according to my informants. The qualifying word "real" I believe refers to the mother's father's "one-granny" siblings, conceptually one person in the minds of my informants. In any case by marrying a mother's father, ego's co-wives are both her long-way and "one-granny" siblings, thus the extension of the sibling terms regardless of matrilineal and genealogical relationship. Ego's co-wives' children are classified with her own children, but her own daughter's daughters will be distinguished from her sister's daughter's daughters, who could in time become her younger co-wives.

According to my informants a girl can also marry her father's mother's brother, her father's sister's son, her mother's mother's father's sister's son, or her mother's father's sister's daughter's son, all of whom are called *amini* by ego. As I show in Figure 10 a girl may be able to trace her genealogical re-

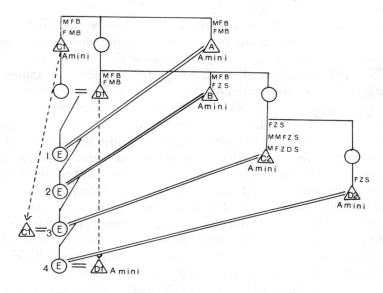

Fig. 10   Marriage and extension of term *amini*

lationship to her husband in a number of ways. For example, A, the husband of 1, is both 1's MFB and her FMB *(amini)*. B, the husband of 2, is both 2's MFB and her FZS *(amini)*. C2, the second husband of 3, is 3's FZS, MMFZS, and her MFZDS *(amini)*. In all cases the husband is two generations removed in actual fact if not in kin-type designation. The need for the simplicity achieved through the use of alternating generation terminology for long-way kin is apparent. I believe it acts primarily to simplify the relationships that *result* from such arranged marriages and not in order to facilitate the *arrangement* of such marriages, which are, I believe, made by close kin in the majority of cases.

If two men who belong to the same matrilineal sibling set, the same father's father's sibling set *(aminiyati),* or the same landholding group, exchange their daughters as mothers-in-law, a woman's son-in-law is her father's close brother. The obligations of coresidence and continual economic support that the *ambrinua* relationship demands of a son-in-law appears in an entirely new light when we see that such an exchange causes a man to assume these obligations for his close brother's daughter. When we view the various rules of residence and culturally preferred patterns of behavior among kin types and among members of culturally recognized social groups separate from this type of marriage exchange, they do not appear to be related in a functional sense. However, this type of marriage exchange appears to eliminate all the ambiguities and awkwardness that the residence rules and economic obligations inherent in the *ambrinua* relationship pose for a son-in-law. Thus I feel that Type A marriages were often, if not preferentially, made in this fashion if at all possible. All other marriages of a girl to other long-way kin-types, while possibly the result of a Type A contract, were, I believe, of secondary preference or the result of a different type of contract made by a father, brother, or son.

Hart and Pilling (1960) have illustrated with many excellent examples the complexity of the B, C, and D types of contracts leading to a woman's secondary marriages. I can add little to their discussion either by supplying the missing data on kinship and genealogy underlying such transactions (virtually impossible, I believe) or by adding significantly to their recorded cases of Tiwi political intrigue that involved women as political assets. I do, however, want to mention two types of secondary contracts, just to complete the record.

One male kin type classified with those a female could marry (but only as a secondary husband) was rarely alive to be married to ego. I was told that a girl could marry her father's father *(amini)*, but only if regular exchange of matrilineal descent groups had *not* occurred, so that he was a member of a different matrilineal descent group from his son's daughter. Since men did not have legitimate children until they were thirty to forty years old, a girl's father's father (real or his close sibling) would be seventy to eighty years old by the time his son's daughter was old enough to be given to him. In this case the relationship of the two contractors would be close kin FF and SS within a patrilineage or long-way *amini* or *inimini,* men who belong to no common important social unit. I know of no cases of such a marriage contract.

If a woman is married to a father's mother's brother *(amini)* who is not also a mother's father's brother, I would suspect that this too is a result of a secondary contract arranged by a girl's father, with the real expectation that *his* mother's brother—an important man in his matrilineal descent group— would agree to arrange a reciprocal contract, giving his daughter to his sister's son in exchange for a Type A wife.

The actual genealogy that I managed to collect in 1962 (Fig. 11, p. 128) is my only proof that ego's first husband is usually a man her mother's father calls close brother, a man born two generations before his promised wife. This is the only genealogy for which I was able to fix most of the matrilineal generations adequately, an essential process in demonstrating this type of marriage contract in the form of meaningful diagrams. I have, however, also included a connecting aggregate of genealogies (Fig. 12), in order to demonstrate some of the exchange principles. Detailed contract histories are given to the extent that they are known to me, the contracts identified by numbered mother-in-law relationships. Refer to Figures 11 and 12, pages 128-29.

Genealogy 1: Explanation of Contracts

Case 1: Y, Mother-in-Law of B

Both Y and B are members of the Turupi corporate group, as were their mothers and fathers. B's father belongs to the Turupi-Koraka (D3) sib, as does Y, his mother-in-law. B belongs to the Turupi-Kudalui (C2) sib.

Y first entered into a Type A contract with X, a Turupi-Kudalui man, and Y's first daughter M, born in 1900, was married to X. X died, and B inherited not only M but also the contract with Y, her mother. Y subsequently had two more daughters, each by a different husband, and both F and P came to B as wives in what I suspect was a Type A2 contract.

B made another Type A contract that resulted in his marriage to MA, a Mandiupi-Miatui (B1) girl.

Although B, when I knew him, counted all of these women among his wife assets, he had actually given one of his wives, M, to a non-Tiwi man BG, whom he had adopted as a "brother" when BG was quite young. I never could determine the exact circumstances that resulted in BG's adoption by B, but it is interesting to note that neither B's corporate group, Turupi, nor his sib, Kudalui, acknowledged BG as a member; thus it was only through B's generosity that BG could acquire a wife. While BG is himself still considered a non-Tiwi in all respects, his son has been adopted and acknowledged as a member of his father's "brother's" corporate group, Turupi, as well as, of course, his mother's sib, Kudalui.

B's wife F was barren, but his wife P produced a daughter N in 1930. P's son-in-law BF was a Turupi-Mandubawi (B2) man born in 1890, who was still alive to receive N as his wife in 1940 (and indeed to be one of my informants in 1954).

Case 2: N, Mother-in-Law of J

When N, the daughter of P and B (see Case 1) reached puberty, her father B selected an *aminiyati* (same father's father) brother, J, to be N's son-in-law. J, a Turupi-Wilintuwila (A2) man born in 1910, eventually acquired N's daughter H, born in 1944, through a Type A contract. J, however, already having a wife (and four children, see Case 3) has agreed to "give" H to a man of her choice, retaining, however, the right to veto the choice should he so wish.

Case 3: H, Mother-in-Law of R

H is the daughter of N and BF (see Cases 1 and 2). However, before H reached puberty, her mother N had married LC, a Turupi-Kudalui man, her father's (B) sister's son. (BF, her first husband, evidently raised no great objection, but I have no data on what actually took place concerning this affair.) LC was N's husband and H's "father" when H became a *muriŋgaleta* and, therefore, LC arranged for his "one-granny" and "one-father" brother, R, to receive the spear and become son-in-law to his "daughter" H. H "married" to J (see Case 2) is, however, not a member of J's domestic group, and as yet has not produced a daughter for son-in-law R.

Case 4: C, Mother-in-Law of JY

C's father OJ, a Turupi-Koraka (D3) man, married two of B's sisters. My data are not too clear on the relationship of OJ to B, or of OJ to JY, the man to whom he gave his daughter C as a mother-in-law. I believe that OJ and B are *aminiyati* (one FF brothers), and that JY is therefore his close father's sister's son. JY, born in 1925, is a Turupi-Koraka (D3) man and a "one-granny" brother of B's wife P. Although I have no factual confirmation, I would suspect that the contract in Case 4 is the exchange/reciprocal contract to that in Case 1. The marriage resulting from Case 4 contract, that of C's daughter A (born in 1948) to JY, a man fifty-seven years her senior, did take place in fact as well as in contract. (JY had two co-resident wives in 1962: A and an old widow only five years his junior. He had, however, contracted with another mother-in-law for a wife born in 1962.)

Case 5: A, Mother-in-Law of BH

A, the daughter of C and M2 acquired BH as a son-in-law at the time of her puberty. I do not know the relationship of M2 and BH except that they are both Turupi-Koraka (D3) men. This contract was, however, not arranged by M2 directly. Rather, B (see Case 1) arranged the contract between his own son and his "one-granny" sister's daughter's daughter. This contract could be regarded as reciprocal exchange for either contract 1 or contract 4, or perhaps both. It could even be regarded as reciprocal to contract 3.

Case 6: R's Mother, Mother-in-law of D

R's mother, one of three sisters from the Munupi-Takariŋui (A2) sib married to JN, a Wileraŋgu-Kudalui (C2) man, was given D as a son-in-law by her Munupi father. D is a member of the Mandiupi-Miatui (B1) sib (whose sister MA is married to his "wife's" father's mother's brother, B). R's mother died shortly after R's birth. D did not have a contract with his deceased mother-in-law's co-wives and "one-granny" sisters, and a problem arose. This contract was a reciprocal one, the other side of which I do not know, aside from the fact that parties to the other contract considered their contract in jeopardy if D's contract (now lapsed) was not honored.

In 1962 the situation was this. JN had just died, but for a number of years he had been supporting his daughter's (R) preference for a husband, a young lad her own age (YM), the son of JN's "one-granny" sister. JN considered that with the death of R's mother, the original contract with D had become void. As father of R he therefore had inherited the right and duty to arrange his young daughter's marriage. R, with the support of her father and numerous other paternal kinsmen, openly acknowledged her lover YM as the father of her two-year-old daughter, and father of the child she would soon bear, but she still had to remain a member of her father's domestic group until the problem of her first Type A contract could be resolved. Regardless of how this case is resolved, R's two-year-old daughter is considered the promised wife of a Munupi-Tapitabui (D1) man born in 1920.

Genealogy 2: Explanation of Contracts

Case 7

R2 is a member of the Malau-Miatui (B1) sib who is married to J, a Turupi-Wilintuwila (A2) man (see also Case 2). I do not have any information regarding this contract. When R2 reached puberty her father (unknown) arranged a Type A contract by which P, a Mandiupi-Purilawila (A2) man became R2's son-in-law. R2 has produced three daughters, all of whom have been given to P as wives. However, when the youngest of his wives, B, reached adolescence, P decided that two wives were enough, so he "gave" B to F, a young Munupi-Wilintuwila (A2) man of B's choice. F is B's father's sister's son, and although J (B's father) may have had a hand in the new arrangement, B's second marriage to F was conceived by my informants (P and H, J's other promised wife) as being of the Type A3 contract, rather than a father-arranged contract (Type B).

Case 8

J has, however, arranged his daughter's daughter's marriages. Two elderly "one-granny" brothers belonging to the Mandiupi-Purilawila (A2) sib became J's first and third daughters' sons-in-law, while JE, the second daughter, became the mother-in-law of AL, a Wileraŋgu-Wilintuwila (A2) "brother" of J. J's son, S, has been given AL's sister as a mother-in-law by LP, a Wileraŋgu-Uriubila (C2), a man indirectly related to J. Although this seems to be a "brother-sister" exchange of *ambrinua* relationships, the arrangers of the contract are not close brothers.

Case 9

Although LP, a Wileraŋgu-Uriubila (C2) man, has received five marriage contracts (four of which are shown here), only one of these is a Type A contract, arranged for him by PB. PB is a Palauwiuŋa-Uriubila (C2) man, whose great-grandfather (FFF) was a close brother of LP's great-grandfather. These two great-grandfathers were originally famous men who accumulated large numbers of marriage contracts, wives, and children. Since their country Palauwiuŋa was not large enough for both men to maintain their domestic group within its boundaries, LP's great-grandfather moved across Snake Bay and settled in the then unoccupied Wileraŋgu country. Relations between the two famous brothers remained cordial, and this close relationship is maintained among their descendants today. PB gave his brother LP a Type A contract with his daughter, and just before he died, PB also gave LP his wife D. LP received another wife from a "one-father's father's" brother, PO, a Wileraŋgu-Koraka (D3) man.

Both of LP's inherited wives are "one-granny" sisters whose common father arranged for both of them to have the same son-in-law, BJ. BJ is a Turupi-Kudalui (C2) man, who has married P and M, the daughters of S, and A, the daughter of D.

Case 10

This case represents an interesting adoption arrangement. BJ and FA are a brother and sister sharing the same mother and same father. FA and her husband have no children of their own. BJ gave FA his daughter D by his wife M for adoption, not as a daughter but as a daughter-in-law. In 1954, when I first became aware of this arrangement, I noted that young D did not call FA (her "acting mother") by the term "mother," but by the term she would have used had she not been adopted, *intiŋaniŋa* (FZ). I postulated at that time, and verified in 1962, that since D already had a promised husband, YB (a Munupi-Tapitabui [D1] man) arranged for her by her mother's father (a Munupi-Uriubila [C1] man), YB would join his wife in her adopted household when the time came for him to claim her. This had happened by 1962. YB called FA "mother," and he and his wife D were expected to "look after" his mother and her husband as long as the old couple needed their support. Furthermore, D's sister (M's second daughter) was expected to join D as a co-wife in a few years. BJ, in arranging for his sister's security, did not upset any marriage contract previously made; he merely allocated part of his own domestic group to that of his sister's husband. I was told that this kind of arrangement between close brother and sister was fairly common when either had no children to care for him in his old age.

Although it is an almost foregone conclusion that und€ this system of Type A marriage contracts, a woman's firs husband is considerably older than she by reason of generatior removal, I have included in the genealogies the recorded dates of birth of the key individuals in order to demonstrate this age factor more clearly. In my 1959 analysis of Type A contracts, I worked on the erroneous assumption that preferential marriages were to cross-cousins; that is, individuals on ego's own generation level. I reasoned that the stated preference of a mother's father's sister's daughter's son (a patrilateral second cross-cousin) for a girl's first husband was explainable only on the basis of the unavoidable age difference of at least twenty years between the girl and her Type A husband, resulting from the time at which this contract was made at her mother's puberty. A mother's mother's brother's daughter's son (a matrilateral cross-cousin) would not normally be born in time to make such a contract with a girl's mother (his mother's father's sister's daughter). The effect that the Type A contract has on the age structure of Tiwi kinship relations should not be underestimated, but I do not think now that this is the only explanation of the preferential patrilateral arrangements for a girl's first marriage. From the data presented here, I tend to view Hart's explanation as more correct, that Tiwi marriage is governed or structured by the monopoly that "big men" control over the market supply of women. Close brothers form an almost closed corporation *within* which their woman-wealth is circulated at least in the form of marriage contracts, if not always in actual wives.

Despite this quite rigid control over the distribution of women, the Tiwi do not feel that they have a limited choice of marriage partners. In fact, they openly express the opposite: "We can marry anyone who is not in our phratry, whom we call cousin." This statement should be qualified, however, to read, "After puberty we can marry anyone who is . . . etc.," for once a woman has reached puberty she has acquired a son-in-law, and primary marriage arrangements for all her daughters have been rigidly preset for the next generation. Her husband cannot under normal circumstances alter the course of events until *his* daughters reach puberty, and he can allocate his granddaughters according to his wishes. The built-in delayed effect that nonpreferential or alternate second marriages have on the system as a whole allows a considerable amount of individual flexibility of choice within a rigid framework of preferences.

The resiliency of the Tiwi marriage system is apparent in the present situation at Snake Bay. The two genealogies presented show Type A marriage contracts still being made in spite of the multiple forces at work that should have ended them. These forces include pressures of imposed Western morality and values (working against polygamy, against marriage between individuals vastly different in age, and against marriage of young girls before their late teens or completion of school), and the desire for freedom of choice on the part of both bride and groom. The mission and settlement administrations have supplemented "old-age security," a function provided by multiple wives in the past. Tiwi men have new means of gaining prestige, which they are accepting enthusiastically. The young girls and women are also finding new occupations; some, like my informant, prefer a career before settling down in marriage. Why then should the system continue with such apparent strength and vitality?

The answer, I believe, lies in the fact that it was never the *result* of the contract, the bride and groom relationship, that was the most important, but rather the other two diadic relationships involved in contract making: the relationship of the exchangers of contracts, the two men, and the resulting relationship of mother-in-law and son-in-law. It would seem that although in the marriage "game" men thought of women as so much capital wealth to manipulate as they wished, in reality it was through the *ambrinua* relationship that women gained a balance of power over a male. A man might lose his temper at his mother-in-law's husband, but he usually maintained his control with his mother-in-law, no matter how hard-pressed he might be to fulfill her demands.

The real functions of the Tiwi marriage system—acquiring new contracts for prestige, the formation of a special relationship between two contractors, and the formation of a special relationship through which women could exercise their independence from males in a way that complimented their dependent relationship on their male close kinsmen—are functions that do not conflict in any way with complete acceptance of Western culture and values. At the same time they serve to preserve the traditional values that make the Tiwi society a dynamic and ongoing entity.

KEY TO GENEALOGICAL CHART SYMBOLS

Symbols common to anthropological charts of genealogical relationships are used here in their usual context. In addition I have used a number of different symbols to indicate special relationships.

Common Symbols

△ man; ◯ woman; = married couple.

◯ (vertical or slanting single lines) connect parent(s) and children.

△ ◯ (horizontal lines) connect siblings.

Special Symbols

~ same; ~∤ different (together with kin type indicated); qualifies the "sibling" type of relationship according to Tiwi principles (for example, ~ MM = "one-granny"; ~ FF = *aminiyati* or "one-grandfather" siblings; ~ M ~∤ F = same mother but different father).

~PS~ phratry section siblings.

△——◯ (slanting double solid lines) connect mother-in-law and son-in-law. [2] case number for discussion.

△ = ◯ (broken line) indicates same individual in his consanguineal and affinal genealogical position.

△01 Small numbers indicate year of birth.

Note: All individuals are identified by a unique initial; the same initial always indicates the same individual. Numbers above the marriage sign indicate number of marriages for wife involved. Sibs are indicated by shading.

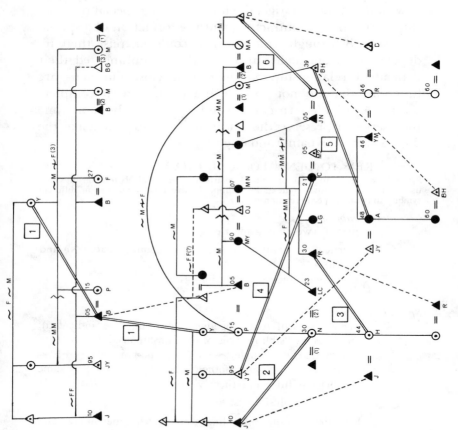

Fig. 11 Genealogy 1

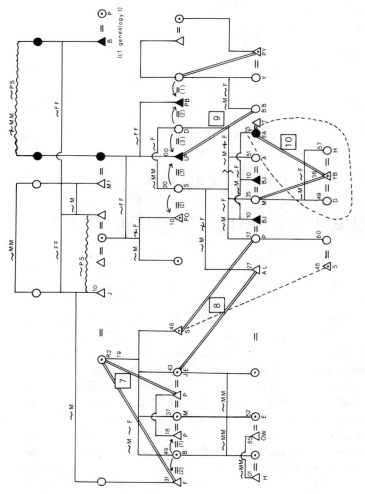

Fig. 12 Genealogy 2

CHAPTER FIVE

Pregnancy and Motherhood

Four months after a girl reaches puberty she ceases to be a *muriŋaleta;* she is now referred to as a *murukubara,* a young woman. She is considered to have graduated from both economic and sexual "schools" and is expected to assume full responsibility in these activities. She is also expected to play a responsible role on all ceremonial occasions. She has, however, little social standing. She is no longer a child to be indulged, but she is not yet an adult to be listened to. She has borne no children to give her prestige in the eyes of her husband or of other women. If her lot is hard at "home," with little outlet for her individuality, she is, however, of an age to attract the attentions of young men and to arrange meetings with them in the bush at times when she should be hunting for food for her elderly husband. If she is going to accept a lover, this is the age to do so, for as my informants commented, "Children make such bush meetings difficult."

I do not believe that in the old days, or even today, extramarital love affairs were a completely sanctioned custom. From the husband's point of view, they were a source of constant concern, but from the young wife's point of view they were often very desirable. For the young unmarried men, certainly, they were something to achieve whenever possible. According to my female informants, it was "proper Melville Island way" to have both a husband and a lover as contemporaneous sexual partners. Choice of a lover was made among those young men in the vicinity of the wife's residential group who could be sexual partners of the woman without violating incest taboos. Typically they were her husband's close or long-way "younger brothers."

Go-betweens, usually close siblings of the lovers, aid them in arranging meetings in the bush, for the two should not be seen talking together. When lovers walk together, the boy is careful to walk in the girl's footprints, obliterating them so that her husband cannot follow her. Such attempts at secrecy are designed to conceal the actual meetings of the young lovers and not the affair itself. The young women compose love songs that they "present" to their lovers, but which only they can sing. I collected only one of these love songs, an ancient one, the composition of which was ascribed to Bima, the errant wife of Purakapali, both important mythological characters. Bima sang this song after her lover, the moon, had been killed by her husband:

> *Biliwaŋiya tiŋatia*
> I am a bad girl.

This song is still sung by a woman when she has met her lover frequently enough to goad her husband into some overt and public action.

The action that a husband may take on such occasions is legally defined. It must be remembered that under normal circumstances the husband is a resident member of his wife's natal domestic group, and thus he acts under the supervision of her close kinsmen. He may verbally express his displeasure within the earshot of all his wife's resident kinsmen, an action that is considered a "formal growl" by the Tiwi. In response to such a "growl" his wife's kinsmen may take action and direct their sister or daughter to behave herself and not make her husband angry.

A husband should not take physical action against his wife. A small-scale "beating" may pass unnoticed by his wife's kinsmen, but should a husband beat his wife too much or too often, her kinsmen (father or brothers) will take her away from him and he cannot "growl," for they are still considered her "boss."

But the husband can take physical action against the lover, and this is considered the proper way to handle such situations. One such fight took place while I was gathering information in the settlement. A man with three wives had received information that his youngest wife, aged twenty-two, had been seeing too much of a certain young man, and in particular they had been seen on the previous day going off to the bush together. The two men started wrestling with each other, then retired to get their fighting clubs (*muraguŋa*). They circled each other, shaking their clubs violently in the air but striking no blows. The lover was then handed a sharp metal-tipped mainland-type spear by his brother, but immediately the husband's brothers shouted that this was not right, and they sent a young boy to fetch the superintendent of the settlement. The threat of the superintendent intervening immediately resulted in the lover's laying aside the spear. The two men returned to wrestling, and the messenger to the superintendent was called back. All within hearing had now surrounded the two men, and a discordant chorus of opinions loudly offered by nearly everyone present accompanied the fight. The young wife of the angry husband stomped up and down beside the fighters yelling her side of the story to all present, but her "one-granny" brother stepped in, grabbed her by the arm, and told her, "Shut up, be quiet. You are the cause of all this trouble."

Occasionally one of the combatants would be knocked to the ground, at which point he would be helped up by his wife, in the old husband's case, by his eldest wife. Although each man had close brothers among the spectators, they did not come in to help, but I was told that they would have done so had the fight reached serious proportions.

An old woman threw a bucket of water over the two fighters, and they immediately separated, but they continued with a verbal exchange. The old man crouched with one hand held behind his back, the other supporting his chin, as he raved at the lover of his wife. My informant pointed out that he was acting in an "old-fashioned" way, for when the men used to wear long beards they would clench these beards between their teeth while fighting.

After five minutes of this verbal exchange, the fight ended. It was hard to tell at that moment who had won, and even my informant could not answer my question. However, by next morning the old man had left the settlement with his three wives, and he remained camped across the bay for ten days.

Eloping is considered a serious offense which, in the past, usually led to pursuit by the offended husband and his kinsmen, and often to battle between the kinsmen of the husband and lover. While women were often the cause and perhaps the victims of feuds and battles, these were the activities of men, and I did not collect many case histories of such events. Pilling (1957) gives such case histories, and I will add here only one woman's description of a "formal" battle. As a woman's impression of a battle, this account should be considered to have validity, but as an actual description it leaves much to be desired.

According to my informant (a middle-aged woman), the husband whose wife had eloped would call a meeting and ask for help from his local sib and phratry members. If necessary, he would send a messenger to invite distant members of his sib and phratry to join the battle. The "enemy" (the lover's "people": his sib and phratry) would also be sent a message. The messenger was painted red, white, black, and yellow, and carried a single unbarbed "mangrove" spear. He announced the time and place for the battle. Everyone prepared his mangrove spears and assembled at the appointed place at the designated time. When everyone had arrived, my informant continued, they lined up on opposing sides and the battle began.

First a young boy from each side advanced and threw a spear. Then two more youngsters exchanged spears, and then a third pair. After this exchange of spears everyone threw his spear. When one side decided that they had had enough, an old man carried a white flag between the two lines and said, "You have won, we lose." Then they all camped. Next morning they had a little fight and went home. My informant finished her description at this point, and I had to ask her who got the wife, the husband or the lover, in the case either side won. She informed me that in either case the lover kept the wife, for the fight was not over who got to keep the woman but only for the husband's "honor," and after the fight the trouble must be forgotten. I suspect that my informant's account of the legal outcome of such a battle may have been personally prejudiced, as she had eloped three times successfully!

Today murder and battle are frowned upon by both the mission and government officials, but they have, probably unconsciously, provided an alternate way to settle illegal elopement by making available certain valuables used to make satisfactory financial compensation and by providing social security for old men. The old men do not need young wives to feed them, and are often quite willing to have a young wage-earning man supply them with all the fancy things they never needed or thought of in the past and for which they themselves cannot obtain the necessary money. In view of the fact that his young wife was probably deceiving him at every opportunity anyway, the old husband today has little to lose and much to gain by agreeing to a financial settlement.

A story of such a case was told to me by the wife stealer, the girl's lover, a man in his early forties.

D's first husband, an old man, died in Darwin, and her *aɲamani* (MMB—restricted genealogically) took her away and said, "No one can have this girl. She is too expensive. If anyone tries to get her, I will murder him." [I do not know by what "right" D's mother's mother's brother justified his statement and actions.]

D sent her brother to me with a ring. "Who sent this?" I ask her brother. He says, "My sister sent it to you. She likes you." I told her brother that I couldn't marry D because her *aɲamani* didn't like me. D's *aɲamani* took D away from the settlement, but D then met brother of mine and gave him a bracelet to give to me. I ask him, "Who sent this?" and he says, "D sent it to you. She likes you."

So we three go, my brothers and I, in a canoe and in two days we come up to D and her *aɲamani*. Again the old man says, "I can't give you D. If she had a younger sister, O.K."

I told the old man, "Well, I don't want her anyway," and we went away and camped. We were only three, and we had no people so we couldn't fight the old man. We followed them. At sundown, I took a spear and a knife and went close to the old man's camp. I threw a stick into the camp. D heard it and came up to me and stood along side of me and said, "Well, I'll follow you."

"Right-oh," I said, "we've got to go away." We walked back miles and miles and swam across a large river and met my two brothers. One brother say, "Did you bring her back?" and I say, "Yes," and he say, "Oh."

We sleep for a little bit, but at three in the morning D and I get up before old man and his mob come after us. We went to Tiparaimi and hid for three months. By and by, I think all right to come to settlement. Across the bay from the settlement some people come up and say, "You got big trouble. Going to be killed." I say, "I don't care," and go and get my spears.

Next morning we go to the settlement in a canoe. I go first so

I get killed first. We land. No one come. I walk up and say, "D
get off canoe." I anchor canoe and go up to compound. No one
fight. Meet old man and he say, "All right! Give me flour,
sugar, tea, tobacco, calico, jam, cheese, pants, singlet, razor,
mirror, tins," and plenty more. I give him these things. No more
trouble, plenty expense that's all.

Conception

A woman will remain in the *murukubara,* young woman,
classification until the day when a certain food "no longer
taste good." Having been well instructed in the facts of life,
she knows that she is carrying a child, and she becomes known
as a *poperiɲanta,* a pregnant woman.

Much has been written about aboriginal conception beliefs.
Knowing that this was an "important question," I approached
a group of men and women one day early in my investigations
and quite seriously asked them, "Who makes babies and how
do they get inside the mother?" I was entirely unprepared
for the reaction. The men and women stopped their talk and
looked at me questioningly. When I said nothing, they looked
at each other and began to giggle, then broke into uncon-
trolled laughter. They paused only to repeat my question to
each other and to those who, hearing the uproar, came to
investigate. Each time my question was repeated, the laughter
resumed with renewed convulsions. Finally, one woman dried
her streaming eyes and caught her breath enough to answer
my repeated question. "Boy make him," she said and looked
so contemptuous at my innocence that I feared for my future
ability to get any useful information from these people. I did
the only thing possible and joined in the continuing laughter,
hoping that they would think that I had meant the question
as a joke in the first place.

After a while I said defensively, "I know boys make babies,
but in America we tell little children a big bird brings them
to the house." A lengthy and quite serious debate ensued.
Finally the woman who had given me the first answer said,

"They reckon Purakapali makes children." "Where does he get them from?" "Oh, from anywhere." "What does he do with them?" "Reckon he tells his wife Bima to bring them down to the women."

I knew I had literally and figuratively asked for it, and it was six months before I asked a direct question again. However, by this time I had considerable information concerning Tiwi conception beliefs, and the direct question was merely to put the various facts in their proper perspective.

Without a doubt, the Tiwi today know that sexual intercourse between a man and woman is likely to result in pregnancy, that husbands and lovers both can *make* babies. Two instances will illustrate this. Accompanying the expedition to the island was a man who had been in Darwin for over a year. He was returning to see his wife whom he had left on the island and his newborn son. When I asked his wife who was the father of her child, she replied with the name of her husband, but when I asked her who *made* the baby, she gave me the name of another man. I asked a number of other women the same set of questions separately, and each gave the same two names in the same order of relationship. I asked the other women how they knew the name of the man who *made* the baby, and they said, "That is easy. The baby looks like B, its mother's lover," and indeed the infant was the image of its biological father.

The case of the only "single" girl in the settlement is another instance. A was in her late teens in 1954. She was classed as "single" by my informants, not because she did not have a husband (she had two, both of whom she had deserted), but because she preferred to live with her parents and accept the love of three young men simultaneously. The other women considered her to be very foolish, for they said it was hard enough to stay out of trouble with one husband and one lover at the same time, but with three lovers at the same time there was plenty of trouble in the bush. Lovers are considered to be more jealous than husbands, and they said that all three

boys were following her in the bush and there was no opportunity to "do business." But evidently A and one lover did
find time to be alone, as she became pregnant.

Again I asked the two questions, who was the father and
who made the baby. The women said, "She got no husband.
By and by when that baby get born, we see who make him,
then she marry that one." A solved this particular problem by
having a miscarriage, whether induced or by accident I was
unable to determine.

Although the Tiwi recognize that either a husband or a
lover can make a baby by having sexual intercourse with its
mother, they also assert that such activity cannot alone
create a *Tiwi* child. A Tiwi must be *dreamed* by its father,
the man to whom its mother is married, before it can be
conceived by its mother. To the Tiwi there is no conflict
between the two beliefs concerning conception. In fact there
is only one belief, while there may be two "fathers."

According to Tiwi belief, individuals exist in the universe
before birth into Tiwi society. Unborn individuals are called
pitapitui, and if conditions are right, groups of *pitapitui* may
sometimes be seen by both men and women, playing about
the locality with which they are associated. An interesting
contrast was found between male and female informants'
descriptions of the appearance of *pitapitui* in general. Male
informants described the playing *pitapitui* as small individuals
with human shape, while invariably my female informants
told me that they looked like little birds that live in the pandanus. One woman, when given the opportunity, selected
without hesitation a picture of the brown honeyeater from a
book on tropical birds as representing the appearance of these
unborn *pitapitui.* I thought it particularly appropriate that
the proper designation of the brown honeyeater is *Glicophila indistincta!*

Regardless of the difference in appearance perceived by
male and female Tiwi, both sexes agreed on the social characteristics of the *pitapitui.* The principal activity of these

unborn children seems to be either playing or hunting for their parents. When I asked what was their life if they were never found by their fathers and thus not born into Tiwi society, my informants suggested that they undoubtedly married other *pitapitui* and had babies, hunted for their food, fought, and eventually died: in other words, lived a life similar to that of the living.

Individual *pitapitui* are affiliated with one or another of the matrilineal sibs and thus must be born to a mother who is a member of its own sib. But evidently there is no direct communication between *pitapitui* members of a sib and female members who will become their mothers. *Pitapitui* do not know which woman in their sib is their particular mother and can only obtain this information from their father, whose identity they do know.

A *pitapitui* lives in the country of which his father is an owner (not necessarily a resident). Each country has a number of known localities inhabited by *pitapitui*. As part of my census data I asked individuals to name the place in which they had lived as *pitapitui*. Many of them had no idea, but others were very definite in giving the geographical location and adding, "That place is alligator, or flying-fox, or pandanus *dreaming*." In every case obtained, the sib name given was not that of the informant's own sib, but rather the name of his or her father's matrilineal sib. In this instance, the word "dreaming" is used in reference to a place owned by particular matrilineal sibs and inhabited by the children of *male* members of the *owning* sib.

The word "dreaming" is also commonly used as a synonym for one's father's matrilineal sib in such statements as "one should marry one's *'dreaming'*" as an alternate to "one should marry a member of one's father's sib," having exactly the same referent. It was some time before I became aware of this equivalence of an individual's *dreaming* with his or her father's sib so that in my data collection I asked information separately until one day an informant, with whom I had been checking much of the data collected up to that time, turned to me and said with some impatience at my evident stupidity, "But they are the same: one's dreaming and one's father's sib!" But they are not exactly the same. An individual is not a member of his or her father's matrilineal sib, nor are they owned by that group. They rather *possess* an essence of that sib as their *dreaming*.

Unborn Tiwi *(pitapitui)* do not possess a *dreaming,* and this is the essential difference between the unborn members of a matrilineal sib and the living member of that sib. A *dreaming* is the catalyst that transforms a Tiwi from the world of the unborn to that of the living. A *pitapitui* gets a *dreaming* by being found by, or finding, a father. The act of "finding" is also called *dreaming,* and it occurs typically while the father is asleep. According to some of my male informants, a father can only "find" a *pitapitui* while he is resident in his own country. If this is true—and exceptions to this occur in my case histories—then *pitapitui* have a pre-existent local corporate group affiliation as well as a sib affiliation. This concept is strengthened somewhat by the belief that should a man have difficulty in "finding" a *pitapitui,* the man's own deceased father will locate one and bring it to his son. No living man can locate a *pitapitui* to send or bring to his son. Ideally, that is, if the son has married into his father's matrilineal sib and if there has been local corporate group endogamy, a man's father is a member of the same localized matrilineal sib segment as is the *pitapitui* that he finds for his son. My informants did not consider it necessary to explain the help that a deceased father may give his living childless son in terms of sib and local corporate group affiliation, but they were emphatic that only a deceased father's ghost was in a position to communicate with and dictate to a man's unborn children.

The Tiwi today say that the *pitapitui* are "stories" from *palinari* (dream) time, the past. As such they strengthen the position of an individual in his *ideal* social relationships with

his local corporate group, his localized matrilineal sib segment, and his father's, mother-in-law's, and spouses' matrilineal
sibs. It is for these reasons that fathers still dream their
children, in spite of the fact that many of my informants could
recognize conflict of this belief with their traditional knowledge of biological conception and with what knowledge they
have acquired through contact with Western science and
beliefs. The apparent conflict between the biological and
sociological beliefs concerning conception are neatly resolved
by discriminating between men who make babies and fathers
who dream children, both of whom are necessary to conception and creation of a new Tiwi life.

Cases of father's dreaming their children were related to
me in 1954.

> My father been die when I little boy. By and by I get wife.
> Father see I no got *pikanini*. He get *pitapitui* from Karslake
> Island in my country and bring them to me. One day I was out
> with Pablo. We are crossing a mangrove swamp, and the water
> was deep. Pablo go ahead. I couldn't cross so I go sleep in
> mangrove. Five girls come up. "Papa," they say. (I had five girls.
> Four been die. Rosemary was behind.) I say, "Come along." I go
> back to Darwin. One night I be asleep. A spear hit me on the
> head. I wake up. I think wife hit me on head. I slap her. "You
> been kill me," I say. "No," she say, "I been asleep." I point to
> my head and say, "Look here, I got hurt." She say, "No, no. I no
> hit you." I think then maybe *pikanini* and next morning I got
> *pikanini*.

Ali had a dream in which he saw his unborn son in a canoe,
killing a turtle. Ali then went to Darwin without his wife, and
his dream son followed him and said, "You are my father, but
who is my mother?" If a man has several wives and particularly if they are members of different sibs, this is an important question. Ali told the *pitapitui* that his mother was Polly.
Later, Ali told me, he received word from his wife, Polly,
back on the island, that she was pregnant.

Women never see their children in dreams before they

know they are pregnant, and so I questioned several women on whether they really believed husbands saw their children in dreams *before* their wives told them they were pregnant. One elderly lady related the following story as proof that husbands did indeed dream their children before their wives conceived.

> Bos saw his son in a dream. His son was in an airplane fighting in the sky. The son was shot down receiving wounds in his arm and leg. The injured *pitapitui* came up to Bos and said, "You are my father, but first I go to America to get good medicine. I send my sister to you first; I will come behind. In six years I will come back and you will know me." Six years later Bos's wife gave birth to a son. When Bos first looked at his son he said, "What is he? He is a man, but he has a crooked arm and leg. This is the son I dreamed."

The relationship among dreaming localities, localized matrilineal sibs, and landowning groups is definitely not a simple, unambiguous one. Direct questioning of informants on localization of *dreamings* elicited a myth and a list. "Back in *palinari* time, Tokombini was the big boss. He called a big meeting at Muripianga in the Yeimpi country. He say to each one, 'What are you going to be?' and they would say, 'alligator,' 'water,' and so on. Then Muripiaŋganila said to his sister Uriupianila, 'You go make that place, Uriupi.' And he went on and gave places to each one." Mountford (1958:35) continues this myth and states that each was also instructed to "create the aboriginal foods belonging to each place and then change themselves into the particular bird, reptile, fish or inanimate object with which that locality is now associated." The list that was given corresponded with separately obtained listings of localities associated with *pitapitui* and *dreamings* (father's sib), rather than origin places for particular matrilineal sibs. However, if sib marriage exchange and local endogamy were strictly followed, each locality should contain two *pitapitui* centers, each belonging to one particular sib and inhabited by unborn members of the alternate affinal sib. I have discussed this postulated aspect of Tiwi sib distribution in the previous chapter, and it is unnecessary to do more here than to point out the discrepancy between the myth and reality as it exists today. Although Tiwi social structure has obviously changed over time, Tiwi mythology does not reflect these changes. We should not expect to see a complete congruence between mythology and fact, but it does seem that among the Tiwi there is far less acknowledged relationship of the past with the present than has been reported for other aboriginal peoples. Tiwi beliefs of conception *dreamings* appear to be almost completely disassociated today from mythology and philosophy concerned with the origin of life, activities of *dreamtime* ancestors, or continuity of descent through time. I do not believe that this disassociation is a recent result of the breakdown of Tiwi culture and loss of traditional philosophical teachings and faith. In Tiwi culture, there is little recognition of or dependence on the past as validation of the present, and this factor emerges as a dominant characteristic of Tiwi life.

Pregnancy

Once a *pitapitui* has been dreamed by its father and been told who is its mother, the women say that it enters their body through their vagina and goes into a little "egg" located in the placenta *(anera)*. There it grows big until it bursts out of the egg, at which point birth takes place.

When the baby begins to grow inside its mother's body, it makes some food taste bad to its mother, and by this sign women know they are pregnant. (A husband evidently does not tell his wife he has *dreamed* a child and sent it to her.) A pregnant woman must observe certain precautions. Because she might offend the *maritji* (rainbow spirits), she cannot bathe in the sea or in large bodies of fresh water, particularly those in a strange country. Placing food on a fire (cooking) or spitting into the flames will cause a child to twist in the womb and give pain. Certain foods are also taboo. Pregnant women may not eat carpet snakes, fish, or hawksbill turtle, nor the eggs of crocodiles or snakes. During all of the rainy season and for most of the dry season, pregnant women may not eat yams. Yams begin to grow during the wet season, and only when they have reached their full growth late in the dry season are they harmless to the unborn child. The women explain that new yams have sharp-pointed tips filled with an invisible sickness called *tarni*.[1] If a pregnant woman eats these yams, the end of the yam will pierce the womb and *tarni* sickness will kill the baby.

"In the old days," I was told, a pregnant woman was not allowed to walk in the bush after dark. Another *pitapitui* might pass into her body and two babies would be born at the same time. In 1954, my informants insisted that this had never happened in the past, and that today only mission girls had twins. I cornered a visitor from the mission at a funeral ceremony and got the admission that twins were sometimes born in the past, but they choked the second born because "Old people didn't like twins." In 1962, my informant confirmed the practice of killing one of a pair of twins but added that in the case of a boy and a girl pair, the boy would be choked regardless of the order of birth. She said they did not like twins because "it was shame for the mother."

This belief that a "walk in the bush in the dark" will produce twins is, I think, further proof of the recognition that sexual intercourse can result in pregnancy. The phrase "walking in the bush" is most commonly interpreted as "meeting a lover." Sexual relations between husband and wife were said to be suspended during pregnancy. No reason was given, but this seems to be consistent with the belief that menstruation is caused by sexual intercourse. Although a father will

[1] All yams carry this sickness at all times, and during the wet season initiated men can eat no yams; women, unless pregnant, are not so restricted. More about this sickness and its connection with yams will be given in Chapter 9.

dream of several of his children at one time, he never sends them to the same wife at the same time. A *pitapitui* theoretically cannot get into its mother's womb without being sent by its father, but multiple births have occurred. Since a father is entirely innocent, a lover must have been responsible; hence, the "shame" and probable concealment of the event from the mother's husband.[2]

Some Tiwi women, practice abortion, and all women past puberty know the methods. Drinking the milk of the milk-wood tree will cause an abortion, as will eating or drinking something very hot, including today strongly seasoned food prepared in the settlement. Jumping from a tree to the ground or hitting the womb with a stick will also produce an abortion, I was informed. When one of these methods proves effective, the mother will be all right if the *anera* (placenta) wherein resides the *pitapitui* is discharged, at which time the bleeding will stop. However, if the placenta is not discharged, the bleeding will continue and the mother will die, for there is no known cure.

It was difficult to find out just why some women deliberately tried to abort their child. One woman told me that if a wife became pregnant too soon after having reached puberty, it was not good for her to continue the pregnancy. The baby if allowed to be born may be too weak to live. But I think an equally strong reason to abort a pregnancy when the mother is young is the desire of some young wives to postpone their motherhood so as not to interfere with their love life. This was the dominant reason given in 1962 by young female informants who frankly admitted that they had induced sometimes several abortions and would do so again should they become pregnant before they had decided on which of their boy friends they would eventually "marry." I think, however, that the willingness to abort a pregnancy has become more common in recent times than it ever was in the

[2] The obvious phallic shape of the new yams, whose pointed ends are filled with sickness, may be the reason for their being tabooed at this time.

past, for then it was only by becoming a mother that a woman gained any real status in the society.

Birth

As soon as a woman knows she is pregnant, she starts to "follow" moon. "Moon makes baby come," I was told. When the moon is full the woman knows her time is near, and she goes into the bush with a "big mob of people, father, mother, in-laws, brother, sister." Anyone may accompany her except her husband, for "maybe he get too frightened."

One afternoon, as I was chatting with the wife of the superintendent, Barbara came up to request some castor oil for Glenda, whose "pikanini was close up, but too slow." Most of the women considered Barbara to be the most skilled midwife in the settlement. We followed her back up to the top of the hill above the settlement. Near the top we passed by a small clearing with a fire smoldering in the center. Close by this clearing was another, where we came upon Glenda and her attendants. Glenda was kneeling with her legs folded under her. Behind her sitting on a log was Doris, whose legs supported Glenda's back. Two other women sat on either side of Glenda, and Barbara squatted down in front of her.

Truly a "big mob" of people were present: over a dozen women and many children of all ages, but no men were in the group. When a brother of Glenda's husband appeared to ask a question of the superintendent's wife, however, no one seemed to regard his presence as other than normal. As he turned to leave, this man paused to give Glenda a few reassuring pats on her head. The children played about under no restrictions and were even encouraged to make lots of noise, for the baby would "hear them and would come out quick to join them having fun."

As each pain began, Barbara and Doris pressed hot leaves against Glenda's back and groin, and the two side attendants pressed their thumbs against her closed eyes. Barbara massaged Glenda's swollen abdomen with swift short movements, while

Doris pressed downward on her back. When the pains were particularly severe, close to the end of labor, Barbara supported Glenda. She continued her massage and pressure on Glenda's stomach. In the intervals between pains, Glenda was given sips of water but no food, for eating food "would make the baby come slowly." Hot leaves were applied to Glenda's back, groin, and legs to relieve cramps, for throughout the two hours that I observed her, Glenda did not move from her kneeling position.

Just before the baby was delivered, the children were told to move a short distance away. Jenny, a cohabiting wife of thirteen, sat nearby, but did not take part as did the other women. The baby was allowed to drop on the ground unsupported. Glenda was helped to shift a few feet to the right and her left foot was placed on the umbilical cord. While Barbara continued to assist the new mother in discharging the placenta, one of the other women placed some calico under the infant's head and with another cloth began cleaning her. When the afterbirth had been discharged the cord was cut with a razor blade; it was not tied, but allowed to bleed. In the old days, I was told, before they had razor blades, they crushed and severed the cord between two stones.

A small depression was made in the ground close to the log. The afterbirth was placed in it and covered with dirt and ashes, and some burning logs were placed on top. Only then was the infant picked up and placed on some calico. One of the women then assisted Glenda to her feet and supported her as everyone moved to the other clearing close by, where the fire had been kept burning. The fire was removed, and Glenda squatted over the warmed earth. More warm earth was wrapped in a bit of calico and held against her abdomen.

Meanwhile, the baby girl was placed on her left side on a blanket spread on the ground. She was wiped off some more and dusted all over with warm earth to "dry her." Barbara used her little finger to remove mucus from the infant's throat, for otherwise, she said, the child's voice would be hoarse like a willy-wag-tail (a bird). She asked the women to bring some urine *(pagini)* with which she would wash the infant's eyes, but the woman handed her a little water instead, inside a folded leaf. The infant's eyes were washed and a little of the water was forced down her throat. Then Barbara took the baby in her lap, and after warming her hands near the fire, she molded the infant's head by pressing on the back of the skull and up on the underside of the chin. "By and by her head grow too long if we not do this," she informed me.

For the rest of the day the newly delivered mother is given nothing to eat, but afterward she may receive bush foods in any amounts and kinds she desires. She camps at this place for five days. During this time her husband may not see her or the infant. If he should break this restriction, the baby might die of *tarni,* the invisible sickness. However, the father receives a message from his wife's attendants informing him of his child's sex. For a girl he receives a short stick, for a boy, a long stick or spear.

At the end of the period of isolation, but before returning to camp, the mother and baby are painted. The baby is rubbed with milk and then covered with charcoal. The mother is painted as she was when she became a *muriŋaleta,* with a red stripe down the center of her body, both back and front, and down her upper arms. The lower half of her face from the bridge of her nose down is painted black, while the upper half is red.

By becoming a mother, the woman has reached another period of life. If she is the mother of a girl, she is called *pernamberdi,* or if the mother of a boy, *awri-awri.* These terms last until she produces a child of a different sex from the last one, and until she reaches menopause. The term applied to barren women is the same as that for a woman who has passed child-bearing age—*parimariŋa.*

With the birth of her first child a young wife becomes an equal among the other women of the camp. No longer is she given the most tedious housekeeping tasks to perform. No longer are her opinions tossed aside as being inconsequential. The older women will still give her unasked-for advice and help when requested, but the young mother can refuse to follow the advice and begin to give some of her own. By giving birth to a girl she gains status in the eyes of her son-in-law and her husband. By giving birth to either sex the wife has begun to insure that she and her husband will be looked after in their old age.

Some women are, however, barren, and although they gain some status with age, in all respects this status is limited. The women I knew who had never had children of their own were, with rare exceptions, social nonentities. Their only value was in being counted as wives by their husbands. Although these barren women were close classificatory mothers to their co-wives' and sisters' children, their role as second mothers did little to relieve their disadvantageous position. The only solution was formal adoption. I have already related the case of a brother giving his childless "one-granny" sister his daughter for adoption as a "daughter-in-law."

Although adoption may be worked out between close siblings of opposite sex, as in the case above, more commonly a sister will give her sister a child to adopt formally. Usually the women are resident in the same camp or district and are married to the same man or close brothers. There were a number of these cases among the Snake Bay group in 1954, but it was often hard to discover such adoptions, for the close proximity of both the natal and adoptive families allowed the child to divide her time between the two quite equally. In one case I observed, I was quite sure the child herself chose her adoptive parents—her mother's younger sister and her husband. Once she fell and hit her head quite severely on a rock. The little girl's older sister ran to her aid and called not to their real parents, who were close by, but to their mother's sister and her husband, who were some distance away but who came running and comforted the injured girl. When I asked the older sister why she had not called to her own parents,

she told me that her youngest sister had been given to Agnes
and Albert because they had no children of their own. The
young girl, however, still slept with her real mother and
father, and accompanied them whenever they left camp, but
whenever she hurt her pride or her body, she ran to her
adopted parents, and in particular to her "father," who always reciprocated with a great deal of comforting attention,
lasting sometimes for several hours. It was obvious to me that
the close mutual affection that existed between this child and
her adopted parents grew out of something more than the
formal adoption, the close proximity of the two households,
or the relationship of the two mothers. I expect that the
adoption came after, and sanctioned, the attraction and affection that grew up between the young child and the childless
couple.

CHAPTER SIX

The Economic Role
of the Tiwi Wife

The Tiwi have no single term to denote the period of a woman's life during which she assumes her full economic responsibilities, preferring to emphasize "motherhood." Nevertheless, Tiwi women play an important role in the island economy.

Division of Labor

Under the settlement conditions today,[1] there is little evidence of any division of labor by sex in hunting and gathering. Husbands and wives and their children form the daily hunting parties when they are in the bush. But in the old days, when men had plenty of wives, this was apparently not

[1] In 1962 I noticed that the Tiwi at Snake Bay had almost completely abandoned their traditional hunting and gathering activities. The ethnographic present for what follows is therefore restricted to 1954.

151

always so. Today there are still some foods that are exclusively hunted by only one sex, and when informants gave me a list of foods, they distinguished between those foods usually collected by women and those hunted by men. Even a casual glance at the list reveals that women's foods are all land foods, while those hunted by men, with one exception, belong to the sea and air.

In the list[2] of "women's foods" those in group A are also collected by men today; foods in group B were always collected by both men and women; and those in group C are still collected mainly by women. The second list contains those foods hunted exclusively by men, in the past as well as today.

WOMEN'S FOODS

Group A

bandicoot *(ibobu)*
blanket lizard *(kuperani)*
blue-tongued lizard *(tunuŋa)*
carpet snake *(iliŋa)*
cockle *(muludaga)*
crab *(uluŋga)*
honey *(iŋwati)*
iguana *(muani)*

mangrove snake *(puliarliŋa)*
mangrove worms *(irwili* and *wakitapa)*
opossum *(ununga)*
oyster *(arau)*
snails *(piruŋa* and *uteriman)*
tree rat *(ururatuka)*
water rat *(alintini)*
white-tailed rat *(itamuŋga)*

Group B

turtle eggs *(kuduka)*

Group C

cabbage palm *(tulini)*
cycad nut *(korka* and *iŋala)*

[2] Minor items of diet are omitted from this list.

fan palm *(mipari)*
a sweet root *(tugula)*
white clay *(tudianini)* "which they
    eat at the mission"
yams *(dioni, moruŋa,* and *ubona)*

FOODS HUNTED EXCLUSIVELY BY MEN

brolga *(tjilati)*
cockatoo
crocodile *(irikupe)*
dugong *(manduiŋini)*
fish *(maputi*—all kinds)
flying foxes
geese *(urukiliki)*
turtle *(tarakalani*—loggerhead
    and greenback)
wallaby *(taraka),* the one land
    game animal
whistle duck *(turinduri)*

It is questionable whether buffalo should be included in
the list of men's game. Certainly women do not hunt buffalo,
but I do not believe that men "hunt" them either. In 1954 it
was estimated that there were perhaps a dozen head of buffalo
still roaming Melville Island. The day before I left the island,
word was brought to the settlement that a buffalo had been
killed by a timbering party at the head of the Tjiberabu
River. According to the messenger, the buffalo had attacked
the party, who immediately took to the trees. For two hours
a battle raged with the buffalo charging and the men
striking back with their axes whenever they had an opportunity. Eventually the men won, but this is not hunting.[3]

That there has been some division of labor in food collecting is unquestionable, but it was probably most pronounced

[3] Cf. Basedow (1925:144-45) for another description of a buffalo "hunt."

in connection with vegetable foods, birds, and sea life. If a man had a lot of wives there was no need for him to help his wives in the bush collecting. His many wives could provide him and his nonproducing dependents with a balanced diet of meat and vegetables without his lifting a finger. But in the past young single men and those with only one or two wives almost certainly either accompanied their wives into the bush or went alone to hunt for opossums, bandicoots, and the like, as they do today. It is not considered "wrong" for them to hunt these small game animals, as it is considered "wrong" for them to collect vegetables or for women to go turtle hunting or goose killing. If women happen to be along on men's turtle hunts or goose-killing expeditions, nothing "bad" will occur, but they do not take part in the actual hunt or kill.

Women's Hunting Equipment

If women received little help from their men folk, they got a great deal of help from their well-trained hunting dogs. The dingo *(diamini)* is referred to as "the boss of the island." In the past, the natives say, they captured young dingo pups and trained them. The present-day hunting dog is a mixture, but dingo blood is undoubtedly a dominant part of the breed. These breeds are called *waŋgini*. One cannot keep the puppies born of one's own hunting dog, but must give them to another to raise and train. Women call their dogs by the same kinship terms as they call their own children. Dogs are also given sib membership. They have personal names that must be unique. A dog that gets too old to hunt is never killed but is retired, and another pup is trained to take its place. When a hunting dog dies, he is buried, and his owner's family weep and often cut themselves in mourning.

Another indispensable aid to women is the ax. In 1914 Spencer wrote,

> Fig. 4 which came from Melville Island, represents the crudest hafted axe that I have ever seen in Australia. It is simply a

roughly shaped block of ferruginous sandstone, measuring six and a half inches in length, four and a quarter in width, and two and a quarter in greatest thickness. It has been very roughly flaked so as to reduce it to its present shape and to form, also what must have been a very unservicable cutting edge, but there has been no attempt at grinding. It is the only example that I have seen in Australia of a hafted axe which has been flaked but not ground [Spencer 1914:355-56].

Today all the Tiwi use steel axes, the introduction of which probably began before the Fort Dundas settlement but did not reach any large distribution until the turn of the century. During the course of our bush travels in 1954, many stone axes were picked up from the surface. The older natives all said that these axes were used by their parents. Many had seen them in use, and some of the older men and women said they themselves had used the stone axes when they were small. All except two of the axes in our collection corresponded to Spencer's description, but of varying sizes and weights. Two showed some evidence of grinding. One old lady told me that the ground ax was a "proper good one and a proper old one," and that the chipped ones were "made quick feller and not so good." The same informant said, "In old days, I can't make proper ax so my aunti (FZ) make me good one. She make lots of good ax. Ax belong woman, no more men."[4]

Bush hunting requires an ax as a primary tool, whereas sea and air hunting require an ax only in order to make secondary tools, such as spears and throwing sticks, and to administer the death blow if necessary. Axes are absolutely necessary for cutting funeral poles, a job usually delegated to the men, but one in which their wives can and do sometimes help. Undoubtedly axes were used by both sexes and perhaps both sexes made them as well. We had several of our collected

---

[4] The ax situation in Melville contrasts markedly with that described by Sharp among the Yir Yoront of Cape York Peninsula, where stone axes acquired by trade were owned exclusively by older men and were an important symbol of their authority over women and young men. See Sharp 1952:69-81.

axes hafted, and the women who did this work showed no hesitation in preparation. The result is exactly the same as described by Spencer (1914:356).

The women stripped the bark from a vine *(ununduŋa)* and then split the vine in half. After heating the vine in a fire, they measured it around the butt of the ax. Then it was removed and beaten with a stone on the underside of the curve, after which the bark was braided into a small circular band. A paste prepared from crystals of bloodwood sap softened with water was put around the stone ax butt. The vine handle was then bent carefully around the stone over the sap, and the woman used her teeth to compress the vine while she worked the braided band up the handle until it was tight against the ax. The resulting haft was strong enough to hold up during a test in which a small sapling three inches in diameter was cut through. Informants said that one ax might last throughout the cutting of a whole funeral pole, but when the hafting sap gets brittle with age, it must be replaced.

Containers were also necessary for woman's hunting and collecting in the bush. Today, cast-off tin cans (billy cans), flour and rice sacks, and lengths of calico are used as containers, with the latter doubling as a change of clothing. Before these were available, the Tiwi women made baskets from the bark of the stringy-bark tree. This bark is best removed during the wet season, when the sap is running. First the woman makes two cuts top and bottom encircling the tree, then one longitudinal cut. Working the ax or the fingers into the long cut causes the bark to pop off. The outside shaggy bark is trimmed off with the ax, after which the whole sheet is soaked in water for approximately twenty-four hours. The sheet is heated over a fire to make it pliable, then folded end to end. The woman uses a sharpened and polished wallaby bone to make holes along the sides, through which she threads strips of pandanus, and she sews the sides together. While the basket is still damp, cross sticks placed inside hold the bark apart. When it dries the sticks are removed, and the basket remains permanently open. The basket is carried over the shoulder on a stick placed through a small, braided pandanus loop worked into the top edge. "Work" baskets are rarely painted. Baskets vary greatly in size; the largest are reserved for funeral ceremonies.

Water containers may be among the everyday hunting equipment, depending upon the location of water supplies and the season. The traditional water containers were made from the dry cabbage palm *(tulini)* leaf. The ends of the leaf are folded over and sewn tight with pandanus. The stem is bent over and sewn to the opposite end to form a handle. The resulting water-tight container, which measures approximately twelve inches by six inches and is about six inches deep, is called *tulini* and is rarely seen today. In 1954, I made a three-day expedition with a Tiwi couple and their daughter up the Tjiberabu River in order to gather some of these *tulini* leaves, this being the nearest source of supply. The *tulini* containers that were made to show us the technique were subsequently used at one of the funeral ceremonies to carry the water that the mourners washed themselves with at the grave site at the conclusion of their taboo period. This certainly was a traditional occasion that necessitated portable water. There were, however, few other occasions requiring the portage of water, and since the *tulini* palms are one of the few resources distributed unequally throughout the islands, these containers were probably comparatively rare, even in the past. Today tin cans made into "billy cans" by attaching a wire loop handle to the top are used not only to carry drinking water but also to boil tea, a staple in the contemporary "bush" diet.

The Tiwi woman hunter carried one other indispensable item with her—fire. Although matches are widely used today, fire brands are usually carried from the camp and kept burning throughout the day's hunt. The cone of the Bankshire pine is a preferred form of portable fire, but any slow-burning stick taken from the night fire will be carried in preference to making a fire when needed in the hunt. In 1954 all Tiwi knew how to make fire with a simple fire drill, despite the fact that matches were commonly distributed; however, it was rare indeed that we saw fire being made from "scratch."

Women's hunting equipment, in summary, consisted of a dog, an ax, a bark container, and a fire. With these items she was fully equipped to hunt, kill, collect, and cook any animal or vegetable food found on land or along the mud banks of creeks.

Men's Hunting Equipment

Men carry a spear when hunting and perhaps an ax, and if they are hunting inland game like the women, a dog and a fire. Today hunting spears are equipped with wire prongs, but in the old days a simple unbarbed "mangrove" spear with a fire-hardened tip was used to hunt wallaby, fish, and larger sea dwellers. The Tiwi do not use spear-throwers, and the basic technique was to approach as close as possible to the quarry so that the spear could be thrown at almost point-blank range. Wallabies were sometimes run down and killed with an ax or a stick. Today a harpoon with a detachable wire-pronged tip is used to capture both turtles and crocodiles, who are then dispatched with an ax blow or shotgun. I did not obtain descriptions of the traditional equipment or techniques for hunting these quarries.

Canoes were a part of the traditional material culture. Today, rather crude dugout canoes are carved from the kapok tree or bought from mainland natives who, the Tiwi say, "make more better canoes." The introduction of the dugout canoe to the northern coasts of Australia by the Malays is fairly well documented (Berndt and Berndt 1954:16; Harney 1957:77). Whether the Tiwi were taught the technique directly by the Malays or indirectly by the mainland natives is not known. Probably it was a combination of both.

The old style canoe was made of the bark of the stringy-bark eucalyptus. Basedow (1925) and Spencer (1914) both mention having seen these bark canoes in use in the early part of the twentieth century together with the dugout. A small model bark canoe was made in 1954 for use in a dance. These traditional canoes were essentially huge bark baskets with the main fold being lengthwise rather than crosswise. Basedow (1925:161-63) describes in detail the folding and sewing of the two ends with lawyer vine and the final caulking with beeswax, clay, or resin. The canoes varied from twelve to fifteen feet in length (Spencer 1914:398), and according to my informants were most unseaworthy; however, Basedow reports that the Tiwi occasionally traveled in them to the mainland (Basedow 1925:163).

Paddles are (and were) made out of ironwood. Extraordinarily heavy, they sink (I regretfully discovered) if lost overboard. The Tiwi make no attempt at artistic elaboration of the strictly functional paddles. Today's canoes have a short mast lashed in place between two close thwarts, and a square calico sail stretched between two booms which are permanently attached to the mast. The Tiwi sail their canoes only with a following wind that is not too strong.

The men used canoes in turtle, crocodile, and dugong hunting, and anyone who had to cross a span of water over a few yards in width and with any depth also traveled by canoe. All the Tiwi learn to swim at an early age, but the ever-present fear of crocodiles prevents anyone from swimming across such water barriers except in dire emergency.

For hunting geese each hunter cuts a set of special throwing sticks (*miliŋani*). The hunter measures the length of his sticks from his elbow to the tip of his fingers. He trims the sticks or bark, rounds off the ends slightly, and soaks them in water for about six hours to gain weight. The hunters kill geese at dusk as the geese fly low over the fresh-water swamps to roost for the night. Just before setting out the hunters smoke their sticks on one end to dry that portion which they will hold. As they do this, they cup their hands and direct the smoke to their necks, shoulders, and upper arms, singing in imitation of the noise their sticks will make as they fly through the air and hit the goose on its neck or upper wing, bringing the bird to the ground. Out on the marshes, the hunters arrange themselves in a line, and as the geese fly overhead each hunter fires off his sticks. In one hunt I witnessed, ten men each threw thirty sticks and downed only three geese, but I was told that this was a poor showing due to some unknown interference (fortunately they did not blame my presence).[5]

The men use their ironwood fighting clubs *(muraguŋa)* to down wallabies and flying foxes, although they also throw expendable sticks to knock flying foxes out of the mangrove branches where they roost during the day. When approaching roosting flying foxes, the men often smear the swamp mud over their bodies to disguise their man odor.

Bush Hunting

In the preceding pages I have discussed the hunting equipment of both the men and women and some of the more exotic types of hunting carried out periodically by males. The remainder of this section will be devoted to techniques of hunting small land game, a task usually relegated to women, but one in which young men participated in the past and in which both men and women participate to a great extent today. Bush hunting has always provided the everyday menu of the Tiwi living away from sources of flour, rice, corned beef, and tea.

A bush hunting party usually sets out a few hours after sunrise. Nowadays, they start the day with a heavily sugared cup of tea and a few puffs on a cherished rolled cigarette or on a crab claw, its open end stuffed with trade tobacco and the biting smoke drawn through a small hole drilled in the tip of the shell. During this quiet time some general plan for

[5] I have described this hunt in greater detail elsewhere (Goodale 1957).

the day is made: whether they shall hunt for opossums or bandicoots inland, go to the mangroves for fish, crabs, or cockles, or go along the shore for turtle eggs. If there is more than one nuclear family in camp, decisions will be reached as to the direction and area each family or small group will cover during the day. When I asked one man who was the "boss" of a hunting party, he wordlessly pointed to his feet. Indeed the decision-making process was so subtle that it almost went unnoticed by me.

When it has been decided to go inland, it is necessary to decide whether to hunt for opossums or bandicoots, for the locality of each differs. Opossums are to be found in trees, while bandicoots prefer hollow logs lying on the ground. It is more efficient to walk through the bush directing one's attention either up at the trees or down on the ground, rather than attempting to do both. Tiwi bush hunting techniques demand the least expenditure of physical energy; time is never a consideration.

Making a shopping list is but the first in a long series of energy-saving customs. For example, when hunting opossum, the first step is to locate a tree that shows signs that it has been occupied by this nocturnal animal. The Tiwi study the base of the tree carefully to see if there are any fresh tracks, then they scrutinize the trunk for signs of tiny tears made by the opossum's claws. I was told that these scratches are best seen against the sunlight, but even when they were pointed out to me, I had difficulty in distinguishing any animal-made scratches in the rough bark, much less the relative age of these marks.

If tracks and claw scratches are found to be recent, the hunter stands back to examine the tree itself to determine the easiest method, first, for making sure the opossum is at that moment in the tree and, second, for catching him.

If the tree is hollow all the way from the base to the top, the hunter is in luck, for he or she can use the most energy-saving method and light a fire in the hollow base and wait either for the smoke to drive the animal out or for the tree to burn down, whichever happens first. Should the animal be driven out on a limb, the hunter throws a barrage of sticks and stones at him until he falls to the ground, then chases and kills him with a blow from a stick.

If the tree is not hollow to the base and the animal is suspected to be sleeping in a hollow limb, the hunter must climb the tree. Holding his ax clenched between his teeth, the male hunter circles the tree trunk with his hands and places the soles of his feet against the trunk. Leaning outward, thus increasing the pressure of his hands and feet against the tree, the climber alternates advancing his hands and feet up the trunk and in a series of frog-like leaps soon reaches his goal. A woman tree climber presses her knees against the trunk rather than the soles of her feet. When the diameter of the tree is very large, the hunter (either male or female) cuts a long sapling and rests its top in a crotch where a limb joins the trunk and places its base firmly in the ground a few feet away from the base of the tree. The forty-five degree slope presented by the slender sapling presents no difficulty to a Tiwi as he or she runs up this "highway" on all fours in less than thirty seconds. (Once a Tiwi man demonstrated a tree-climbing method that involved tying the feet together at the ankles and then proceeding up the tree as in the first method described above.)

Once the hollow limb is reached and before any more energy is expended, the hunter breaks off a small branch, trims it with his ax, and inserts it into the opening in the limb as far as possible. If the branch meets with resistance, the hunter twists it gently, then withdraws and examines it to see if the rough end of the branch has picked up telltale opossum hairs. Rarely will a hunter persist if this final evidence is not obtained.

If the opossum is close to the opening in the limb, the hunter inserts a hand into the limb and grabs the quarry with no more ado. With one continuing movement he pulls

Above: Men hunt crocodiles mainly for the cash value of their skins.
Below: Children accompany their parents on the hunt. Carpet snakes are the only variety that the Tiwi eat.

Left: Cycad palm nuts are an important resource for the Tiwi. Dolly carries a bandicoot which she has killed in the day's hunt.
Below: Topsy and her dog Tober make an efficient bandicoot hunting team. Topsy inserts a stick into the hollow log to test it before chopping a hole where Tober indicates the bandicoot is sleeping.

Upper left: Some of the final painting for the *pukamani* ceremony is deceptively simple, such as Jack's striking use of solid colors. *Upper right:* Such elaborate designs often take as long as five hours to execute, but are considered necessary to disguise the close relatives of a deceased Tiwi from his ghost as they approach the grave to carry out the final rituals. *Lower left:* Joe painted for the final singing of the *apa* songs in the *kulama* ceremony. *Lower right:* A young woman (a *murukubara*) wears simple paint for a funeral ritual.

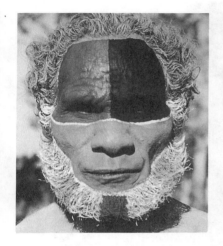

Father and daughter. The father is under mourning taboos and wears a feather ball (*tokwiiŋa*) around his neck and ochre on his face.

the animal out of the hole and swings it hard against the tree to kill it before it can bite. When the opossum is sleeping far down inside the limb, the hunter may chop a second small opening closer to the animal. If this is not possible, he will chop through the whole limb close to the trunk, and alert the ground crew—the hunter's companions—to chase the opossum if it wakes and runs when the limb falls to the ground.

Only when these methods are unsuccessful is the entire tree chopped down; and this drastic action is taken only if the hunter is both very desperate and certain that there is an opossum in the tree.

Of all the land game, only the opossum is gutted immediately upon killing. The hunter uses a small stick to lacerate the belly skin and open the inner abdominal cavity. The intestines and gall bladder are carefully extracted, for if they were not "it would make the meat taste bad." Although knives are readily available today, I only saw sticks used for this operation.

Since bandicoots spend their days sleeping in hollow logs resting on the ground, a good hunting dog can save the hunter a great deal of energy. As the hunter walks through the bush, her dog darts from one fallen log to another, investigating all in a broad line of march. A good dog is a beautiful thing to watch as he approaches a log, going first to one end and then to the other, giving each a careful sniff. Then he quietly works his way down the length of the log until he has located the exact position of the animal. Only then will he raise his voice to summon his owner, and he sits down close to where the animal is sleeping. The hunter may or may not test the log further by inserting a long trimmed branch down the inside of the log and twisting it to obtain the evidence of hair. Whether she does this depends on how much she trusts her dog's judgment. Once the bandicoot is located, the hunter cuts a hole in the log just large enough for her to insert her hand and pull the animal out. I never could figure out why the bandicoots slept through this activity as most of them did, but occasionally one did wake up and try.to escape. If the dog was well trained and on his toes, he detected this movement, waited for the bandicoot at the end of the log, and caught it as it emerged.

The Tiwi also use axes to cut out honey nests from hollow trees or fallen logs. And honey may be found in ground deposits, where nothing but a stick is needed to obtain it. Honey is usually eaten on the spot, for it is hard to transport unless one has an empty water-tight container. Usually considered "trail" food, honey is not looked for, but collected whenever located. Iguanas and carpet snakes are also incidentally gathered game. The hunter who spots one will grab any available stick and strike a killing blow before the reptile sees her and runs.

In collecting inland vegetable foods, an ax is necessary only in cutting down the fan palm and cabbage palm. Digging sticks necessary for yam gathering are usually made on the spot, sharpening the point of a strong stick with the ax. Cycad nuts are merely gathered from the ground or picked from the low tree.

Collecting shore and mangrove swamp food requires little but one's hands and available sticks or stones. The mangrove worms must be cut out of the mangrove roots with an ax, and a long stick is used to probe the sand for turtle eggs before digging them out by hand. Crabs are annoyed by touching them with a stout stick, which they grab with their powerful claws and foolishly refuse to release as they are pulled out of the shallow water. Cockles are hunted in the mud flats of the creeks at low tide, where their location is detected by noticing two faint lines of the edge of their shells as they lie just under the mud's surface. They need merely to be picked up. If the day's hunt is poor, the woman will often return to camp early, collect a container, and go to a mangrove swamp, where in a very short time she can gather the dependable and plentiful cockle in sufficient quantities to satisfy her family.

Although wallabies are properly men's game, the only one

I actually saw killed was attributed to a woman. Topsie's dog, Tober, flushed a dozing wallaby, chased it, and caught it by one leg. Although savagely cut by the hind feet of his quarry, Tober held on until one of the men in the party was able to catch up and strike a killing blow with his ax. Since it was Topsie's dog that caught the animal, she was considered the "boss," an important consideration in distribution the food, a subject that will be discussed shortly.

The outstanding characteristic of Tiwi hunting is related both to the abundance and to the nature of the fauna of the islands. There is no land animal, with the possible exception of the wallaby, that cannot be killed with a minimum of physical strength, skill, and equipment. Thus, the women not only could but did provide the major daily supply of a variety of foods to members of their camp. Children too could learn the necessary techniques at an early age, and since strength and energy were minor requirements, they began early to contribute to the larder. Men's hunting required considerable skill and strength, but the birds, bats, fish, crocodiles, dugongs, and turtles they contributed to the household were luxury items rather than staples. Hart describes a joint wallaby drive using fire and women beaters to drive the wallaby toward the men (Hart and Pilling 1960:41-42), but says these were spasmodic affairs, and I heard no reference to them during my stay.

Food Preparation and Distribution

There are two principal methods of food preparation, roasting and baking. Some foods are always roasted, others always baked, and still others are cooked by either method according to individual choice. A roaring fire is used only in cooking the fan palm. Otherwise roasting fires are all small and are usually allowed to burn down to glowing coals. In cooking small game animals and wallabies, there are usually two steps. First the animal is placed whole on the fire and frequently turned. When the skin and fur, if present, is charred and crisp, the animal is removed and easily dismembered. (In the old days a cockle shell, the only small cutting tool, was used for such tasks, together with the ax if necessary.) The separate parts of the animal are now replaced on the glowing coals and occasionally turned until well roasted. For a large wallaby, hot coals are placed on top of the joints as well as in the rib cavity to speed the cooking process, but animals are rarely completely buried and baked in what would be an earth oven.

Fish, cockles, crabs, and some forms of yams may be roasted or baked. The choice of method seems to depend to a large extent on how hungry the hunters or their dependents are, for baking takes quite a bit more time. Cockle roasting is interesting, for it is sort of a reverse roast. The cockles are arranged in a circle with the open edges of their shells facing down. Then a large fire is built on top and lit. After only five or six minutes, they are raked out of the fire and removed from their opened shells.

The cockle oven is equally interesting. A ring is cleared, and a fire is built using a few sticks of wood but mainly strips of fast burning bark. A large quantity of discarded cockle shells, the remains of past meals, are gathered and tossed on the fire. When the fire has almost burned down, the few remaining flaming pieces are moved, leaving only the hot shells and ashes. Upon this bed the cockles are carefully and evenly spread and immediately covered with strips of clean paperbark and then warm sand from around the fire. After about twenty minutes, the cooks will feel the top of the sand and if it is quite hot, they know that the cockles have cooked long enough. The sand is scraped off with a stick, the bark carefully peeled away, and everyone helps himself.

The very act of cooking distributes the food to others beside the hunter and his or her immediate family. Only if a hunter is hunting alone and not as one of a party, as is usual, may she cook the food she obtains in order to sustain herself through the day. But if she is returning to the camp, she is expected to bring some of her cooked catch back to the others. Under most circumstances a hunter—male or female—is not alone, and she gathers with her companions at some designated spot, where they either cook their food together before returning to camp, or decide to wait to cook at the camp itself. It is against custom for the hunter to cook what she has obtained; it must be given to another cook, even in cases where two hunters have made identical catches. The hunter is considered the "boss" of the animal, and the other, naturally, is called the "cook." In the case of an animal catch, the boss always receives the forequarters and brisket, and the cook gets the tail. Even in the case of a snake, these areas are determined and so distributed. Actually the choice of a cook depends on who first yells, "That's my tail." The first to call must always cook. Where there are more than two to be involved in the initial distribution, or in the case where the animal caught is a large one, others in the camp may lay claim to portions. The second person to yell claims the head and the third, a leg. This order is invariable. Those who make such claims help the first claimer in the cooking process.

The initial distribution of crocodiles and turtles seems to correspond to the men's positions in their canoe. The paddler in the stern, who is also the owner of the canoe and captain, gets all four legs. The man in the center, whose job it is to bail, gets the body, while the spearman positioned in the bow gets the head of the animal.

These two methods of initial distribution of animal portions are not necessarily governed by kinship, but they represent only the beginning of the distribution of any significant amount of food. One is obligated to give food to kinsmen in the order of priority: (1) the immediate family, spouse, children, parents, and mother-in-law; (2) "one-granny" brothers and sisters, with the restriction against handing it directly to them if they are of the opposite sex; (3) mother's brother and maternal or paternal grandparents. As the informants say, "You work for old people, not the young ones who can work for themselves." If an old person has no immediate family (a rare condition in the past), anyone belonging to the same sib is obligated to look after him. If the hunt has been very successful, the food will be distributed among all present, regardless of degree of relationship or age. However, if there is only a small amount, those not in the preferred ranks will not "growl" or be angry if they do not receive any.

Beliefs

Wasting food is considered to be dangerous to the person who does so. He is likely to be bitten soon by a poisonous snake or a crocodile. I was told a story of a man who had claimed the head and back of a wallaby and had gone away briefly while it was being cooked. He returned to find that only the head had been saved for him. He threw the head away in his rage. The next morning he was out fishing at the settlement fishnet. A big crocodile was in the net, and it caught the man, "who had to have thirty-six stitches taken in his leg."

A crocodile that has tasted or consumed human flesh is taboo for human consumption. A revenge hunt is undertaken, and if the animal is killed it is hacked to bits. If the animal is suspected of having consumed a member of the tribe, an attempt is made to recover enough of the victim to bury and hold a proper funeral. An animal killed by a hawk is also taboo for human consumption, for it will bring illness to the consumer.

There are times in an individual's life when certain foods are taboo, as during a woman's pregnancy and during part of the *kulama* initiation procedures. Aside from these individual food taboos, there are seasonal ones for fully initiated men, who may not eat yams from the beginning of the wet season until the conclusion of the annual *kulama* rituals held at the beginning of each dry season.

Unlike many societies where there are totemic sibs, there seem to be no taboos against eating the animal or vegetable food whose name is given to the sib to which one belongs. Not all the Tiwi sibs are named for edible things or even useful ones. There was only one instance in which I could find any connection between the avoidance of a certain food and sib affiliation. This was an individual case where a man was said to be avoiding the consumption of crocodile flesh, for "his father bin die last year and he still feel too sorry alonga him. He alligator dreaming." In other words, this man was refusing to eat the animal identified with his father's sib, his dreaming, not his own sib.

Members of a sib identified with an edible or useful substance have no special rights or obligations pertaining to the use, conservation, or increase in the supply of that substance. The only customs concerned with maintaining the supply of food pertain to two vegetable foods that are not identified with any sib, at least according to the records. In order to preserve the supply of cycad nuts, one cannot cut down a cycad palm. To my question, "Why not?" women answered, "If we cut down, then *korka* (cycad) have no more pikanini." They also reported that this custom had never been violated,[6] although no beliefs of evil or bad luck sanctioned the cycad law.

It was the custom when digging yams, particularly the new yams found at the beginning of the dry season, always to "leave little bit behind so more yams come up." Leading the women on, I asked why they did not take that "little bit" back to camp or settlement and plant it close to their homes. They replied, "Too much bother. We leave little bit where we find him, we know where he is alla time. By and by we want yam we find him easy." Again, no other explanation was given to sanction this custom. The Tiwi today have been

[6] Pilling (1957:264) cites only one case occurring on Bathurst Island between 1930 and 1932, which resulted in what appears to be a minor intercountry battle with unspecified results.

introduced to agriculture in a small way at the settlements, but I do not believe that it has had any influence on these incipient horticultural attitudes regarding cycads and yams.

Success in hunting appears to be a strictly personal matter. A long run of bad luck is usually attributed to an interfering *mobuditi,* a deceased Tiwi's spirit. If in life the deceased was closely associated with the hunter, and in particular if it is the spirit of one but recently buried, the ghost may follow the hunter in death as in life, and this will usually cause bad luck. But occasionally, by prearrangement, this expected result can be reversed. Two hale and hearty young men told me that they had made such an arrangement, agreeing that the one who died first would help the other in hunting. He would make some kind of signal, such as knocking on a tree, to indicate the presence of game. He would also warn his friend about sleeping crocodiles, so that he would not accidently put himself in danger.

Spirits of the dead appear to have some control over game in the area surrounding their place of burial, but only in extreme cases are they invoked to give aid to the living, for they are more likely to cause bad luck or even illness if their names are called. I heard such an invocation on only one occasion, during the goose-killing expedition, when after five days of poor luck the hunters called out to the ghost of a famous man buried in the locality many years previously. "Baŋgri, give us some geese," they called and pressed the point no further. The hunting improved only slightly, and no mention of Baŋgri was heard again. No promises are made to a ghost and no thanks tendered nor is any part of the catch shared with the ghost by placing an offering on his grave or by other means.

There is one class of spirits or mythological beings who can bring luck to an individual—the *paramanui. Paramanui* are small (about three feet tall) and look like men; but they are very "cheeky," and people are afraid of them. Whole families of them—men, women, and children—live together in big ant hills. They eat raw mangrove snails, for they have no fire. They have all kinds of weapons, and they are to be found everywhere.

A *paramanua* will follow a man and make his presence known, but when the man tries to hit him, he is not there. The mischievous spirit then jumps in back of the man and tickles him. The man turns quickly, but again the *paramanua* vanishes. The spirit then hits the man on the ear with the flat of his hand, causing the hunter to become "deaf" (unconscious) and to forget everything. The *paramanua* carries the man to his home in the ant hill—"nice places; got tucker (food) and house like hole in ground"—where the hunter lives with the *paramanua,* who makes a friend of him and gives him a daughter for a wife. If children are born, they are little fellows, for like the Tiwi, they "follow mother." The man may stay with the *paramanua* and thus disappear forever, which is the reason the Tiwi fear capture by these spirits. But sometimes he is allowed to return, and, because of the friendship, the *paramanua* gives his former captive a gift of phenomenal luck, but always with the condition that he must never tell where he got it.

A young woman told of her friend, a young man called Mani. One day Mani met a *paramanua* who said to him, "I'll give you something good," and, having become friends, they both sat down. *Paramanua* said, "No matter where you go I'll follow you and look after you, but if you call my name, you die." Mani never said anything for a long while. The *paramanua* had given him a small bone, like a child's bone, which Mani held in his hand, and every time he saw a wallaby he "catch him quick." He was lucky in cards, "Alla time get big numbers," and he won ninety pounds worth of clothing, calico, knives, and tobacco. One day someone said to him, "Someone bin give you this thing, what name?" and Mani, forgetting the words of his benefactor said, *"paramanua."* The *paramanua* was close by and heard him. The next day Mani

got sick, and about six o'clock he died. "He only about seventeen years old, poor fellow," my informant concluded.

Control of Resources

Although all those whose fathers are buried in a country
inherit rights to the products of the country, there is internal
control over who may exercise these rights and when. The
leading "big man" or his descendants—a group of one-
grandfather brothers—are considered the boss of the country.
The extent of their authority appears to include all co-owners
of the property as well as all nonowning residents, but today
this authority involves only permission to burn the grass. I
can say little about such leaders of the past.

During the wet season the grass grows about four to six feet
tall and provides effective cover for wallabies and dangerous
poisonous snakes, as well as bandicoots in fallen logs and
ground-dwelling iguanas. Hunting these animals at this time
is not only difficult but, because of the snakes, potentially
dangerous. When the rains diminish in March or April, the
tall grass begins to brown and dry, and when it is considered
to have dried enough the "boss" of the country gives permission for the first burning and, in effect, opens the hunting
season. The hunting parties start the fires early in the morning, and the flames rush through the countryside. Because
this is done every year, there is no accumulation of dry
tinder, and the flames are mainly confined to the grass alone,
merely charring the tree trunks and setting a few fallen logs
on fire. The fire goes so rapidly that it does not seem to drive
the game away permanently. Both animals and man can side-
step the flames without much difficulty. The snakes are
driven away, and should they return they are easily spotted
on the bare ground. The dense smoke is a sure indication that
someone is hunting in the vicinity, and as it can be seen for
miles it provides a good check on the hunting activities going

on in one's country, both authorized and unauthorized. The grandsons of Banjo, who were the bosses of the country Wileraŋgu in which the settlement was located, gave permission to all Snake Bay residents to burn the grass shortly before our arrival in April 1954, and I often heard them complain of "poachers" from the Bathurst Mission when unaccounted fires were to be seen in the distance.

A bush fire burns only until the heavy evening dew falls; a few logs may smolder through the night. The hunting party that set the day's blaze has temporary right to the game found in the burned area. This right may last as long as a week or more, or until the new shoots of grass appear. The game will be temporarily exhausted after this length of time, and the party will move on to a new area.

Individuals may also put their marks on certain finds for future collection or use. Such items usually include honey deposits or turtle-egg nests. The marks will be respected, but if someone is particularly hungry or is a close member of the original finder's family and violates the mark of ownership, no one can be angry. However, marks put on kapok trees that are to be made into canoes reserve that tree for the marker and his descendants. No one else may make a canoe from that tree without causing a great deal of trouble. Such a marked tree had been chopped down by a man a number of years before our visit, and the sons of the man who had originally marked the tree many years earlier were still arguing the case. Meanwhile the tree lay rotting in the forest.

The boss of a country has the authority to deny the use rights to any resident or owner of the country should he deem it necessary. One locally famous case took place some time ago, and was related to me by two grandsons of Banjo, present joint bosses of Wileraŋgu.

Banjo was the founder, big man, and boss of Wileraŋgu. He is said to have had as many as "a hundred wives." Many years ago three of his sons were walking at night on a beach near

Punkatji in Mandiupi country. They saw a man with whom they had a grievance, and one son said, "There is that man, let us kill him." Another replied, "We can't kill him. We know him." Nevertheless, they drove a spear through their enemy, and as he lay dying the victim asked, "Why did you kill me?" The sons of Banjo replied, "We are sorry, we thought you were someone else."

Then, as was the custom after a murder, the men painted themselves with white clay in order to disguise themselves from the dead man's ghost. In one day they walked back to their country, Wileraŋgu.

When their father Banjo saw them, he asked, "Why did you kill?"

"It was all a mistake," the boys replied. But Banjo didn't believe them. He told them to sit away from the camp under a certain tree and instructed the women to give them no food.

The next morning he called them up, fed them, and then said to them, "You can no longer camp in this country. Go!" When they had left, he said to the others in the camp, "When I die you may do what you want with these boys."

In due time Banjo died, and as the people gathered for his mourning ceremonies, relatives of the murdered man, who belonged to the Malau country where the murderers had taken refuge, plotted to kill the three. However, one of the murderers had a friend among the Malau plotters, who went to Banjo's son and said, "we are going to kill you and your brothers, but I will warn you by pressing my spear against your leg just before we strike."

When the group was holding a preliminary dance, an *ilanea,* at a place on the west side of Shark Bay just outside the Wileraŋgu boundary, the signal was given and the fore-warned murderer sped for the mangroves while his brothers were killed and spears were thrown after him. One of the spears wounded him in the side, but he escaped and hid in the mangroves until the ceremonies for his father were over.

He then returned to his own country and all was clear. In time he became a big man of Wileraŋgu. (See Pilling 1957: 326-29 for another version of this case.)

The story of Banjo's life is interesting, for it illustrates another factor in land ownership and use, and in intercountry relationships. Banjo, by rights of inheritance through his father, owned and resided in Palauwiuŋa country to the east of Snake Bay. Banjo had a brother, Baŋgri, who like Banjo became a big man with "a hundred wives." The Palauwiuŋa country became too crowded, so Banjo went west across Snake Bay, found that the Wileraŋgu country was without claimants, and took possession of the area. Palauwiuŋa is famous for its large fresh-water swamplands that attract migrating geese on their way south to Australia for the summer, but this country has only a few miles of beach and mangrove-lined creeks. Wileraŋgu, however, has many such beaches and creeks and a plentiful supply of excellent sea and shore foods. Rather than amalgamating the two areas into one country, geographically rather difficult, the two close brothers made a mutual agreement that whenever Baŋgri and his household wished crabs, cockles, or oysters, he could hunt and fish in Wileraŋgu waters, and when the geese began to gather to feed in the Palauwiuŋa swamps, Banjo and his group would be invited in for the kill. Descendants of these two men still honor this agreement.

Specially Considered Food Plants

Aside from the secular laws governing who may hunt in a country, the Tiwi believe that some foods will cause illness to those who are not owners of the country in which they are found. The foods that were mentioned to me were the cycad nut and the wild cashew. These two foods, as well as the variety of yam called *kulama,* are all toxic in their natural state. The cashew fruit can only be eaten at a certain time of the year, and presumably the people who live in an area where it is found know when it can be eaten, while those to whom it is foreign do not, and may well "swell up about the face."

The cycad nut is something different. It requires special preparation to remove the poison, which can be fatal if consumed. After the nuts are gathered, a large fire is made. When it has burned completely down the nuts are placed in the ashes very carefully, in a single layer. Hot ashes and hot sand or dirt are mixed in with the nuts and placed on top, covering them completely. During the half hour cooking time the nuts are gently stirred and turned over several times, after which they are removed and set aside to cool, usually overnight. They are then "cracked" with a crude but specially fashioned ironwood mallet. The meat is removed from the shell and crushed with a single blow of the mallet. The crushed nuts are taken to a fresh-water billabong or swamp and placed inside a "cage" of cycad leaves planted upright in a ring in about two feet of water, which "keeps them from running away." They are left there for two or three days, then are removed and eaten with no further preparation.

The Tiwi distinguish two kinds of cycad: *korka* and *iŋala*. The *iŋala*, which is larger and less widely distributed, is said to be poisonous to anyone not belonging to the country in which it grows, and even the people of that country must have the cooked and soaked nuts rubbed on their heads by their fathers, else eating them would cause fits. M. G. Whiting of the Harvard School of Public Health has suggested to me that the Tiwi, like many others who use the cycad for food, might regard the toxic nuts as either famine food or as medicine (Ancient Seed Plants 1955:65-80), two factors which had not occurred to me in the field. It does not seem to be considered as curative medicine, but a case could be made for its being a preventive medicine.

The cycad may be considered a famine food, but it is unlikely that real famine conditions ever existed on the island. Today, however, the cycad is not considered very good eating, in fact my informant went so far as to describe its taste as being quite bad. The only time I ever saw the settlement natives prepare and eat the cycad was when food supplies had run very low, both in the settlement and in the neighboring bush. The preparation takes a long time, but large amounts can be prepared at one time. All these factors seem to indicate that the nut is not a food particularly relished by the Tiwi, but one that is regarded with respect, for there exists the "never broken" law that no one may cut down a cycad and thus destroy the constant supply. The cycad nut is also prepared and eaten during part of the initiation procedures that take place when great quantities of the nuts are available, thus providing food for large numbers of otherwise occupied participants, but its consumption is not restricted to this time.

A third toxic plant, the *kulama* yam, is one of a number of varieties of wild yams distinguished by the Tiwi: *dioni, ubona, moruŋa, uruŋara,* and *kulama.* Only the *kulama* is botanically toxic. However, the Tiwi consider other varieties to be toxic for men during the rainy season and for pregnant women when the yams are new and small. Yams contain a sickness called *tarni,* which is controlled by Rakama, the boss of mosquitoes. *Tarni* is present in all varieties of yams and during all seasons. A major ceremony, called the *kulama,* is held annually at the very end of the wet season, and after its conclusion initiated men as well as women and noninitiates can eat yams.

A few weeks before the ceremony is to take place, the women dig some of the small new yams, called *moruŋa,* for the first time in the season. They cut off the "head" of the yam and replant it. Several days before the ceremony they go back to collect what has grown, called *uruŋara,* and take it to the ceremonial ground. Later the men, as well as the women and children, eat the *uruŋara,* together with the prepared *kulama* variety of yam, at the conclusion of the *kulama* ceremony.

All the yam varieties are part of the regular diet except the *kulama,* which is eaten only at the conclusion of this ceremony. No reason for this restriction was given other than "It's Melville Island way." However, Mountford and I sampled this yam after its ceremonial preparation, and we agreed that no further explanation was necessary: its extremely bitter taste and tissue-burning qualities seemed enough reason for not eating it regularly.

Why the Tiwi should single out the *kulama* yam as the only element in their physical environment to emphasize in a major ceremony is both interesting and difficult to explain. In the following chapter I examine this ceremony in detail.

CHAPTER SEVEN

The *Kulama* Ceremony[1]

The *kulama* ceremony is a major part of a sequence of events by which men and women become fully initiated adult members of Tiwi society.[2] But a *kulama* ceremony can take place with no initiates. It is an annual event, held at a certain time of the year in a certain place; it is organized by a group of fully initiated men, and all the residents or owners of a certain area participate. The mythological background states that originally there was one *kulama* ceremony for the whole tribe (Mountford 1958:123) held in only one place. However, today there are a number of *kulama* grounds—one per country, as far as I could determine.

All my information concerning initiation procedures comes from informants. We did, however, observe one three-

---

[1] Cf. Goodale 1963 for a less detailed account of this ceremony.

[2] Unfortunately, during our stay on Melville Island, none of the initiation procedures were undertaken. Many men and women of initiation age were objecting to the lengthy procedures. During the funeral ceremonies, however, I observed several events which appear to be related to initiation.

day *kulama* ceremony that involved no initiates. In 1912 Spencer also witnessed a *kulama* in which several grades of male and female initiates took part. Since much of my information conflicts in details with what has been published by Spencer (1914) and Mountford (1958), I shall divide my discussion of the ceremony into three parts. First I shall describe the actual events that took place during the *kulama* we observed in April 1954. Then I shall present what my informants said about initiation procedures. Finally, I shall make comparison with Spencer's report of the same ceremony forty years previously.

The 1954 *Kulama* Ceremony at Banjo Beach

This ceremony began on the evening of April 30 and ended the morning of May 3. It was held at the south end of Banjo Beach a mile away from the settlement at Snake Bay. Mountford, Harney, and I observed this ceremony and took notes and photographs. During the ceremony a number of nonparticipants gave us song translations and made explanatory comments. After the ceremony we obtained other comments. These comments are incorporated into this description set off in quotation marks. The description itself represents the collective observations of all three observers.

1. *Seclusion of men*[3]
2. *Women gathering* uruŋara *yam*

Parts 1 and 2 of the *kulama* ceremony were not held at this time. This is what should have happened:

1. Four days before the ceremony, the men who will take part are supposed to leave their women and go hunting in the bush about eight miles away from the main camp.

2. During this time the women collect the *uruŋara* yams.

---

[3] In order to facilitate a later comparison of the 1912 and 1954 ceremonies and the discussion of the role of initiates in the ceremony, I have isolated and numbered forty-one separate ritual events which occur during the three-day ceremony.

The men send an old man as a delegate into the main camp
to find out when the women are ready. When all is prepared,
the men return. Stopping some distance from the main camp,
one man throws a fire stick into the air. Where it falls is designated the "lying down place," the *muramiramili,* of the men.
APRIL 30, 7:30 P.M.

3. *The* muramiramili,
   "lying down" of the men
   and singing

3. About 6:00 P.M., visitors from the main settlement began to appear on the beach, and shortly afterward the expedition members were escorted to the far end of the beach. A
small area, about fourteen feet long by six feet wide, had been
cleared, and inside it four men were lying on their backs:
Ali (a Wileraŋgu-flying fox [B2] man), Jacky Navy (a
Wileraŋgu-fire [C2] man), Black Joe (a Turupi-fire [C2]
man), and Tuki (a Munupi-housefly [B2] man).[4] Also in
the cleared area were two smoldering logs; no flames were
visible. Around the outside, the families of the four men had
their own small campfires in among the trees. Some of the unattached and uninitiated young men and women sat together
close to, but not inside, the small clearing.

When it grew quite dark, the singing began. It started with
a beating together of two *muraguŋa* (fighting clubs) to fix
the rhythm. Ali began with a soft humming "clearing the
voice"; and then, still softly, he began his song. "Ali is best
singer, that's why we wait for him and that's why he is a big
man in *kulama.*" The singing is like a plain-song chant,
with a regular sequence but very small range of notes. The
song is in verse form with a regular meter, except where an
extra beat is necessary to accommodate an extra syllable or
word. At the end of each verse, there is an interval during
which the singer hums and maintains the beat with his clubs.
Ali was lying down when he began, but after the first verse

---

[4] None of these men was Ali's close brother. Two of Ali's close brothers were
residents of the settlement, but neither was yet fully initiated.

he stood up and sang facing first to one side and then to the other:

> My father, you were a king and you died.
> I want to be like you, my father.
> Be rich and have lots of money.
> Have a flag, all blue, white, and red.
> Have a warship with me and live in a big house.
> This song is for you—the dead man.[5]

Ali ended his song with a high-pitched wail that was picked up and continued by the females outside the area. Ali's father had recently died and been buried, but his *pukamani* (mourning) ceremonies had not yet begun. "The ghost *(mobuditi)* of the dead man, as well as all the local *mobuditi,* come to the *kulama* to listen. They would have been displeased if Ali had not referred to his dead father and not stood up and sung directly to them as they circled the area."

At the end of his song, Ali sat down and the conversation, which had been generally stopped, was renewed. Suddenly one of the small campfires burst into flames, and a man shouted, "*Ikwani* (fire)! *Tarni* (sickness)!" and someone quickly smothered the fire "lest *tarni* catch one of the children."

The next singer, Jacky Navy, then began, as had Ali with a beating of the sticks, then humming, then the song:

> There was a *pukamani.*
> You went first, I came after.
> Old people came in first from Cape ———.
> I was late because I had a *kulama.*
> Why didn't you wait for me?

Then he sang "about the dead man": "Where the shark's tail is lying down." One of the men shouted from outside the area, "I was there and that is right."

---

[5] Harney collected all song translations cited here.

Then Ali sang again:

> The Queen was talking in England:
> "I would like to see a blackfellow dance."
> When I was in Brisbane, the Queen said:
> "I would like to meet a black boy,"
> And I went up.
> King Philip, he had a good look at me.
> He was watching a lot as I danced.
> I was singing into a loudspeaker.[6]

The next singer, Joe, stood up.

> I am a goose wading through the swamp.
> Old Wanganui[7] shouts, "Look out.
> Someone is going to hit you with a stick."
> Someone tried to hit me, but only hit on the feathers.

During this song the children became noisy, and someone shouted, "Be quiet so we can hear the words." In the interval after Joe's song, a man on the outside said, "Sing my song of Fanny Bay Jail (in Darwin)," and another said, "Sing about a bottle of beer."

But Tuki had his own song to sing about his mother-in-law:

> When Dory have baby girl the old man said,
> That's for you.
> Dory, my *ambrinua,* she burns me.
> I would like to kill her.

There were other songs until late in the evening, when the camp retired for the night. For the duration of the ceremony

---

[6] Ali had just returned from an aborginal dance exhibition in Brisbane held to honor the Queen during her tour of Australia in 1954. The *kulama* had been delayed until he could participate.

[7] The oldest resident of Snake Bay in 1954, Wanganui died in 1959 at the estimated age of eighty-nine years. In 1962, my informant, after telling me of his death, added, "He nice old man, kind to everybody."

the men had to sleep on the opposite side of the campfire from their wives.

One important feature of the *kulama* ceremony has been illustrated by this description of the *muramiramili* phase, and it will become more evident as the ceremony proceeds. The songs concern a great variety of subjects. A song can only be sung once and then must be thrown away, for people would laugh scornfully if a song were repeated. The songs are composed for the occasion by their singer; they belong to him and may not be sung again by anyone. Throughout this evening, the audience chanted, "Oh, oh, oh, oh," in approval at the conclusion of a song they thought particularly good, and all songs were discussed and commented on during the intervals. Ali was considered the best singer, not only because he had a good voice but also because his words were well composed. Since there is a preset style for the *kulama* chant, many archaic words are used if they will fit the rhythm better, and extra syllables will be added or dropped from words for the same reason.

Like the bards of the Middle Ages, the Tiwi singers compose poetry for the occasion, distributing news of current or past events, describing lyric scenes, defending a certain personal action that was contrary to social custom, or airing their grievances before the assembled group. This is a time of ceremonial truce, and the singer's words go unchallenged. What he might not have the courage to say at other times, he may now say without fear.[8]

MORNING OF MAY 1
4. *Making of yam sticks*
5. *Spitting and throwing water*
6. *Cleaning ears*
7. *Painting with white*
8. *Digging yams*
9. *Placing yams by tree and return to camp*

---

[8] Pilling (1957:98-99) lists five types of grievance songs traditionally sung during the first night of the *kulama*.

4. Early in the morning the *kulama* men made the special digging sticks *(alaguni)* to dig up the *kulama* yam. Each man must make his own *alaguni,* sharpening the point nowadays with a knife, but in the old days with a clam shell. When fashioned, the sticks were painted red. The men then stood waiting at the rear of the clearing where they had sung the previous evening.

5. One of the women brought a container of water and placed it just in front of the clearing. Ali, Joe, Jacky Navy, and Tuki individually approached the water, cupped their hands in the container to collect a small amount of water which they threw over their heads, then over their bodies. Then they took some water in their mouth and blew it out in a fine spray, first in one direction, then another, until they had covered the four points of the compass. While they did this, they shouted and called "in imitation of thunder, 'oh, oh, oh, oh.' " By throwing the water over their bodies, they make the clouds go away, and when they call and spit, *tarni* (the sickness) will be frightened away.

6. Each man then took two small twigs, which he used to clean the wax out of his ears. This not only enables them to hear any approaching enemy during the coming year, but also keeps their memory clear so they will not forget what should not be forgotten.

7. Meanwhile, a paperbark container filled with white clay mixed with water had been brought up to the men. Each in turn placed both hands palm down in the paint, then patted the paint on his hair. They then held their paint-covered hands up toward the sun, "so that *tarni* will not kill them." As they did this they called out again, "oh, oh, oh, oh," imitating thunder.

They then placed some white paint around their eyes, "so that when they grow old, they will have good eyesight." Next they painted their arms, "to keep them from being broken," and their legs, "so that they will walk straight, and so that sticks will not break them," and finally they painted their chests.

8. When all the men were painted, they stood together. A quiet signal was given, and they moved toward a bark basket that had been freshly decorated with color. Jacky Navy was the first to pick up the basket. He held it in the air, calling out in a low voice, and hit the basket, which with a drum-like sound "spoke in the voice of thunder." He did this four times facing north, east, south, and west. Then the other men did the same. The last man led off toward the place where they would dig the *kulama* yam, and all the *kulama* men but Joe followed.

Joe said that he was too tired to go, a remark that alarmed the people, who said that he, particularly, should go to chase *tarni* for the sake of his young son Chrisy. Did he not know that *tarni* might kill Chrisy, as it had his infant daughter just a few months ago and another son just last year? Joe merely shrugged and remained in camp.

The other three men located the vines of the *kulama* yam at a place about a half mile from camp. Before digging they patted the ground, saying softly, "Wake, wake." "*Kulama* is a big boss and would make them sick if they did not do this." The yams were dug very carefully, and as the men worked they pretended that they were women, for they were doing woman's work. However, during the digging a point of one of the sticks broke. Immediately, the man whose stick it was handed it to another man, who exchanged sticks with him. The stick was repaired before it was used by the new man. Another accident occurred as Jacky Navy was carefully removing a yam from the hole. The yam was slightly damaged, and Jacky raced away through the bush carrying the yam. Then he returned and placed the yam in the basket. "He ran to escape *tarni,* and it was lucky that the yam broke only a little, for had it been broken in half a *big* sickness would come."

The yams are always held carefully in the palm of the

hand, never with the fingers alone. They are round and about
the size of a medium potato, and are covered with many short
rootlets "like a man's beard." As each yam was removed from
its hole, it was placed carefully in the basket and the hole
refilled with sand, "so that the yam will come again." As the
hole was filled, the diggers called again in imitation of thunder, "so that the rain clouds will come in the evening."

9. When all the yams were collected, the men filed back
through the jungle toward the camp. They did not enter the
cleared area but circled it until they reached a tall bloodwood
tree between the camp and the fresh-water billabong. Standing beside this tree, designated the *permajigabruŋa* ("stand-
ing-up-of-the-basket"), Ali spoke, "At this tree I was made
mikigula" (the last grade of initiation).

The men set the basket up, leaning it on a stick a short
distance from the tree, while they cut some branches and
cleared the grass around the base of the tree. Next they took
the yams from the basket, laid them carefully on the cleared
ground, and set the basket beside them against the tree. They
planted the branches upright, covering both the yams and
the basket. Then they returned to camp and rested until late
afternoon.

LATE AFTERNOON AND EVENING, MAY 1
10. *Preparation of kulama*
    ceremonial ground: the
    milimika
11. *Preparation of the fire*
12. *Taking yams from tree to*
    billabong
13. *Washing in water by men*
14. *Return to camp*
15. *Singing*

10. At about five o'clock, the four men stood up and together shouted, *"Yoi, yoi!"* ("Dance, dance!"). They
scratched the ground before moving a short distance from

their camps. As they did this they said, "I am here in this country," and beat the earth with short sticks. Next they pulled up grass from the earth and threw it into the air, first toward the west and sunset, then toward the east, yelling all the while, "This will make them live a long time."

Where the uprooted grass fell, the men assembled and discussed how big to make the *milimika,* the ceremonial ring. In the center of the designated area, a small circle was drawn in the sand. "This is the *tumaripa,* the navel." The *kulama* men then cleared a circle about fifteen feet in diameter of all grass, sticks, and stones. Using their feet, they pushed up the sand around the ring, setting it off from the surrounding area with a low encircling mound. When they were almost finished, they decided that fifteen feet was too small, and some of the other uninitiated men helped in enlarging the circle.

11. When the ring was finished, the four men gathered a number of yard-long dry sticks, which they set upright in the ground encircling the *tumaripa* (navel) in a two-foot circle. As Ali helped build the fire, he hummed a song in a low voice, the words of which neither we nor our informants could hear. After the upright sticks were in place, other shorter pieces of firewood were gathered and laid across each other horizontally between the uprights until the "fire" was about two feet high.

Meanwhile, the women, children, and "outsiders" were preparing their night camps around the new *milimika* and gathering wood for the night fires. The children played as usual, and they were not restricted from entering the cleared *milimika.*

12. When the laying of the special *tumaripa* fire was completed, the families gathered together outside the *milimika.* The *kulama* men asked, "Ready?" and then filed off down the path to get the yams that had been resting under the boughs at the base of the big bloodwood tree, about a hundred yards from the *milimika.* When they arrived at the tree, they all gave a long sustained call, "oh, oh, oh, oh," as they threw

away the bushes covering the yams. Still calling, they picked the yams from the ground and replaced them in the basket, then proceeded to the billabong.

There they scooped a hole in the soft bottom of the shallow pool, making a basin in which they laid swamp grass. In this watery bed they carefully placed the yams.

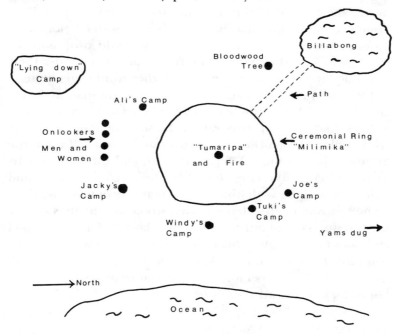

Fig. 13   *Kulama* ceremonial ring and surrounding area

13. When this had been done, the men splashed their bodies and heads with the fresh water from the billabong, calling and shouting all the while.

14. Then, with Ali as leader, they returned to camp, each beating a slow rhythm with their throwing sticks. Ali hummed a slow chant as they neared the *milimika*. The men stepped inside and circled the ring counterclockwise. All joined in the low chant.

When these chants were concluded, they began to talk of
"*tarni, ikwani*," (sickness, fire) and, at these words, the family
campfires were lit around the *milimika*. "It is safe now, for
this is the end of *tarni*."

15. As during the previous night, the men took turns singing. Each man entered the ring when it became his turn, and
as he sang he circled the ring counterclockwise as men have
done ever since the first *kulama*. "If they walked clockwise,
kulama would become angry and they would drop and become sick." As they sang, they rested one arm across their
forehead "to give them more wind so they would sing better."

Joe sang first. His song was about a white man at Snake
Bay who had had a row with him. Then Jacky Navy sang of
a shark that killed a sting ray in the sea. Joe sang again, "A
wild apple *(binyama)* ripens its fruit and lets it fall upon the
ground." Jacky sang, "A boat runs fast, and the waves hit its
side." When Tuki sang, his wife "followed him up," and
helped by singing with him while remaining outside the ring:
"The salt water puts plenty of driftwood for our fires on the
beach." Joe sang about his mother-in-law: "That she is good
and does not take away his promised wives." (Joe's *ambrinua*
had already given him two wives and had produced a third,
now about four years old.) The singing went on until about
ten o'clock, when all retired for the night.

Morning, May 2, 6 a.m. to Noon
16. *Lighting the fire*
17. *Painting bodies red*
18. *Singing*.
19. *Yams and grass collected*
20. *Yams and grass by fire*
21. *Making the grass ring,*
    the imbini

16. At sunrise the following morning, the *kulama* men
gathered some of the brick-like ant bed and broke it into
small pieces. They placed the pieces on top of the cross wood

of the *tumaripa* fire in the center of the *milimika*. As each
piece was placed they said, "*Yeatse ambrinua*" ("We are here,
mother-in-law"). When a piece of ant bed accidently fell to
the ground, it was picked up and replaced on top of the wood
with the same words.

Jacky Navy then lit the *tumaripa* fire, using a fire stick
from one of the surrounding campfires, and as the flames
rose the four men circled the fire beating their clubs. Windy,
a man nearly eighty years old, entered the ring and sat on the
ground. From this point on he joined the four other men in
performing the ceremony. As they circled the fire some of the
men sang, while women and children looked on and talked
among themselves. One of the songs told of "the shining new
iron of the new school house" being built in the settlement.

17. The *kulama* men started to paint themselves with red
ochre mixed with water, covering themselves completely
from head to toe. When they had finished, Ali and Jacky
called to their children, a boy and a girl both under eight
years old, and started to paint them. As the painting proceeded, the men discussed among themselves how "the people of the island are small in numbers, because the white
people brought other tribesmen into this land who sang
magic songs of poison, which caused the Tiwi tribe to die."

18. When the men were completely painted, they began
singing again and beating their throwing clubs. These songs
were all concerned with how "they have now been changed
into women," and they called jokingly to each sister on the
outside that now "they are her." Joe sang, "I am my sister,
Dolly, and I am combing my hair." The women laughed as
their names were called.

19. About ten o'clock, the painted men went to the billabong to collect the yams that had been left soaking overnight.
Some of the small children followed along behind. At the
swamp Ali pointed out the place where they had left the
yams, and they all assisted in collecting them and placing
them in the bark basket. Some water was put in the basket

with the yams. Then Jacky placed the basket on his shoulder and went in the lead. On the way back to the *milimika,* Ali collected some swamp grass.

20. Jacky led the procession into the ring. Then he handed the basket to Tuki, who carried it on his shoulder as they circled the fire in the center. All chanted together. Then Tuki set the basket, with the swamp grass on top, upright near the fire, "to warm it up." The chanting continued. Old Windy entered the ring, picked up the basket, held it on his shoulder briefly, and then replaced it on the ground.

Ali then sang alone. His song was of "money and cards and how he drew ten pounds from the Native Affairs account in Darwin." Ali's wife, Polly, helped him by singing with him from outside the ring. Then Ali picked up two double-edged barbed ceremonial spears. With these over his shoulders, he struck a fighting pose and sang, "I have two spears in my hands now, and I would like to kill someone." As a finish to his song he shouted out the name of his recently deceased father and beat himself on the back with a club. The people of the camp cried out, wailing, "to help him in his sorrow."

After a pause, Joe also sang of Ali's father, "my stomach flares like fire for you my uncle." A woman wailed anew as Joe concluded his song.

21. While the singing was going on, old Windy took the swamp grass from the top of the basket of yams and braided a special ring about two feet in diameter, the *imbini.*

AFTERNOON, MAY 2, NOON TO 2 P.M.
22. *Throwing away the fire*
23. *Putting yams in oven*
24. *Dancing*
25. *Singing for the cooking*
26. *Uncovering yams*
27. *Placing hot sand on body*
28. *Placing hot yams on body*
29. *Peeling yams*

22. By noon the *tumaripa* fire had burned down well. The *kulama* men picked up the few remaining fire sticks from the fire and with loud calls threw them in all directions "to push *tarni* away." The remaining hot ant bed and ashes were carefully brushed with clean leafy branches "to see clearly." The grass ring *(imbini)* was laid around the circumference of the mound of ant bed, and the water in which the yams had been soaking while in the basket was sprinkled on the hot ant bed.

23. Ali, "the boss of the basket," removed the yams, one by one, and handed them to each of the other men to place on top of the ant bed. When all the yams had been placed, they were covered with newly gathered paperbark. Great care was taken that nothing went wrong and that all the yams were entirely covered, for otherwise "some of the *kulama* men would go blind." (It was said at this point that Windy had never done wrong in a *kulama* and that was why he still had good eyes even at his age.)

The *tumaripa* oven, "now called *iŋnerti*," was covered with warm sand from the surrounding area. When all was completed, Ali patted the oven while the others chanted "*nimbaŋi kulama, nimbaŋi imeraniŋa*" ("Good-by *kulama*, good-by daughter").

24. The men discussed the next move. Then they called on the outside non-*kulama* men to dance their individual dances and sat down to watch. (As these individual dances are a major part of the funeral ceremonies, they will be fully described later.)

Tuki's brother began dancing the *tjiruwa* (bird) dance. Then Jacky Navy rose and placed a goose-feather pompon *(tokwiiŋa)* in his mouth and danced the *irikupe* (crocodile). Ali and his *iŋgalabini* brother then crawled on their bellies into the ring from opposite sides, also imitating *irikupe* fighting in the water.

They called then for a woman to dance, and Dolly, shy at first, entered the ring and danced in imitation of a buffalo, after which Alice danced *irikupe*. The final dance was a turtle dance by a young man, Strangler.

25, 26, 27. About one o'clock Ali entered the ring and called for "the cooking of the yams," and half an hour later the *kulama* men gathered around the oven, felt the sand with their hands, and debated whether it had become hot enough to indicate that the yams were cooked. They decided that it was indeed right and carefully began to scrape the sand away to expose the bark. As they were doing this, they picked up handfuls of the warm sand and placed it on their elbows, chest, shoulders, head, and knees, "to give them strength in the future."

After this, the paperbark was carefully removed, sheet by sheet, to expose the cooked yams, and the women sitting outside the ring chanted softly, "Ah, *kulama,* ah, *kulama."*

28. Each man picked up the hot yams. As he removed them he touched them to his arms, legs, head, and chest so as "to acquire the same strength-giving properties provided by the oven sand." Children of the men were sent by their mothers into the ring, where their fathers placed the hot yams on their heads.

29. The men peeled the yams and exposed the yellow flesh. As they worked, each sang his own words but in unison. Ali sang that he was "cutting a piece of bread for a feast." Tuki imagined that he was "cutting up a bullock and roasting it on the coals of the fire," and old Windy sang of "eating corned beef."

The peeled yams were left exposed on the paperbark beside the remains of the oven, and the men retired to their camps to eat and to rest before continuing.

LATE AFTERNOON, MAY 2, 3:00 TO SUNDOWN
30. *Slicing yams*
31. *Yam mash rubbed on body*
32. *Painting for* apa
33. Apa *songs and dances*

34. *Fight over yam basket*
35. *Yams taken to billabong*
36. *Dance in water and return*

30. At three o'clock the men began to slice the cooled yams, first using knives, but switching to the traditional cockle shells to show us how they did it in the old days.

31. They placed the sliced yams in the bark basket, reserving a few that they dipped in water and mashed between the palms of the hands. Mixing the mash with some remaining red ochre paint, the men rubbed their hair, face, whiskers, and body with the mixture, all the time chanting in a low voice some jocular song. Our usually cooperative informants declined to translate this song, saying only, "Him about nothing. Him funny one." The explanation for rubbing themselves with the yam mash was to "make them healthy and strong."

32. From half past three to five o'clock the *kulama* men painted for the *apa* songs. The elaborate multicolored design is always the same and cannot be executed alone, unless one is the proud possessor of a white man's mirror. Joe painted Ali, first his hair and then his face. Then Joe painted Jacky. Joe had a mirror and so painted himself, but Ali helped by painting his hair. Meanwile, Tuki painted Windy, and Windy then painted Tuki. The result of all this activity was something to behold. Their hair, which is curly and worn short, was painted half white and half yellow, with a dividing stripe of red, running back from the forehead to the nape of the neck. One half of the face was black with horizontal rows of yellow spots across the forehead, cheek bones, upper lip, and chin. The other side of the face was yellow with corresponding white spots. The beard, like the hair, was half red and half white with a center yellow stripe. The upper body was completely red, with one arm yellow and the other white. One leg was yellow to below the knee cap and striped white on the calf, and the other leg had white stripes on the thigh.

33. At five o'clock the painting was finished, and Ali began the *apa* songs:

> The big steamship, "Marella,"
> Was beside the Brisbane jetty.
> There were motor cars and trains.
> The boat went under the big bridge.
> The motor cars went over the bridge.
> The ship's flags were flying.

Joe helped Ali in this song. At the mention of the flags the audience cheered and clapped their hands. Then Joe sang, also of flags:

> The *tapalinga* (stars) are like those in the
> American flag.
> They lifted it up each morning.
> They lowered it at night.

Joe stayed in the ring and sang about "a shark, it swims about looking for stingrays." As he sang he danced the shark dance, and the audience encouraged him shouting, "*pira*" ("go on"). When he finished Ali asked him to dance some more, and Joe continued his dance while the onlookers beat out the rhythm, slapping their buttocks with their hands.

Then Ali sang again: "I am a wireless and have sent a message to Brisbane. / My message was heard by Native Affairs in Darwin." Joe followed with: "Leo Hickey's boats race over the sea with cargo from Darwin." And finally Jacky sang his *apa* song:

> A canoe is being made in the jungle.
> First they cut the tree.
> The canoe is this [demonstrated] long.
> The canoe is shaped like this [demonstrated].
> Finally they roll it to the sea on logs.

There was then a period of brief rest.

34. As the sun began to set, the painted dancers took their places at four equally spaced positions on the edge of the *milimika*. Lying on their stomachs they crawled around the basket of yams resting in the center of the ring, then they turned toward the basket itself. The women on the sidelines beat sticks together and beat on tin cans, crying, "brru, brru," in "imitation of Purakagini," the owl. While the women cried, the dancers grabbed the basket and pretended to fight over its possession. Ali and Windy danced the crocodile dance and ended it with a shout. Then all five men marched with the basket down the path to the billabong, all the time continuing their shouting cries.

35. At the swamp a grass bed was made for the yams in the shallow water, and with long drawn-out shouts, the men tipped the yams out of the basket and onto the grass bed. The basket was laid beside the yams.

36. Ali patted the surface of the water with his hand and began to jump about, crouching in the water while the others chanted and trilled, finally ending the "dance" with the cry, "*Yoi*." Then they marched back to the *milimika*.

EVENING, MAY 2, 7:30
37. *Songs and dances* apa
38. *Songs and dances*
   kakaritjui *(children)*
   imunka *(spirit)*

37. When the men reached the *milimika* they marched around the ring, again beating their clubs and humming softly. Shortly Ali began a new song:

> The government plane flew me to Brisbane
>   to see the Queen.
> It flew through the clouds.
> I went to the pilot's room in front.
> The wireless told me Brisbane was only
>   seven miles away.

This was followed by Jacky's song: "A ship which brings cargo to Darwin." Then Tuki sang: "A kite on a long string it flys into the sky." Joe's song concluded the *apa* songs:

> An enemy plane flies low over Melville Island.
> The men on the ground at the word, "Stand by,"
> Shoot it down with a cannon.[9]

38. Without a pause, the men began the group of songs called *kakaritjui imunka. Kakaritjui* is a term used to refer to small children (under five years old), and *imunka* is an individual's living soul, the one that wanders about during the night. However, I suspect that these songs may refer to the unborn spirit children, the *pitapitui,* but unfortunately I did not check this in the field.

Once again Ali began the singing: "All my children have gone to Karslake Island[10] and are playing there." Jacky Navy then sang: "My children are dancing on a sand bank by the sea." Joe sang next: "My children are in a canoe paddling about looking for fish, turtles, and turtle eggs."

Tuki then sang an *apa* song, for "he had not sung a proper one before, which he must do before singing of his children's spirits." "A tractor pulling trees out of the ground to make a big airfield." Tuki did not sing well. He forgot his song, and the girls and other onlookers commented on this in loud voices and laughed at him. To his credit, Tuki also laughed at his poor performance. He then continued with his *kakaritjui* song: "My children have gone to the other side of the island. / But they must come back as they are hard up for tobacco." As Tuki sang this song, Joe entered the *milimika* and sang along with him, but with his own words:

[9] During the Japanese attack on Darwin, during World War II, the attacking planes flew directly over Bathurst Island. Throughout the duration of the war, planes from both sides were occasionally ditched on the island.

[10] Karslake Island is a small island lying just off shore to the north of Ali's country, Wileraŋgu. It is a home for *pitapitui.*

My children will wear clothes and shoes.
They will go to school.
They will learn to write.

Tuki's song continued: "My children have now come back. / I know this for they have taken the tobacco which I have held in my hand." Joe sang again and concluded the evening's songs: "My daughter died because I did not sing at a *kulama*."

DAWN, MAY 3
39. *Wake and collect yams*
40. *Take yams to camp and eat*
41. *Placing the ant bed around* milimika

39. At dawn the next day the *kulama* men went to the swamp. Close to where the yams lay the men picked some swamp grass, softly calling, "weari, weari," in order to awaken the yams. "Should they not do this, the yams would cause a sickness to come upon them." Some of the yams were left in the water so that those who were not present could go and eat them during the morning.

40. The men then carried most of the yams back to the camp, where they were eaten by members of the camp. As we were not awakened in time to observe this eating, arriving only in time for the final act, I do not know whether or not children were given the yam to eat. Our informants said everyone ate at least a little bit; however, the fully initiated *kulama* men ate first, in order to "tame" the yam for the others.

41. The men placed pieces of the ant bed used in cooking the *kulama* yam around the circumference of the *milimika,* leaving the rest of the ant bed and the grass ring in place. The *kulama* ground, the ring and the camping area, was deserted shortly after the eating of the yams. Should anyone later make a fire in the *kulama milimika,* "they would become blind."

Our informants, commenting on the placement of the ant bed on the edge of the ring, said that an initiated *(kulama)* man could, if he chooses, take a chance on obtaining good luck in the hunt by taking a piece of the ant bed and throwing it at a tree. Should he hit the tree, his spears and throwing sticks would always go straight for the kill, but should he miss, he would always be unlucky in the hunt.

Should a *kulama* man be so unwise as to toss any of the ant bed or cooked *kulama* yam into the sea, a big sea will rise up. It was said that Karslake Island was separated from the main island during a storm induced by throwing a *kulama* yam into the sea, which made *maritji,* the rainbow, very angry. Karslake Island used to have a *kulama* ground, but after the storm the Tiwi could no longer dance there.

Kulama Initiation

Tiwi initiation has been discussed in varying degrees of completeness and with varying degrees of accord by Spencer (1914:91-115), Hart (1930b:286), Frey (1949, 1950), and Mountford (1958). It was indeed unfortunate that we could not observe at least some of the initiation procedures in 1954, for it might then have been possible to question our informants more closely and with greater reward.[11] It was also unfortunate that the period of our investigations coincided with the end of the Tiwi's concentration on the *kulama* and the beginning of their concentration on funeral ceremonies. I found it very hard to get any informant interested in explaining their initiation procedures, while I had no such difficulty when I began discussion of the funeral. I do not attribute my difficulty to any inherent reticence in discussing initiation with a female foreigner. Rather, I believe it was primarily due to a preoccupation with the *pukamani* (funeral rituals)

---

[11] Initiation procedures were still being carried out for some of the young men (at least) in 1962, according to information received during my visit then.

during the remainder of my stay on the island, by my informants, and, I must admit, by myself as well.

Noteworthy aspects of the Tiwi initiation procedures are: (1) both males and females are initiated by the same formalized procedures—they must pass through a series of "grades" until they achieve the status of fully adult *(mikigula, mikiguliŋa)* members of the society; (2) the late age at which initiation is begun and the length of time it takes to complete; and (3) the intimate association of initiation with instruction and participation of the initiates in the annual public yam ceremony and the fact that there are only a few other rituals for initiates. Tiwi initiation is thus quite unlike that reported for other aboriginal tribes and deserves far better treatment than I am able to give it here.

There are seven status grades that an initiate must pass:

	Male	Female
1.	*Marakamani*	*Marakumariŋa*
2.	*Kulpaniati*	*Kulaminatiŋa*
3.	*Wadjineti*	*Wadjinetiŋa*
4.	*Mikinatriŋa*	*Mikinatiŋa*
5.	*Mikidara*	*Mikidariŋa*
6.	*Mikiaterima*	*Mikiateramuŋa*
7.	*Mikigula*	*Mikiguliŋa*

According to my informants it takes six years or six annual *kulama* ceremonies to pass through all grades. Grade 2 lasts only a month before the second participation in the *kulama*-yam ceremony, while all the other grades last one year, from one ceremony to the next. Each of these grades have associated customs involving symbolic identification by means of special body painting and wearing of ornaments, physical isolation, food and behavior restrictions, and differential roles in the *kulama*-yam ceremony itself. The exact association of these customs with the various grades is where my data are most incomplete and contradictory, and therefore I shall not attempt a grade-by-grade discussion of initiation. Rather, I shall discuss the nature of these various procedures,

and only where I am sure of the association will I indicate
the grade distinctions. Male and female informants said that
there was no sexual distinction in the various procedures, that
they were the same for initiates of both sexes.

Age of Initiation

According to my informants, initiation begins when a man
or woman is approximately thirty years old. However, forty
years previously, according to Spencer's account, the initiates
were in their teens—and some of them were already in their
second or third year of initiation when he observed them
participating in the *kulama*-yam ceremony. Either the total
length of time it takes to progress from the first to last grade
is in fact far longer than "six years" as given by my informants or there has been a significant change in this aspect of
the initiation since 1912. All my male informants said that
they were already married before they were "caught" for the
first grade, and none of them were married before the age of
thirty. In 1954 one thirty-two-year-old young man was pointed
out to us by the men who would be involved in his initiation
as being the correct age. He was considered ready to be
captured so that he could begin his advancement to adulthood. This man had inherited elderly widows from an older
brother, and although we heard much talk by others that he
would soon be captured, this had not happened by the time I
left. However, by 1962 he had progressed as far as the *mikidara,* as had six other young men, who had not begun in
1954. The average age of these seven men in 1954 was thirty
years, and all but one was married at that time.

At least today, the criterion that decides whether young
Tiwi are ready for initiation appear to have no relation to
puberty. Our informants said, "We watch to see if a boy has
got a good voice." I would like to suggest that this should be
interpreted to mean that they are able and willing to play
responsible and leading roles in the ceremonial life, rather
than merely participating as apprentices, a role they have

been encouraged to take since they learned to walk and talk.

During the third-year participation in the yam ceremony, the big event for the initiate was his first original composition and presentation of an *apa* song. One man (who possessed dual tribal citizenship and had therefore been circumcised and initiated as a young boy on the mainland) said that he was not looking forward to being captured for Melville Island initiation, for it was far more frightening and difficult to compose and publicly perform the required song than it was just to sit back and endure a little pain inflicted by others.

Special Rituals of Initiation

Each initiate has a director who guides him or her throughout the entire sequence of special rituals and participation in the *kulama*-yam ceremony, grade by grade. A girl's director is usually someone she calls mother *(iŋnari),* but not her real mother, for reasons left unexplained. Her father's sister *(intiŋaniŋa)* and husband's mother *(timandiŋa)* were also said to help guide a girl initiate. If Spencer is correct in his kinship identification, a girl's father takes part with her in the *kulama* ceremony itself, but a girl is always captured by and isolated with these female directors at times other than the actual ceremony.

A male initiate is captured by someone he calls sister's husband *(amini),* probably his mother's father, or his father's father, but it is unlikely that a boy's father's sister's son *(amini)* would be enough older than the initiate to be his director. My informants also said that their father's people, mother's father's people, wife, and mother's brothers all come to help in their initiation. However, there are special terms by which an initiate refers to his principal director and by which the director refers to his initiate. The initiate calls his chief director *aŋintumurili,* and in turn he is called *apakuli-tupa.* I do not know whether these terms are used by female initiates and their directors, nor did I obtain any translation or explanation of these terms.

The initiate is captured by surprise at a time when there are many people present, usually during one of the preliminary dances before a final funeral ceremony, or during the final ceremony itself, but never at a *kulama*-yam ceremony. One man described this capture in a song, comparing it to the Japanese surprise attack on Darwin: "The Japanese are like chicken hawks, they won't send wireless to let us know they are coming."

During a preliminary dance before the end of one *pukamani,* we witnessed the ritual of *irampumuni,* where five young men were tossed into the air by older men. The five young men were referred to as *malikaniui.* Without our informants' drawing it to our attention, we may have seen a capture. Or it may have been a regular part of a first-grade initiate's ritual activity during his first year. These same five young men were also participants in a tree-climbing ritual that took place before a number of preliminary dances for the funeral rituals, and in 1962 my informants lumped both the tossing-up and tree-climbing together under one ritual term, confirming that it was something first-grade initiates must do.

For a period of two to three weeks after this capture the initiate is isolated from the main camp, sleeping in the bush with his wife and his director and observing a number of food and behavior restrictions. He is also elaborately painted in a distinctive pattern and color, and he wears distinctive ornaments. For the next three to four years, until he becomes *mikidara,* he is periodically isolated and restricted in actions and variously painted and ornamented in distinctive ways. Fourth-, fifth-, and sixth-year initiates do not seem to have any special restrictions other than those applying to all fully initiated men: pre-*kulama* isolation and prohibition of sexual relations during this and the following ceremony. It is not certain whether the prohibition against eating the edible yam during the rainy season applies to these initiates as well as the initiated. Uninitiated men, like nonpregnant women, may eat yams at any time.[12]

During the first three years of initiation nearly all the special initiatory procedures are carried out. During his first period of isolation after his capture, the initiate must not look at water except when it is in a container. He must not make fire; his wife does this for him, and at sundown he must throw his fire away. At night he sleeps with his director while his wife must sleep "fifteen feet" away. He must not eat carpet or water snakes, and he must avoid breaking any animal bones. He must wrap all such bones in paperbark and place them carefully in a tree. He may not feed himself; his director places the food directly in his mouth. Nor may he scratch himself with his fingernails, but must use a stick for this purpose. Although he is isolated for several weeks, he observes these food taboos only for three to four days at the beginning of the period.

A second-year man is again captured, isolated before the yam ceremony, and ornamented for a month afterward. During this time he must not make fire nor cook his own food "lest the flames singe the hair on his arms and cause injury to someone." Neither may he cut up his own food, but he may feed himself. He cannot hunt, nor may he give food to his daughters. He must not call out or speak in a loud voice. His wife must sleep on the opposite side of the fire, and he cannot "hunt girl friends."

A third-year man is captured again, isolated before and, according to my informants, during a major part of the *kulama* ceremony until the *apa* songs, when he makes his singing debut. During this period of isolation he may not eat opossum, iguana, honey, or flying foxes; but these seem to be his only restrictions.

---

[12] Pilling (1957:159-61) lists a number of other taboos for fully initiated men, such as touching a child and eating from the same container as wives or his children.

Decoration

From all accounts the decoration of initiates with paint, and at times with special ornaments, is a most important aspect of initiation. The first design is quite elaborate and was demonstrated to us by two fully initiated men who devoted an entire morning to being painted with this design executed in yellow ochre over the entire body. Our obliging informants did not, however, have any stingray fat, which they said was traditionally first rubbed on the body to hold paint. Mountford (1958:121, facing) illustrates this design as well as a number of other initiation-grade designs. The painted initiate may not wash for a month after his first painting. After this he is at times painted all black, or black and red, or black, red, and yellow, or again all yellow, with varying lengths of time that he must abstain from washing. The prohibition against washing obviously had some connection with the taboo against looking at or associating with large bodies of water, wherein dwell the *maritji* spirits.

Some of the ornaments are made and worn exclusively during the various stages of initiation. Others are worn by anyone during the funeral ceremonies as well as by initiates during their initiation. Those that are worn during both events are the *tokwiiŋa, priplederi, bulubuŋa,* and perhaps the *pakabino.* The *tokwiiŋa* is a pompon of goose feathers and down, with the feathers stuck in a ball of beeswax making a two- to three-inch ball. This is suspended on a rope of braided human hair and is worn around the neck with the pompon resting on the chest or sometimes held between the teeth. The *priplederi* is a headdress made of cockatoo feathers set with beeswax on a wallaby-bone hairpin. These two ornaments are placed on the first-grade initiate when he is first captured and painted.

The *bulubuŋa* is a belt of braided human-hair rope. Many single strands of this rope are bound together at both ends and occasionally fastened in the middle by weaving some material (today, often dyed wool) across and through the strands. The "belt" is worn either around the waist or around the head, the natural hair of the wearer being twisted into the *bulubuŋa*. The *pakabino* is a false beard made by sticking goose down and feathers into a semicircle of beeswax. Hair ropes are worked into each end and are tied over the head to hold the beard in place on the chin. These two ornaments seem to be part of the second-grade initiate's costume, as well as being commonly worn during the funeral ceremonies. One of our performers fastened his false beard on the chin of his small red-painted daughter during one of the rest periods of the 1954 performance of the yam ceremony. I have also seen all these ornaments worn by women during the funeral ceremonies, and I am inclined to believe that here, as in the rest of the initiation procedures, no sexual distinction is made between female and male initiates.

There are two special ornaments that are made for and worn by second-grade initiates and, with one exception, only at this time. The first of these is the *ilangini*.[13] This ornament is made of a strong, springy jungle vine bent into a half-circle and placed around the back of the initiate's neck and then fastened in such a position by tying the two ends about two inches apart with a hair string between them. From the center of the string dangle a number of hair strings to which feathers have been attached. When the initiate swims, my informants said, this neck ornament chokes him, and during the yam ceremony, his director uses the neck ring to pull him through the water. According to Spencer (1914:111) the initiate's mother wears a similar neck ornament while her child is wearing one, which may be the only exception to the exclusive wearing of these during the wearer's initiation.

The second kind of special initiation ornaments are called *waŋgini*. These are three-inch-wide armlets made from strips of stringy bark. Attached vertically to this circle of bark is

---

[13] Also referred to as a *wadjinati* by my 1962 informants, which the initiate calls his *imerani* (my son, male speaking).

an "H" of wood, to which cockatoo feathers have been fastened on the free unattached ends. The bark itself is painted in elaborate designs.

These last two ornaments, the *ilangini* and *waŋgini,* seem to be regarded as something quite special. In 1913 Frey (1949) met Joe Cooper's half-Iwaidja son, Reuben, who was being initiated into the *kulama.* Reuben secretely showed his arm-bands to Frey, which created quite a stir in the native camp when Frey innocently mentioned the event. Both Frey and Spencer report the "removing ceremony." Spencer's inform-ants placed it in September, while Frey observed it in March. My informants, both in 1954 and 1962, said that it occurred during the initiate's participation in his third *kulama*-yam ceremony, specifically on the afternoon of the second day when the yams have been cooked, pealed, sliced, and placed in the basket resting at the *tumaripa* (navel) of the ceremonial ring. The third-year initiate, who has been secluded for a period of time, is brought in and ceremonially washed. His *ilangini* and *waŋgini* are removed (by his sisters according to Spencer; by an old man according to Frey). The two ornaments are placed first in the basket with the *kulama* yams. When the yams are placed in the water, the ornaments are removed and put on a special platform built in a tree, where they will remain. This might be the significance of Ali's remark during the 1954 *kulama* ceremony, "By this tree I was made *mikigula,*" but this remark might equally apply to the hiding of the initiates by such a tree, as reported by Spencer (see p. 215).

The ceremonial eating of the cycad nut, according to Mountford's informants, is an integral part of the removing ceremony, which, he writes, takes place in September when the nuts become ripe for eating (Mountford 1958:129-30). My informants said that the ceremonial eating of the cycad nut was before the seclusion of the men at the beginning of the *kulama* ceremony. They said nothing about the removal of ornaments on this occasion. However, the cycad nut does play some part in initiation. The women collect and prepare the nuts, which are then placed in separate baskets according to who collected and prepared them. The directors bring the initiates to the area, where they are washed, and everyone sings. Each woman then distributes her cycad nuts to her son-in-law.[14] The initiate, however, gets his from his wife.

The Role of the Initiates in the *Kulama*-Yam Ceremony

In 1912, Spencer observed a *kulama* ceremony in which two first-grade boys and four first-grade girls, one second-grade boy and one second-grade girl, and one third-grade boy participated.[15] When I first read this account, I was struck by the fact that in the sequence of ritual events there has been no significant change over forty years, while apparently significant changes have occurred in two areas—the role of the initiates, and the stated purpose or reason for "making a *kulama*."

The apparent difference to be noted in the role of the initiates in the ceremony must be viewed with caution, since in the 1954 ceremony no initiates were present. There does appear to be a direct correlation between what the men did with the yam in 1954 with what Spencer records was done to initiates in the ceremony he observed. I have no evidence by which I can state that the differences are due to fundamental changes in procedure or are but normal variations in the ceremony to be found whenever it is held without participating initiates. The ceremony must be performed each year by fully initiated men, and the lack of initiates may not be a strictly new element, but one that sometimes occurred in the past and for which traditional ritual variation was provided.

The apparent interchangeability of initiates' role with the

[14] A reversal of the usual *ambrinua* food exchange.

[15] Spencer gives the first-grade girls the term *mikijeruma* (my fifth-grade term) and he calls the second-grade girl, *mikinyertiŋa* (my third-grade). His informants, however, identified these initiates as first- and second-grade initiates.

yams' role is an interesting factor in itself, regardless of whether it represents a ritual change or merely a ritual variation. It deserves careful comparison, for perhaps it will provide some clues as to the "meaning" of this important ceremonial complex.

The 1912 *Kulama* Ceremony

Spencer's (1914:91-115) account begins with the first day's ceremonies, equivalent to my Part 4, thereby omitting the "lying-down" songs of the opening night.

First Day—Morning

1954		1912
4. *Making of yam sticks*	4.	*Not reported*
5. *Spitting and throwing water*	5.	*Singing and*
6. *Cleaning ears*	6.	*Yelling*
7. *Painting with white*	7.	*By men (see 9a)*
8. *Digging yams by men*	8.	*Digging yams by men accompanied by women*
9. *Placing yams by tree and returning to camp*	9.	*Yams taken to swamp*
	9a.	*Return; painting with white paint and bird down*

Role of Initiates, 1912

8. During the digging of yams, the first-grade initiates remained in camp. The second-grade male initiate was taken to a mangrove swamp and plastered with mud. The third-grade male initiate accompanied the yam-digging men.

9 and 9a. During the time that the yams were taken directly to the swamp and the *kulama* men returned and painted themselves with white clay and bird down, there is no mention of initiates' role, activity, or location.

FIRST DAY—AFTERNOON

1954	1912
10. *Preparation of* milimika	10. *Preparation of* milimika
11. *Building* tumaripa *fire*	11. *(See second morning)*
	11a. *Singing and dancing by* kulama *men*

Role of Initiates, 1912

10. During the preparation of the ceremonial dance ground (*milimika*):

First-grade (male) initiates remained in camp for part of this activity but were then taken away by an old man and hidden under bushes around the base of a tree between the camp and the swamp. (In 1954 the yams were so placed, see 9.) The first-grade female initiates remained in camp, and for a short time they joined the men in clearing the *milimika*.

The second-grade boy remained in camp.

The third-grade boy helped the men throughout the preparation of the *milimika*.

11a. During the dancing and singing by the *kulama* men, the second-grade boy was painted black and given his armlets by his "*Yauamini*" and led around the ring.

FIRST DAY—EVENING

1954	1912
12. *Taking yams from tree to swamp*	12. Kulama *men go to swamp*
13. *Washing by men in swamp*	13. *Bathing in swamp*
14. *Return to camp*	14. *Return to camp*
15. *Singing*	15. *Singing*

Role of Initiates, 1912

12. The *kulama* men left the camp and went to the swamp. On the way they stopped at the tree, uncovered the first-grade boys who had been hidden there, and took them to the swamp.

They were accompanied by the second- and third-grade boys and also by women.

13. During the bathing in the swamp, the first-grade boys had their heads and chins rubbed with yams that were soaking in the swamp. Then they were bitten by old men, and had their chins rubbed in mud. The second-grade boy was dragged through the water by his hands and feet.

14. On the return to camp, the first-grade boys were put in seclusion in a hut on the side of the ring.

15. While the men sang and danced, the first-grade boys remained in the hut, the second-grade boy sat by himself and watched, and the third-grade boy joined the *kulama* men.

SECOND DAY— 6 A.M. TO 3 P.M.

1954	1912
16. *Lighting fire*	a. *Building fire and dancing*
17. *Painting red, including children*	17. *Not reported (it was raining very hard)*
18. *Singing*	
19. *Yams and grass collected, and taken to* milimika	19. *Yams and grass collected and taken to* milimika
20. *Yams and grass by fire and singing*	19a. *Fire lighted by initiates*
	20. *Dancing and singing*
21. *Making grass ring*	21. *Throwing away fire and beating ant bed*
22. *Throwing away fire, brushing ant bed*	22. *Making grass ring*
23. *Putting yams in oven*	23. *Cooking yams*
24. *Rest, then individual "animal" dances*	24. *Rest, then individual "animal" dances*
25. *Singing for cooking*	25. *Singing*
26. *Uncovering yams*	26-28. *Not reported*
27. *Hot sand on body*	
28. *Hot yams on body and children*	

29. *Peeling yams*	29. *Skinning yams*
30. *Slicing yams*	30. *Slicing yams*
31. *Rubbing yam mash on*	31. *Rubbing with red ochre*
body mixed with red ochre	*and yam mash*

Role of Initiates, 1912

First-grade boys remained in their hut beside the *milimika* throughout this entire sequence.

The second-grade boy carried the yams, helped light the fire, then was secluded in a different hut from the first-grade. He was later caught by surprise by a few men who pulled out his facial and pubic hair. When the yams were skinned, he came out of his hut and helped.

The second-grade girl carried the yams, helped light the fire, was not secluded but led around the ring by her father after the fire had been lit. She also skinned some yams, and her father rubbed the mash with red ochre in her hair.

The third-grade boy carried the yams and helped the other initiates light the fire. His father was the only *kulama* man to participate in this event.

SECOND DAY—LATE AFTERNOON

1954	1912
32. *Painting in multicolors*	32. *Painting in multicolors*
33. Apa *songs and dances*	33. *and simultaneous singing and dancing*
34. *Fight over yams in basket*	34. *Attack on initiates' hut*
	34a. *Tug-of-war*
	34b. *Tossing fire sticks*
35. *Take yams to swamp*	35. *Take yams to swamp*
36. *Dance in water and return*	36. *Plucking whiskers and placing them with yams*

Role of Initiates, 1912

This was the period when most of the attention was directed toward the initiates rather than toward the yams.

32. During the multicolored painting of their bodies by the *kulama* men, the first-grade boys had their faces painted black

and then were secluded in a small hut especially built near the remains of the *tumaripa* oven.

The second-grade boy was painted white on his face and hair and had his armlets *(waŋgini)* repainted with red ochre. He was then placed in the hut with the first-grade boys.

The second-grade girl was painted all over with yellow ochre, and later some red was added. Her father then twisted a hair belt into her own hair. On her forehead he placed a semicircular bamboo frame reaching from ear to ear, to which were fixed disks of beeswax with tufts of hair from dogs. Her father then led her to the hut in which the first- and second-grade boys were secluded, and she squeezed inside with them.

The third-grade boy's nose and hair were painted yellow, but he was not secluded.

34. When the *kulama* men finished painting themselves, they attacked the hut in which the first-grade and second-grade boys and second-grade girl lay hidden. First they danced around the hut, then opened it and "showed" the initiates. Then with spears they attacked the hut and "killed" the initiates, pulling the hut down. The initiates left the ring, together with the third-grade boy.

34a. The tug-of-war, which appears to have been between the younger men and the older men, began with them pulling on a stick but ended in a "a wild, excited mass of yelling savages, heads, arms, legs, and bodies all mixed up, until at length, one party succeeded in pushing the other, slowly along, while they yelled 'Brr, Brr' " (Spencer 1914:108).

During the dancing after this, the second-grade boy was led around the remains of the fire.

35. When the yams were taken to the swamp, all the initiates accompanied the *kulama* men, and the second- and third-grade boys carried the yams.

36. Only the *kulama* men plucked their whiskers out and placed them in the basket with the yams.

SECOND DAY—EVENING

1954	1912
37. *Songs and dances*—apa	37-38. *This was not reported by Spencer*
38. *Songs and dances*— kakaritjui imunka	

THIRD DAY—MORNING

1954	1912
	a. *Uncover and collect initiates hidden by tree; dancing*
39. *Wake and collect yams*	39. *Collect yams from swamp*
40. *Take yams to camp and eat them*	40. *Take yams to camp and eat them*
41. *Place ant bed around milimika*	41. *Not reported by Spencer, but observed by Frey in 1913*

Role of Initiates, 1912

First- and second-grade male and female initiates were again hidden by a big tree between the *milimika* and the swamp. The men "discovered" them by "surprise" in the morning and removed the boughs hiding them. The first-grade boy danced a solo dance in a circle of *kulama* men. The second-grade girl's father again placed the bamboo and dog's tail ornament over her forehead and a feather pompon (*tokwiiŋa*) around her neck before uncovering her, and he helped her in her dance as did three of his brothers. Joined by this time by the entire camp, all went to the swamp to collect the yams.

The *Kulama* Ceremony: Summary and Discussion

The problem that faces me now, that of discussing the meaning and significance of the *kulama* ceremony, is compounded by the lack of adequate data to describe the nature of the ceremony and the nature of the underlying world view and philosophy of the Tiwi. I cannot do more than summarize the ritual and speculate on the symbolic meaning of various acts.

There are a number of statements I can make with assurance because they are adequately validated by the data available:

The yam ceremony occurs annually at the end of the rainy season (March or April) and is a public ceremony held by residents or owners of each separate locality. There is some indication that the social unit involved is the one composed of either residents or owners of the smaller subcountry, as there appear to be a number of ceremonial grounds in each country. However, the exact relationship of all individuals expected to participate is not clear.

The *kulama* ceremony is a part of the sequence of events and rituals participated in by young male and female Tiwi in order to achieve the status of full adulthood.

Initiates must take part in the annual public ceremony throughout a number of consecutive years, and by so doing they advance through a sequence of named status grades.

Initiation consists in part of ritual instructions concerning the conduct of the yam ceremony itself.

Continued performance and participation in the annual yam ceremony by all fully adult (initiated) members of the society is considered necessary to the health and well-being of one's self and one's children.

A basic question is whether this ritual is to be considered primarily an initiation procedure or a public ceremony, in which the youth must be schooled so that the elaborate ritual can be maintained. In other words, does the yam ceremony have some important meaning in Tiwi culture other than initiation? I believe that today the ritual does have meaning and value in Tiwi culture unrelated to initiation, and I suspect that it did in the past. Furthermore, the meaning and value of this ritual has changed in pace with the changing world of the Tiwi.[16]

Spencer (1914:103) reported that the Tiwi believed that as a result of correct performance of this ritual, all kinds of yams would grow plentifully, and that incorrect performance would result in illness of the performer (not in the decrease of yam supply).

Unless yams are symbolic of all Tiwi food supplies, it is hard to believe that this is, or was, the generally accepted reason for performing the ceremony. There is no social unit associated symbolically with yams. Yams are an important source of food, but by no means primary. In their normal gathering practice, women make sure that the yam supply will be maintained by replanting some of the yam in the hole in which it was found. If the yam ceremony is to be considered as an "increase" ritual, it is likely that the yam is symbolic of more than itself.

Throughout both the 1912 and the 1954 rituals the *kulama* yam was variably personified. Spencer (102) reports that the initiated men referred to yams (in general) as "Yams, you are our fathers." In 1954 our informants referred to the *kulama* variety specifically as "the big boss," a term usually applied to males. The male personification of the *kulama* variety may result from symbolic association of the "hairy" characteristic of this particular yam, which is covered with many fine rootlets (see picture in Mountford 1958: facing 129). It will be remembered that a major rite in the 1912 performance witnessed by Spencer was the plucking of the men's whiskers and placing them in the basket with the yams, and that the third-year boy initiate's facial and pubic hairs were pulled out.

However, in 1954 the yams took on female personifications when brought to the ceremonial ring. The center of the ring, the *tumaripa,* was called "navel" by our informants. The fire built there was called "mother-in-law," while the oven made from the fire was referred to as "mother," and the yams when

[16] See also an earlier analysis of this ritual change (Goodale 1970).

placed inside the oven were called "daughter" (male speaking).

I have already noted the apparent substitution of yams for initiates in the performance of the ceremony in 1954, in which no initiates took part. The most meaningful substitution took place on the second afternoon when the yams were hidden in the center of the ring near the *tumaripa* fire and were later attacked by the men. At this same point in the 1912 ritual, the initiates were all secluded in a hut in the same locality and were later "attacked" and "killed" by the men. The "pregnancy-rebirth" symbolism of the fire, oven, and yams closely parallels the "killing-rebirth" of the initiates. After this event, both in 1912 and 1954, there was a "surprising" symbolic reappearance of the yam-initiates the next morning at a tree where they had remained hidden overnight. This event in its two forms adequately demonstrates what Spencer called the "intimate association" of the yam ceremony and the initiation of Tiwi into adult life. It is, however, unclear whether the initiated men are intent on increasing or maintaining a Tiwi population of both sexes, or only daughters and wives; or whether they are interested only in making all Tiwi responsible adults.

The instructional nature of Tiwi initiation procedures is marked. My informants told me that even during periods of isolation at times other than the ceremony itself, initiates learned only the form and meaning of the ceremony when they received any instruction at all. In Spencer's account the initiates performed, according to their grade, much of the actual procedure related to the handling of the yam. And the proof that correctness in preparation of the yam is meticulously taught to all members of the society is to be found in the remarkable lack of change that is found in the sequence of events by which this yam is ceremonially made edible.

The very fact that this variety of yam is poisonous in its natural state and, unlike the equally toxic cycad nut, is not a part of the regular diet, may explain why the Tiwi consider it so important to teach all their young people how to "tame" it, so that it may be eaten. If an initiated man does not follow the procedure he will die, an informant told Spencer (1914: 103), and there may be more reality in this statement than faith.

The favorable environment of the islands makes it unlikely that famine was ever a serious problem for the Tiwi, nor even periods of scarcity. I have already discussed (Chapter 6) the role that the toxic cycad nut may play as a famine food, and it is equally possible that the *kulama* yam may play a similar role. However, because of its distinctly bitter taste, it was probably rarely resorted to in contrast to the cycad. Nevertheless, knowledge of this natural resource as a potential food has been handed down through the centuries by means of a ritual.

Toxic, bitter, hot, or biting foods are often considered to have health-giving powers, probably because of the immediate physiological reaction to their consumption. That the *kulama* yams are considered to have health-giving powers when applied externally as well as when ingested, is eminently demonstrated in the practice of rubbing the yam on the body of all participants, including initiates and young children of the performers, with the stated purpose to impart strength and good health to all those so treated.

The final element in the *kulama* ceremony that I wish to discuss is the rationalization that the ceremony in general will protect initiated men from *tarni,* which is found in all yams, and, in particular, that the various procedures will protect them and their families from *tarni* or from accidents. I have left this to the end, for it will introduce the discussion of sickness, magic, and death.

What is *tarni?* According to my informants, it is a "sickness," but it was not (or could not be) described. I got the impression that it was sickness in general, rather than any specific disease. It is controlled by *rakama,* the mosquito, but it is worth noting that malaria is not endemic in the islands. It may help to state here that the Tiwi concern for sickness or illness, either natural or magical, is little evident during the course of everyday life. Sorcery appears to be a recent introduction (see Chapter 8).

In reading through Spencer's account of the yam ceremony, I was struck by the few references to prevention of sickness as a rationalization for the ceremony, particularly since it was so evident an explanation in 1954. True, Spencer did refer to the sickness that would result from improperly following the ritual and to the strength-giving properties of the yams, but the fear of a sickness, like *tarni,* being attracted by firelight and being present in the yams was not mentioned.

Is *tarni* a recently introduced sickness? It will be remembered that during the second morning of the 1954 ceremony, while the men painted themselves with red ochre, they discussed the fact that the people of the islands were now few because the white people had brought other tribesmen into their land who sang magic songs of poison that caused the tribe to dwindle.

In 1913 a medical doctor, H. K. Frey, was asked to go to Melville and Bathurst islands to investigate an epidemic that, as of February 1913, had killed an estimated 143 adults, 43 young adults, and two infants. Because of this age distribution, Frey concluded that the epidemic was not measles, as it had first been diagnosed, for that would have killed many more infants and children. Frey's informants told him that the epidemic was caused by magic brought over by the mainland natives employed by Joe Cooper, and Frey admitted that his investigation "supported the native diagnosis of magic" (1949:80).

Frey came upon a *kulama* ceremony that, probably because of his preoccupation with disease and death, he erroneously identified as a funeral ceremony. The old man conducting the ceremony sang a song "about the *Tarula* [the 'riflemen,' the Tiwi name for the Iwaidja] who had planted magic on the beaches to the north at the beginning of the wet season. The sun heated the magic, and up it went like smoke, and the wind blew it all about. The magic works on the black fellow with a feeling like a snake crawling up his legs. It moves up to his stomach, and when it reaches his heart, he eats no more and dies" (ibid.).

It is tempting to equate the magic planted by the mainland natives with *tarni,* the sickness permeating all yams during the rainy season, controlled by the mosquito, attracted by fire, and counteracted by ceremonial means. If the ritual emphasis on *tarni* is recent, as I believe, it still cannot be the main reason for holding the *kulama* ceremony, for undoubtedly this ritual was in existence for many generations before contact with whites or mainland natives; and it is certainly not a mainland ceremony.

It is unfortunate that I was not able to obtain more information on the yam ceremony and initiation. I hope that the problems I have presented and the questions I have raised will be answered with further investigation. Although my informants told me in 1962 that the ceremony was still being held and young men were still being initiated, there were many indications that this situation would not last for many years. Some of the initiated men chose not to participate annually, and many of the young men were successfully avoiding capture for initiation. Whatever the multiple reasons were for holding the ceremony and for initiation in the past, these are no longer being valued by the present-day Tiwi, who have other sources for health and well-being and other means to obtain the status of adulthood.

CHAPTER EIGHT

Old Age, Sickness, and Death

Old Age

A woman who has passed childbearing age is called *parimariŋa*. She is in no way considered to be at the end of her life, for there is yet another term for old women, *intula*. There is, however, a change in activity and responsibility when she becomes a *parimariŋa*.

Tiwi women believe that menopause is due to the gradual stopping or complete lack of sexual intercourse, just as the onset of menstruation was caused by the "growing up" sexual activities of her first husband. It is easy to understand the cause and effect rationalization the Tiwi give concerning the onset of menstruation, but on what grounds do they rationalize the ceasing of menses? I do not intend to discuss the possible psychological or physiological implications of this Tiwi belief, for I do not have the necessary information. However, let us look again at the husband-wife relationship in the light of Tiwi marriage customs.

On Melville Island there is no such thing as an unmarried woman. A woman is "married" from the day she is born to the day she dies. Premarital sexual intercourse simply does not exist, and the custom of handing over a daughter to her promised husband at an early age negates the possibility of extramarital relationships before the girl reaches puberty. However, by the time a woman reaches menopause she is likely to have had extramarital sexual relationships, and, more importantly, she is likely to have had two or more husbands. As I have shown previously, a woman's first husband may be a man much older than herself, and as she grows older and her elderly husband dies, she is married to perhaps a succession of men, each one younger than the preceding one. Her older co-wives may also die off until she becomes the oldest wife of a young man. If this happens, the young man may have several quite young wives whom he prefers as sexual partners. Extramarital love affairs for the older woman also tend to diminish as the younger men reach the age of contractual marriage. These three facts: relative age of husband and the aging woman, relative age of wife among co-wives, and the declining possibilities of extramarital affairs, may, when taken together, affect the frequency of sexual intercourse for an older woman, and may be the reason for the statement that "stopping of sexual intercourse causes menopause." Some such explanation seems necessary, since I found no evidence that the Tiwi regard sexual relations among the elderly as improper.

If sexual activity diminishes or ceases as a woman approaches menopause, her power and prestige directly increase. I have already discussed the dominant role that a woman plays in the *ambrinua* relationship concerning her son-in-law. I wish to turn now to her position in the domestic group. In Chapter 3 I briefly discussed the three kinds of wives in a domestic group: the *taramaguti,* or first wife, the *niŋyka,* the chosen follower, and the other wives. The *taramaguti* is not only the first wife but usually the oldest, by virtue of which she is given jurisdiction over all the other wives, including a *niŋyka.* One woman, herself not a *taramaguti,* told me, "She can sit all day in a camp and send the other wives out hunting." She can direct the other mothers in her domestic group in what she considers to be the proper management of their children's upbringing. These are her given rights as a *taramaguti.* Whether or not she exercises these rights depends on her own personality. Some women demand the respect and obedience due to them. Others receive it without demand and exercise their power "behind the scenes." And still others are content to relegate their power to another co-wife or at least make no attempt to exercise their rights.

While a *taramaguti*'s powers appear to be restricted to her co-wives, in actuality they may extend much farther because of her control over their children: she is their "supreme" mother. Her daughters and her co-wives' daughters will in all likelihood remain members of her domestic group until she dies and thus continue to be influenced by her. Her sons and her co-wives' sons, however, will not remain members of her domestic group once they have contracted for a marriage and have acquired a nonresident mother-in-law with whom they must reside. Old women are, however, treated with a great deal of respect by their sons. They are not only looked after and cared for but their advice is sought and frequently taken. Under certain conditions a man's mother may be in a position to influence her "brothers" to make a marriage contract for her son with one of their daughters, an acceptable alternative to a Type A contract for her son. As we shall see, women are not considered to be "big bosses" or leaders in a funeral ceremony—this is a man's role—but the men do consult female members of the patrilineage that is in charge of the ceremony, and the women voice their opinions freely.

The nominal male leaders consider these opinions to be important.

In recent years, however, much of the power of older women appears to have been lost. Many of the older women are not being remarried after the death of their latest husband, and they seem to have lost a certain amount of "face" by remaining widows. The large polygamous families have almost disappeared, and so the relative power among co-wives has also diminished. Husbands are considered by the government and mission to be the boss of the domestic group, and should some woman (often the husband's mother-in-law or his mother) step in to "interfere" in a family debate, the officials usually back up the husband's word. It seems rather paradoxical that Western culture, the great "protector" of women's rights today, has contributed to the loss of many of the Tiwi woman's traditional rights. This is not to say that many of the young Tiwi women are not very happy with the present state of affairs, where they are the number-one wife (*taramaguti*) at an early age and in a monogamous domestic group with a husband of their own choosing. If a woman has chosen wrongly, a divorce is easy today. Thus she has acquired considerable control over her husband that she never had traditionally, and she is "free" to direct her own life in a way she never could in the past. But she has lost much of her power to direct the lives of others.

Illness

Every Tiwi expects to grow old and eventually to die of old age. They do recognize that misfortune may strike an individual at any time, rendering him ill or incapacitated, or even causing him to die at an unexpected time of life.

Most misfortunes are considered to be self-induced or indirectly self-induced by personally provoking the actions of an angered spirit. All physical accidents fall into this category and are the result of improper observance of taboos, rituals, or social customs. Consequences of improper observance of taboos have been illustrated throughout the preceding chapters, and more illustrations will appear in the discussion of funeral procedures. However, it is interesting to note that there are few specific misfortunes that are attributed to any particular spiritual being, with the possible exception of the spirits of the dead, the *mobuditi*. Only certain infractions concerning the water supplies will invoke the wrath of *maritji*. And *tarni* does not seem to be conceptualized as a spiritual being at all but rather as generalized sickness, much as we conceive of a virus.

Most infractions of taboo and custom are believed to subject the violator to a possible run of bad luck, which may affect the hunter's ability to obtain food or may cause him to have a series of physical accidents. His sight will fail, he will stumble and fall, or he will happen to meet up with a poisonous snake or crocodile. In most circumstances no one is responsible for the misfortune other than the victim himself. The one exception is that parents are responsible for their children's accidents, for a child must learn about right and wrong before misbehavior can cause personal harm. Here is a good case of what you don't know won't harm you.

Under certain circumstances the blame for accidents, bad luck, sickness, or death is laid on a particular *mobuditi,* a spirit of one who has died. Such action by a *mobuditi* can sometimes be attributed to improper behavior by the living in dealing with the spirits of the dead, but often a *mobuditi* causes illness or death among its previously close companions out of loneliness and a desire for company. *Mobuditi* are unpredictable and, being so, are treated with a great deal of respect. It is important to note, however, that not all bad luck, misfortune, or illness is caused by a *mobuditi* or other spiritual being. Spirits of the dead are likely to receive full blame only if there has been a recent death in the vicinity among a close group of associates. And although all *mobuditi* can cause trouble, no matter how long ago the death occurred, only a long run of bad luck or illness that is unaccountable by any other means will be considered to have been the action of a spirit of a Tiwi whose funeral was some years past.

The important point to stress here is the belief in personal responsibility for sickness and accident. Since the Tiwi consider the cause to be personal, they direct their treatment toward the patient and not toward the cause, for no amount of remorse by the patient will help his cure. There is usually, however, a discussion as to what might have been the cause, for there is a lesson to be learned. The patient may join in this discussion, but not with the idea that confession will speed his recovery, although psychologically it may. Or the patient may wait to confess at a later time, perhaps during a ceremony when he can sing his confession with immunity.

So far I have limited the discussion to sickness and accident. But what if one Tiwi injures or kills another? If the injury or death was justifiable in the eyes of Tiwi law, there may be no retribution taken by either the injured person or his people; but it may also be the beginning of a long series of "troubles."[1] If, however, a person directly causes an injury to another by pure accident or unintentionally, he is personally liable to make some retribution, and this often takes the form of self-inflicted injury on the part of the offender in order to show that there was no cause for the offense. Two illustrations of this may be given. The first case occurred during a dance when one man's spear cut one of his dancing partners in the fury of the dance. Immediately the owner of the spear cut his own hand with the same spear; the dance went on, and no more was said. The second case was a little less direct. During the entire funeral procedure concerning the death of a man's wife, one woman continually criticized the widower in his wrongly assumed role of funeral director. More details will be given concerning this affair later, but

---

[1] Pilling (1957) has made an analysis of 107 cases of "trouble" among the Tiwi in his treatment of law and feud. I shall therefore not discuss this aspect of Tiwi society.

when the widower finally had had enough, he threw himself against a funeral pole and apparently knocked himself unconscious. The criticizing woman, recognizing her indirect responsibility for this self-injury, immediately confessed and apologized by cutting her head rather violently, and trouble was averted for the time being.

Self-inflicted injury is a recognized cause of death among the Tiwi. Suicide is sometimes used as a threat to gain proper respect or behavior, but there are also known cases of suicide among the Tiwi to back up the power of any threat. From a purely detached point of view, it would have been interesting to have witnessed the funeral procedures after a recognized suicide, for in any funeral ritual there is a certain amount of confession of guilt, some of which is ritualized but none of which is considered to be connected with the cause of the death.

Although suicide is generally regarded as a rational act, mental illness leading to irrational acts, including some suicides, is also recognized. I heard many stories of people becoming temporarily and completely disoriented. In my informants' words, "They become deaf, they don't hear and they can't speak." In almost every such case the affliction was attributed to the fact that a spirit of the dead, a *mobuditi,* had been in the process of abducting the victim when it had been scared away by approaching rescuers. There is, however, another form of mental illness for which the spirits of the dead are not considered the cause. Indeed, no cause was given. The Tiwi realize that such a victim is completely irresponsible and consider it their duty to do all they can to prevent accidents or injuries to the patient or to others, but beyond that they do nothing. How frequently this type of affliction occurs and what form it takes I am unable to say, but I obtained a few case histories, and in every case the victim recovered within a few months to two years and was now a fully rational member of the society. I was told of two women who suffered this affliction at the same time "a few years ago." "They talk no sense, they go naked and show ass,[2] they eat meat like dog, dripping with blood, they don't know what they do. We take them bush, my mother and me. We look after them all the time. By and by they get better and we come back."

The one woman with whom we came in contact who was considered a mental case by both the Tiwi and the whites was fully able to look after herself. She had almost completely withdrawn physically from social contact, appearing in the settlement only at irregular intervals to obtain tea and tobacco. Most of the time she spent in the bush hunting alone and very efficiently. No one seemed to pay any attention to her at all, but members of her sib informed me that they were keeping tabs on her, and as long as she was getting along all right they would leave her alone. There was no attempt to heal her mind, even though they knew what had made her sick. She had been a *niŋyka* wife, and although her husband had died, she believed he was still alive and with her. In her madness she violated some of the most important taboos concerning death, speaking constantly to and with her dead husband. Since her infraction of the taboo did not concern them, her living kinsmen did nothing about it.

People are expected to die when they reach old age. "He old man, he close up dead," is a statement of fact, and old age is accepted as a cause of death. However, in any case of unexpected death, an attempt is made to determine the cause, if only to ease the minds of the survivors. If justifiable and satisfactory cause cannot be found on the basis of what I have previously discussed, the word "magic" comes into being. Magical death is considered to be either self-inflicted or invoked by the actions of another. "In the old days," my informants said, "if someone wanted to kill another person, he take paperbark swag or calico belonging to that one person,

---

[2] Before contact, Tiwi males wore no clothing, while females usually held a sheet of paperbark covering themselves in front from the waist to knees but leaving their backside bare.

pick it up with stick, not with finger, put it in tree where branch cut it. When paperbark break the man die. 'Nother way, man he take tommyhawk and cut swag and man die." As far as I could determine, the Tiwi had no methods of counteracting such sorcery nor of determining who had performed it. In fact, their entire attitude toward sorcery suggested that its diagnosis was only as a last resort, often made long after the victim had succumbed.

Murder by sorcery may have been a part of traditional Tiwi life, but its significance appears to have been overshadowed by face-to-face murder and mortal combat. Pilling (1957:122, 197) attributes the increase in the number of trouble cases involving sorcery that occurred after 1930 to (1) the knowledge of new techniques acquired from increased contact with mainland aborigines, and (2) enforced peace and Western law by mission and government, which eliminated traditional sneak attacks as a means of resolving personal differences.

My data from Snake Bay seem to support this view that sorcery is in the main an introduced cultural belief. Frequently during my stay on the island a report would be given to me of the impending death of an old man. He was still alive when I left, but the cause of his periodic weaknesses was attributed directly to the fact that, while he had been on the mainland visiting, he had "dabbled" in mainland magic, which he did not understand and which had turned against him and was making him sick. His friends and relatives could do nothing against this, for it was not of their making and they knew no solution; furthermore, conforming to their basic beliefs, it was all his own fault. While I was there a man who had been long on the mainland died on the island. He paddled alone across the straits to Melville island, landing on the south shore. From there he walked across the island, arriving in the settlement in what the superintendant said was an exhausted state but with no other signs of illness. He died within two days. The woman who sat up with him the last night of his life reported that he had come home because he knew he was going to die. He had, he said, been poisoned on the mainland.

There are no true medical specialists among the Tiwi. Tiwi treatment of illness falls into two categories—first aid and preventive medicine—and every Tiwi is expected to learn and practice the methods known to them.

First aid is quite simple. Bloodletting and heat are both considered to be a cure for almost any ailment. In cases of internally caused pain, either treatment may be chosen, and frequently both are applied. Treatment may be self-administered, or one may ask for and receive help. This treatment applied to a poisonous snake bite is almost as effective as Western first-aid methods. The area of the bite is bled and hot stones are pressed on the limb close to the victim's body and moved slowly down toward the incision. Very hot stones or even burning sticks are applied to bad cuts, in many cases effectively cauterizing the wound. Broken arms and legs are "straightened." Muscle stiffness is treated by beating the stiff area with branches—"the sickness goes into the branch and is thrown away." One's own urine is considered to have strengh-giving powers when taken internally. The only other internal medicine I heard of was a boiled infusion of a certain type of grass, but my informants did not understand its powers.

The only treatment that might be in any way considered ritual is that given to a victim of abduction by a spirit of the dead. In such cases the victim is helpless to do anything personally. The rescuers shout and wave firebrands about to scare the spirit away. Then they treat the patient by applying heat and massage to all parts of his body and by talking constantly to the unconscious patient until he revives and recognizes them.

Every Tiwi is concerned with and knows how to prevent illness. Some of the preventive techniques are carried on privately, either at a specific time of the year or life, or every day. Other techniques are carried on by individuals, but in concert with others who have the same problem at the same time, as we have seen in the *kulama* ritual. Many but not all of the laws and customs of the Tiwi are backed up by a threat of accident or illness, and thus observance of proper behavior is considered preventive medicine. But the Tiwi do not believe that one person's conformity will affect the health of another, except in the case of the very young. So although they hold collective "health-giving" rituals, the benefits only come individually. The *kulama* is held at a time when there is a threat of disease to the entire community. Another time when there is a danger of community illness is when the death of a member of the community releases a new *mobuditi*.

Death and the *Mobuditi*

Death is final. An individual ceases to exist in the world of the living as a person, and a *mobuditi* (male) or *mobudriŋa* (female) spirit is created. The distinction between a living person's *imunka* (soul), which can wander about outside one's body but always returns, and a *mobuditi* (spirit), which rises from the body after death never to return, is clear-cut. A *mobuditi* can never return to the living either as a newborn person or as a part of a living person. The pattern of life after death was laid down in the mythological past.

One day Purakapali went out hunting, leaving his family in camp. One of his wives, Pima, left her small son in the camp alone and went into the bush with her lover, Tjapara, the moon.

When Purakapali returned he found his son dead, and by the time his wife and Tjapara arrived, he was in a rage.

Tjapara, the moon, said, "Give me your dead son and in three days I will return him to you alive." But Purakapali would not listen. He fought with Tjapara from one end of Melville Island to another and killed him.

Then he took his son in his arms and walked backward into the sea, pronouncing the fateful death decree, "As my son has died and will never return, so shall all men."

Purakapali and his son never came back, but Tjapara, the moon, came back in three days.

Every Tiwi from about the age of five knows this story and can repeat the words of Purakapali almost without variation. And not once but several times I heard the comment, "We Tiwi foolish fellow follow Purakapali. More better we follow Tjapara." But if the Tiwi cannot return to the world of the living, their life as a *mobuditi* is little different from the life they have always known. When a Tiwi stops breathing, the *mobuditi* rises out of his body, but it does not go very far away. After the body has been buried, the *mobuditi* stays around the grave except for short excursions back to camp or to the place where it was released, in order to visit those it has left behind. At the time of burial, food, water, and tobacco are left by the grave for the *mobuditi,* and the area around the grave is reserved for the *mobuditi* as a private hunting territory, all in an effort to restrict its movements. After the final ceremonies the *mobuditi*'s hunting territory is no longer taboo for the living, but the *mobuditi* is still there, and, to some extent, the land still belongs to him.

As no living Tiwi can exist alone without the company of his fellows, neither can a *mobuditi.* It is this strong desire for companionship that compels the *mobuditi* to visit with his survivors directly after release. But gradually a *mobuditi* will seek the companionship of fellow *mobuditi* resident in the same locality, who welcome him into their society, in direct contrast to the behavior of the living survivors, who repulse his every move in their direction. The *mobuditi* form social groups just as the living do, based on the same cultural principles with the possible exception, according to my informants, of matrilineal group distinctions.[3] They are also subject to death, after which they return again to the

---

[3] This contradicts my male informants' statement that a man's dead father, being in the same matrilineal sib as his son's wife and children, is in a position to help his son find unborn children *(pitapitui)* (see Chapter 5).

mobuditi world as *mobuditi*. The spirits of the dead follow the activities of the living with great interest. They are spectators at every important social event. They do not join the living in their activities, but imitate their actions during intermissions and directly after the close of activity. Thus a new *mobuditi* is not alone in his grave area when the living are performing the prescribed rituals; he is surrounded by sympathetic beings who help him see to it that the proper rituals are being done. The ritual itself serves in part to introduce the new *mobuditi* to the society of the dead, so that it may assume a social identity and position similar to the one it held in the society of the living.

A number of people have met spirits of the dead, which are generally considered to be invisible. They are described as being of the same size as the living: an adult's *mobuditi* is big, a child's small. They are white by moonlight, black by night, and transparent during the day. One man described a group of *mobuditi* he had met: a woman with three children —one at her breast, one on her shoulder, and the other, a young adolescent *(murukubara)*, standing beside her. They spoke: "Look, Mom, a man from the outside." They were like glass. They spun around and around and disappeared in the ground. Another informant said that although he had never seen a *mobuditi,* he had felt one. While sleeping with his wife one night, he suddenly awoke and felt another woman by his side. He said to himself, "That's not my wife, my wife is on the other side." In the morning he reckoned it must have been a *mobudriŋa.*

And an old woman told me that her dead son had once come to her camp. When he was about thirty yards away, he called, "Ah, ah." When my informant did not speak he came closer and called, *"Iŋari"* (mother). Then she answered and asked, "What do you come for?" And her son said, "Come to see you." With that he said, *"Nimbaŋi"* (goodby), and departed into the bush.

Spirits of the dead usually do their visiting at night, spending the day sleeping or hunting in the shade. If someone is ill in the camp, they visit him and tell him how long it will be before he will join them. They may even make someone a little bit sick by clutching at his throat and giving him a sore throat, but in the morning he is well again. If a *mobuditi* desires to cause a death, he always removes his victim from the camp. There is case after case of such abduction.

A middle-aged man, Peter, told me that when he was thirteen a *mobuditi* had stolen him one day while he was in camp with four women. The women went to draw some water; when they returned they offered him some, but he refused, saying, "I'll get some myself." He went down to the swamp and decided to take a swim. When he came up from the water, someone grabbed him, "killed" him, and then carried him away to a camp of *mobuditi*. The spirits all sat down in a circle with their heads in their hands, placing Peter in the middle. He saw Paddy Bush's dead father light fire in the grass and make a camp with sleeping fires all around. Then he saw the *mobuditi* of his stepbrother, Tibundria, who called out "I've got my brother here. Listen, carry Peter and stand him up." All the wives of Tibundria were happy and cried, "We've got our husband's brother." Peter saw only dead people in the camp. They slept there overnight. The next day all the men in the *mobuditi* camp went hunting geese. When they returned in the evening, they saw that their brother was still there with the women minding him, and they cooked a goose for him. Peter sat again inside a circle of his brother's wives. In the morning they got more geese and cooked one for him. Then they were tired and lay down. One old woman was sleepy, and Peter told her that he would go get water. He jumped over all the sleeping people, grabbed two water baskets *(tulini)* and two geese, left the camp, and went to the water for a swim. There he met his mother, who was out gathering honey and opossums, and she took him back to camp. Charlie Cook's father came up and threw spears at the *mobuditi* following him, and they ran away.

In another instance a child of three was carried off into
the jungle by a *mobuditi,* but her cries alerted her father,
who ran after her and rescued her. Usually a *mobuditi* not
only takes his victim into the thick jungle but also hides the
body under leaves. He hits the victim's ears, making him
"deaf," so that he can remember nothing. Everyone searches
for the missing one; they call his name and yell at the *mobuduti,* and sometimes fight with it to drive it away. They take
the sick man home and put hot paperbark on his ears, eyes,
nose, face, and throat. This treatment makes him better, and
he remembers people and friends. People who have been
abducted were not said to have been sick before the incident.
These attacks are regarded as being entirely unprovoked
and without reason.

In the above cases of visitation among the living by the
spirits of the dead, we see an ambivalent attitude toward the
dead. The whole trouble with *mobuditi* is that they are unpredictable. If in life a person is a close relative or friend, the
Tiwi can more often than not predict his responses, but when
he becomes a spirit, they cannot. Out of feelings of friendship or affection, he may leave his living friends alone or even
help them in pursuit of life and happiness. But out of the
same feelings, he may do everything in his power to make
them join him in the *mobuditi* society. To some extent his
actions directly after death are predictable and quite understandable, and that is why the living must go through certain rituals: not only to protect themselves, but to show the
mobuditi that he is not forgotten and to ask that "he please
be kind to the living and leave them alone."

Everyone who has had any contact with a new *mobuditi*
while he was still a living person must go through the rituals.
But not every such person will be present at the time of
death and release of the spirit. Burial is but the first in a long
series of rituals, and as such is perhaps the least important.
In fact, as we shall see later, the subsequent rituals are carried
out even when there has been no burial, as when the body

was lost at sea or when the death has occurred at the mission or
in Darwin, and burial was under the direction of the church
or the government.

Death and Burial

Over a period of eight months in 1954 I witnessed three
burials—one of an adult woman, one of an old man, and one
of a newborn infant boy. In 1962 within a few hours of my
arrival I watched the burial of one of our chief 1954 informants, Jacky Navy. The burial of the adult woman, in 1954,
has already been published by Mountford (1958:65-67), and
although the theme of my presentation is Tiwi woman, I do
not feel it necessary to repeat this description just for the sake
of a female ego. I propose instead to give brief descriptions
of the infant burial ritual and the adult male ritual by way
of an introduction to the subsequent rituals. I leave it to
the reader to compare these three descriptions, if he wishes;
however, I will state here that the ritual is similar for males,
females, and children in the main procedures, with one major
point of difference—the sex of the *ambaru*.

Ambaru is a term of reference given to the surviving spouse
and his close siblings. The sex of the principal *ambaru* will
thus vary according to the sex of the deceased. As I shall discuss later, the role of the living in the rituals varies according
to sex as well as degree of relationship to the deceased. There
are special *ambaru* songs and dances and, in general, these
take a different form if performed by males or females, but
there may also be a deliberate switch, with males taking the
female role and vice versa. Thus, in the woman's burial
described by Mountford, the husband and his close brother
were the principal *ambarui*. When the old man died, his
brothers' wives performed the major *ambaru* dances. But
when the infant boy died, there was a problem. He as yet had
no wife. His little sister, age two, did have a promised husband
of about sixty-five. This man and some of his very much

younger close brothers danced the *ambaru*. I believe in this case the sex of the infant was hardly a consideration, for he was only thirty-six hours old when he died. Other differences in procedure between the two rituals were dictated purely by circumstances and will be indicated in the discussion.

Case 1: The Death of the Infant Son of Margaret and Patrick

On Friday, November 19, Margaret gave birth to her first son and second child in a birth camp high on the hill behind the settlement. The nineteen-year-old mother was attended by her mother, Ruby, her mother's sister, Agnes, one of her two one-granny sisters, and co-wife, Jenny, and her husband's mother, Nellie. Also in attendance were Maria and Margaret's own little girl of two, Patricia. Margaret's father, Jumbo, and Albert, the husband of Agnes, were in the camp to help build a shelter for the new mother and infant (see Fig. 14). The rainy season had begun, and daily heavy showers, often accompanied by chilling winds, drenched the countryside.

Because of the inclement weather the white personnel of the settlement tried to persuade Margaret to move to the "medicine room" with her child. The medicine room had a tight roof and sturdy walls, but it was built close to the sea bank. Margaret's father was greatly opposed to this move. "Houses no good. This our fashion. Medicine room too close

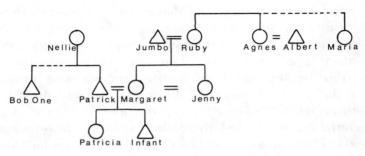

Fig. 14   Margaret's relatives

to salt water. Rainbow kill her." Eventually Jumbo consented to the move, but by this time Ruby had entered the
argument and, backed by the other women, had convinced
her daughter that the move would be fatal to both her and
the baby. Margaret's husband, Patrick, was not consulted
because he had gone to Darwin and had not been able to
return in time.

On Saturday the settlement personnel again tried to persuade Margaret and her infant to move into the medicine
room; they met with even greater opposition from the women, although Jumbo did all he could to persuade them to
move. About 9:30 P.M., after a very heavy rain, the group
arrived at the superintendent's house. They had been joined
by Bob One, a brother of the infant's father, who acted as
spokesman of the group. "Baby cry for milk. Maria been give
him some, but he still cry." There was little that could be
done, for the baby was "close up dead" and hardly breathing.
He died of pneumonia in the early hours of Sunday morning.

At eight o'clock in the morning, the funeral procession
started down the road toward the grave area set aside by the
settlement. Bob One, the baby's acting "father," carried the
little body. All the children of the settlement carried poin-
ciana blossoms. Albert and Agnes left the procession briefly
to come to me to request some tobacco with which they
would pay the workers.

The five workers, men who were sib mates of the baby's
father, were already clearing the area around an old single
grave, marked by weathered poles. Albert joined the workers
in order to speed the work, and Jumbo directed the clearing
and designated the spot for the new grave. While the workers dug the small grave, others from the settlement arrived
and quietly sat down. Occasionally someone rose and sang
alone. Barbara, the midwife, sang, "We were wrong, you were
right, next time we know more better." Then an old man, to
whom Margaret's daughter had been promised as a wife, sang
an *ambaru* song. The *ambaru* song has a special wailing tune,

and the words usually refer directly to the deceased. Bob One sat near Margaret holding the dead infant, but after a while Margaret asked to hold it.

When the grave had been completed and approved by Jumbo, the workers were given a cup of tea prepared by some of the women. Then Bob One collected all the flowers from the children and produced a small wooden box for a coffin. Taking each flower he raised it to his lips then laid it in the box, lining the bottom. Then the mourning began.

One by one everyone, except the immediate family, came up to where Margaret sat holding her dead baby, surrounded by her mother, sisters, and brother. As each mourner stood in front of Margaret, he took a knife and struck himself on the scalp, wailing very loudly as he did so. The knives were handed around until everyone had expressed his sympathy in this manner. Albert, as one of the last to do so, reached down and picked up Margaret's little daughter, Patricia, and with her in his arms and looking directly at her all the while, he delivered a blood-producing blow on his head with the large knife.

The workers then placed a row of sticks lengthwise in the bottom of the grave, while Bob took the little body from its mother and placed it on the flower petals in the box and nailed on a lid. The workers took the box and placed it in the grave resting on the sticks. Branches were then placed over the box, and finally the grave was filled with earth and a low mound raised above the ground. All during this activity everyone wailed loudly and beat his body with club, stick, or knife. Jimmy, a mother's brother to the babe, sang an *ambaru* and told his recently deceased wife to look after the little boy. (Although Jimmy's wife's funeral rituals had come to an end several weeks previously, his *ambaru* was for his wife and not for the baby directly.)

By this time the grave was finished, and the area around it had been brushed and raked clear of sticks and stones ready for the dancing to begin. The men lined up in a semicircle, and Bob One began with the "honey" call, a long drawn out "oh, oh, oh, oh," which was picked up by the other men. Then Bob began his song, which concerned the infant's father's subcountry, Muranappi. As the other men picked up the words, chanting in unison and slapping their buttocks in rhythm, Bob entered the cleared area, ran toward the grave, scooped up some of the earth surrounding the mound and then danced the energetic shark dance, the dust rising in clouds from the kicking of his feet. To the same song another man entered the dance area and danced the bird dance, flapping his arms as his feet stamped in the dust.

Then Jumbo started a song: "I never saw my grandson. / He went a long way away in a canoe." He entered the ring and mimicked paddling a canoe with his hands. Albert, his brother, came in to help him.

Next, three small boys between eight and twelve years of age entered the ring with one of the workers. The worker danced the women's high-stepping type of *ambaru* dance while the small boys danced the shark. The oldest of the boys was left in the ring and danced the shark dance alone, and then another worker took over from him.

Three "older brothers" of the dead infant now all danced together a dance in which they each favored one leg, the dance sign of a sibling. Margaret's young brother, Stewart, under the instructions of his father, danced with his arms cradling an imaginary child (the "mother's dance") then finished with imitating the shark. Jimmy, who calls Stewart "younger brother," helped by joining him in the shark dance.

After about thirty minutes, Bob concluded the ceremony with the high-pitched "mosquito" call, "Ye-e-e-e-e-e," followed with short cries of "Yip, yip, yip." All the young children were carried over the grave mound by their fathers or jumped over it themselves. As some of the fathers took their children over the grave, they called out, "Look you, this my child. Do not harm him." The crowd drifted away

in small groups, leaving a few behind to wail for a while
longer.

Case 2: The Death and Burial of Sizors

Sizors, a man in his fifties or sixties, died in the early
morning hours of Friday, October 15. He was the man referred to earlier, who had been to a ceremony in Darwin,
been poisoned by some "black-fellow magic," and come
home to die.

When I arrived at his camp at about eight in the morning
his kinsmen were ready to move the body to the grave area.
Many of the people had smeared white or yellow paint over
their faces and bodies. Sizors lay covered with a blanket and
a piece of calico, in a small "shade" watched over by his
mother and a brother. Some were wailing and some women
danced *ambaru*.

Three men then lifted the body onto a stretcher and
moved it out of the shade. Wanganui, a mother's brother,
began to dance, and a chorus of female *ambarui* danced in
to meet him in the center of the group. The women held
dancing clubs over their heads, which they shook as they
stepped high to every alternate beat, performing a stately and
ordered *ambaru* dance. They did not keep in line, but turned
around and around as they danced around the body. The
men then called to Little Mik, the eight-year-old son of a
brother of the deceased. With tears in his eyes the young boy
danced the shark dance in the ring alone.

After a few more dances, the stretcher was placed on the
settlement's truck, and as many people as possible climbed in.
The rest followed on foot as the procession moved down the
road to the grave area. The grave "group" in which Sizors was
to be buried included the graves of two of his wives and a son,
as well as Jimmy's deceased wife (whose services had recently
ended), although she belonged to a "different mob" from
Sizors.

The workers were already busy in this area when the procession arrived with the body. Four of them came up to the truck and carried the body to a shady spot under a tree close to the grave. A brother, Brownie, and his wife and *ambaru,* Rosie, sat close by the stretcher with Sizors' mother, Minny. At intervals they were approached by individuals who expressed their sorrow with loud wails and occasional head cutting. Large fires were lit all around the grave area.

One of the workers cut a stick and measured along the body, then took it to the grave, for the grave should be as deep as the body is long. Other sticks were cut, short ones to set crosswise in the bottom of the grave and long ones to go lengthwise over the body in the grave. While this was going on the crowd sat in little groups, smoking, talking quietly, some laughing and some wailing.

When the grave had been excavated, the workers performed a short dance to a song about a boat (inspired by the actual sighting of the long-overdue supply boat coming around the point). Wanganui rolled on the ground backward and forward with his head close to the stretcher, then placed his feather ball ornament *(tokwiiŋa)* in his mouth and lay motionless alongside the body of his sister's son. The chorus of *ambarui* women wailed and beat themselves on their backs with their dance clubs and sticks. Minny still sat alone at the head of the stretcher as the *ambarui* women danced.

Everyone gave the "mosquito" call, and the body was carried to the edge of the excavated grave. Two workers climbed down into the grave to receive the body. Wailing and cutting of heads increased in intensity. Wanganui again lay facing the stretcher and began to crawl on his belly toward the open grave. He was forcibly restrained from crawling into the grave itself. Two workers picked up the body and, together with the two standing in the grave, lowered it until it rested on the bed of sticks. Wailing, beating, and bloodletting increased even more as the long sticks were lowered into the grave, then branches, and finally the earth was shoveled on top and the mound formed: Peter, a son, was restrained from using a knife, while another son, Banjo, danced alone. Bob One, wailing loudly, gathered some sharp shovel-nosed spears,[4] carried them to the grave, and made ready to use them on himself. They were taken away by Charlie. The *ambarui* women were individually singing their wailing songs. Peter grabbed a handful of dirt, stuffed it into his mouth, and ran about trying to elude his friends. It took the combined efforts of ten men to calm him and keep him from swallowing the dirt. A large knife was given to Peter, who cut his head and then passed it on to another. Two men danced with blood running in rivulets down their faces and shoulders.

When the workers finished the grave, the ordered dances began. (Because of the complete preoccupation of every member of the group, I gathered no song translations.) Everyone took part in the dances, one after the other in rapid succession. The women joined the men, often as a chorus, dancing a slow shuffling step. The female *ambarui,* however, danced their high-stepping dance apart from everyone. Even the children, particularly the sons of Sizors' brother, took their turn. The dances ended after half an hour.

Then one group of men started the "mosquito" call. With their women, they rushed to the grave and fell on it wailing; knives were circulated again. Then the second group of men gave the "mosquito" call, rushed to the grave with their women, and joined in the final expressions of grief.

Before dispersing, the children were taken over the grave mound; and Minny, the mother of the deceased, and other elderly women were helped to step over the mound. Water was brought up to the old people, who washed the paint off their bodies, and all returned to the settlement. Sizors had been buried.

Discussion

Many of the elements of ritual performed at a burial are

---

[4] These spears are not traditional to the island culture.

also found in the later rites and will be discussed in connection with them. These include: (1) the roles and kin relationships of the principal groups of participants: the workers,
leaders, and close relatives; (2) the form and content of the
songs and dances; (3) the "honey" and "mosquito" calls; and
(4) the body painting, washing, and so on. Also part of the
subsequent rituals is the showing of grief. However, it is
during the burial service that signs of grief and the ritual
forms it takes are most apparent, and I shall therefore discuss
these here.

The various forms by which one may express grief have
been described in the descriptions of the burials of Margaret's
infant and of Sizors. As I watched the sometimes frenzied cutting of heads, beating of bodies, and wailing, the group
seemed to divide into those who were expressing their grief
directly to the spirit of the deceased and those who were
expressing their sympathy to the close relatives of the deceased. The close relatives directed their grief toward the
grave, and they had to be restrained from doing real bodily
harm to themselves and from joining the body in the grave.
The others were given knives and clubs, which they used
without restraint while facing the immediate family of the
deceased. My informants explained that mourners outside the
immediate kin group felt "sorry for the family" and "helped
them in their sorrow by joining them." In the final ceremony,
however, we shall see that all expressions of grief by close and
nonclose kin of the deceased are directed toward the grave
and the spirit of the deceased that it represents. It seemed to
me that the bloodletting by those not in the immediate kin
group bore relation to the actions taken when a Tiwi has
accidently caused an injury to another. It appears to be a
sign of guilt, and it might be that all the self-injury in the
ritual expressions of grief is to show the deceased *(mobuditi)* that they are sorry if they had anything to do with his
death, rather than to encourage real nonritual tears and wails.

There were two major differences in these descriptions of

burial rituals: first, the use of fires around the grave in Sizors', found also in the woman's burial described by Mountford but not in the infant's burial; and second, the use of the coffin in the infant's burial and the addition of flowers, both of which were, I believe, complete innovations.

The fires are to protect the living from the *mobuditi* and are left burning all day and night, although they are un-attended after people leave the grave at the conclusion of the ritual. Generally it is believed that the fires contain the *mobuditi* in the grave area during the first night after burial when it is most likely to want to return to the camp. The absence of fires at the grave of the little infant can be easily explained in that the tiny spirit could hardly be expected to do much harm by itself. It hardly knew its own mother, much less any other relative.[5]

In order to understand the innovations in the infant's burial, we must anticipate a little the discussion of funeral rituals in the next chapter. Although there is a set sequence of ritual procedure, a great deal of variation and innovation is allowed in the content of the rituals. In a general way the whole ceremony is memorial, but there is also an effort to make it memorable, and by doing so, individual participants gain prestige. Innovations, however, do not ordinarily ac-company a burial service, for expedience together with in-tense personal emotion do not permit its organizers either the time or the wish to do things differently. However, for the burial of Margaret's infant, circumstances plus one man's personality resulted in an innovation, one which had never before been seen or described to me.

The circumstances were that Patrick, the real father of the child and the man who properly should have directed the burial, was not present. The substitution of Bob One in this

---

[5] In 1962 my young female informant said that very small infants do not join the *mobuditi* society but are reborn into the world of the living, and one can tell such a rebirth by recognizing a physical resemblance. However, older male informants in 1962 emphatically denied this and said, "All still follow Purakapali, even babies."

role was quite within the bounds of correct procedure, for he was Patrick's brother, and a "father" to the child. There was, however, one difference in the expected behavior of these two fathers. Emotional reasons would probably have inhibited Patrick, as the real father, from trying any innovation; but Bob One, who was not so closely tied to the mother and child, seemed to be strongly motivated to perform his substitute role more than just adequately for the sake of his absent brother. His direction throughout was orderly, planned, and compassionate, but never emotional.

In many ways Bob and Patrick were alike. Both were between thirty and forty years old and both had two wives. Bob's wives were both much older than he, for he had inherited them. Patrick's wives were "one-mother" sisters, aged thirteen and nineteen. In their marriages both men conformed to the old way of life, and this conformity was reflected in their usually traditional behavior. However, both men were young enough to have had considerable contact with white culture, and both had a great desire for white education not only for their children but also for themselves. They recognized the challenge presented to them by the forces of acculturation and considered compromise to be the best method to meet it. Neither man was considered to be a leader by either the Tiwi or the whites; they seemed content to lead their own destinies and those of their immediate families.

Bob's addition of a coffin and flowers in a burial ritual was undoubtedly inspired by a knowledge of Christian burial. I feel sure that he was not trying to introduce a Christian element, but rather felt that these innovations would make the service a bit different and thus more memorable. Perhaps, also, in the back of his mind, he regarded it as an easy and first step in cultural compromise, and one of which Patrick would approve.

In 1962 I arrived at Snake Bay at 8:30 A.M., and by one o'clock that afternoon I heard that Jacky Navy had just died.

I was told that Jacky had been baptised a few weeks previously, and I include a brief description of his burial in order to illustrate the process of cultural compromise that characterizes Tiwi acculturation.

When I arrived at the settlement area in which the death had occurred, I met for the first time after eight years many of my old friends. Topsy, Jacky Navy's surviving spouse, and their daughter Rosemary made no sign of recognition but sat together near the covered body in a state of near shock. Both were covered with white paint. A coffin was close by the body. A short dance was led by the husband of Jacky's "one-granny" sister and a brother of his, both of whom carried spears. Several women danced *ambaru,* but Topsy did not.

The group then marched to a new Christian grave area. I noticed crosses on four or five graves, and one grave had only a stick with a cloth "flag" tied to it, with a cup and spoon lying on the mound.

Four men were digging the grave when we arrived, and individuals wailed. Topsy still showed no emotion but Rosemary, standing close by a young lad, wept loudly. Ali (sister's husband of the deceased) picked the boy up, comforted him by wailing with him, and then carried the boy about on his shoulders. Several men danced. Jacky Navy's aged mother sat by the coffin. Polly, Jacky's "one-granny" sister, beat her head against the coffin until restrained. As the coffin was placed in the grave, many beat themselves with sticks and knives, and the wailing increased. Then silence, which was broken after a few seconds by the beginning of the Christian burial service led by a young Tiwi man who began the prayers, including the Lord's Prayer. While some of the group followed him in responses and in recitation kneeling by the grave, other nonparticipants stood silently and respectfully by the side of the cleared ground. A child was quickly disciplined for not remaining quiet. The grave was filled while the prayers continued, after which the traditionalists took over again with wailing, beating, and head cutting. There was, however, no formal singing and dancing. The ritual concluded with a number of individuals making short speeches about the deceased—that he was a good man and kind to all people— replacing the traditional songs that often concern the same subjects.

CHAPTER NINE

Pukamani

The word *pukamani* means many things. I have used it occasionally in previous chapters to designate the funeral ceremony that follows a burial. This ceremony is made up of
many parts, the majority of which have separate and distinct
names. The final hours of the ceremony, however, have the
designation of *pukamani*. The word *pukamani* also has the
connotation of taboo, and is used to designate behavior and
ritual paraphernalia as well as objects that under certain conditions are taboo. In other words, throughout the *pukamani*
ceremony, there are people who are *pukamani,* meaning that
they are under certain taboos restricting behavior but are not
in themselves taboo. They wear *pukamani* objects of adorn-
ment that identify the wearers as being under taboos, but the
objects are not themselves taboo. In preparation for the end
of the *pukamani* ceremony, certain objects are manufactured,
and these are referred to as being *pukamani* objects, but these
objects are not taboo either. However, any object owned or

used by the one who has recently died, and the body itself, its grave, and the grave area, are all *pukamani* and considered taboo.

There is some question whether the word *pukamani* is used to designate the taboos found in other rituals, such as *kulama, muriŋaleta,* and pregnancy. I do not believe that it has this wider use, for as these other ceremonial taboos were mentioned to me, the informants would say, "this like *pukamani,*" if indeed they mentioned the word *pukamani* at all.

If we can give such a general definition for *pukamani* as anything connected or concerned with the death of a member of the Tiwi society, then my use of it as a heading for this chapter should be understood as meaning the customs and actions of the living in preparation for and in carrying out the correct ritual procedures concerned with the dead and with the release of a new *mobuditi* spirit.

It is by no means an arbitrary decision on my part to divorce the burial rituals from what I have termed the *pukamani* rituals by placing them in separate chapters. If I had observed this culture in precontact days, I might not have been so ready to do so. However, the present-day situation and its effect on these rites has a precedent in past tradition.

Today the Tiwi population is concentrated in three main areas: the Snake Bay Settlement, the Bathurst Island Mission, and Darwin. A Tiwi may die and be buried in any of these three localities, but the *pukamani* ceremony is virutally banned in all but the Snake Bay Settlement. Snake Bay natives believe that, although a body may be buried in Darwin or in the mission burial ground, its *mobuditi* will return to Snake Bay if its close relatives are residing there, and a *pukamani* must be held. I am not sure what happens to the spirit of a mission Tiwi when his grave and his relatives are mainly residents of the mission and yet remain pagans. I suspect that since the ceremony is banned there, the relatives may well come to Snake Bay to join with some more distant relatives in some sort of ceremony for the deceased, or go across the straits to Melville Island territory and hold the ceremony away from the mission. At every ritual I observed, there were present some kinsmen of the deceased who were resident at the mission. Most of them participated but a few merely observed, considering it wrong in the light of their newly acquired ethics to perform their traditional duties and roles, but considering it necessary to be there according to traditional ethics. Likewise a number of the observed rituals were for residents of the mission who had been given Christian burial there, but whose close kin at Snake Bay carried out traditional rites at the settlement.

In the old days when the Tiwi were dispersed throughout the islands in their separate countries, where a man died and was buried was where his *mobuditi* resided, even if he died in a country other than that which he owned. However, occasionally in the past when someone died at sea and the body was not recovered, it was considered that his *mobuditi* would return to his own country. In such a case his belongings were burned and buried on the shore of his country, and a full *pukamani* ceremony was held there. A slightly different solution obtained when it was suspected that a crocodile had consumed a Tiwi. If possible, they caught the crocodile and chopped it up. If the human remains were recognizable and recoverable, they were buried; if not, the crocodile itself was buried. In none of the above situations is there an actual burial service preceding the main rituals. Thus it is evident that regardless of whether there has been a traditional burial service or not, the *pukamani* must go on. A *pukamani* is dependent on the presence of a *mobuditi*, not on the body of a person in a particular grave.

It is expected and has always been expected that everyone "concerned" will come to the *pukamani* ceremony. Today various external commitments may prevent someone from attending. How often this problem occurred in the past is not known, but it seems to have occurred occasionally, and the solution appears to have always been a part of Tiwi tradition.

The solution is for the absent one to hold what I shall designate as a "memorial" *pukamani* as soon as it is possible for him to visit the grave. A "memorial" *pukamani* may also be held for other reasons more consistent with the connotation of the word "memorial." The "memorial" *pukamani* may vary tremendously in form and duration, depending on many factors, some of which are the closeness of the relationship of the absent one to the deceased, the amount of elapsed time, and the importance of the deceased. The other type of "memorial" service is usually impromptu and may consist of one dance or a short series of dances when some object or event has prompted the memory of the one who has died. It may even consist of only a short ritual wail, which can hardly be called a ceremony.

The dividing line between the main *pukamani* and the "memorial" *pukamani* may well be arbitrary. The Tiwi make no such distinction, which causes me to believe that they regard the *pukamani* ritual as an individual responsibility, the resulting duties of which may be held collectively or separately. But one person alone cannot perform the prescribed rituals. He is always helped by others who have already performed their duty to the *mobuditi,* but who have a duty to the living as well in helping each other perform their prescribed rites.

The distinction between what I am calling the main *pukamani* and the "memorial" *pukamani* is that the former is the first to be held after the occurrence of a death. The main *pukamani* is likely to be a complete and full-fledged ceremony, but a few times in 1954 the first *pukamani* was slightly abbreviated when there was no body for burial.

In a general way the main *pukamani* can be described as containing three principal elements: a series of preliminary dance rituals, the preparation of poles, and a final thirty-six-hour dance ritual held at the grave or place of poles. In Table 17 I have listed all deaths for which some kind of ceremony was held during the period of April to December 1954, and

TABLE 17
PUKAMANI RITUALS AT SNAKE BAY

| | | PHASES OF PUKAMANI | | | |
| | | Preliminary | | Final | |
Person	Burial	Dances	Poles	Ceremony	Memorial
Black Joe's baby No. 1	1953 Darwin	?	Yes	?	Impromptu at baby 2's final ceremony*
Black Joe's baby No. 2	1954 Darwin	None	None	3 hrs.*	
Sugarbag (Waniamperi)	March 1954 Snake Bay	12*	Yes*	36 hrs.*	One at grave*
Bob One's mother (Makapini)	June 1954 Mission	4*	Yes*	36 hrs.*	
Ruby One (Nulatini)	August 1954* Snake Bay	15*	Yes*	36 hrs.*	One at grave*
Billy P.'s daughter No. 1	August 1954 Mission	6*	Yes*	36 hrs.*	
Billy P.'s baby daughter	September 1954 Darwin	Included with daughter No. 1			
Rosemary's mother	Several years past, Snake Bay	? (Completed before 1954)	Yes	?	Impromptu at grave*
Peter's father	?	?	?	?	Impromptu at preliminary dance for Ruby One*
Sizors	October 1954* Snake Bay	(Not held before I left)			
Patrick's baby son	November 1954* Snake Bay	(Not held before I left)			
Paddy One	1962 Snake Bay	1 (observed)*	Yes	Anticipated	
Jacky Navy	June 1962* Snake Bay	1 (observed)*	?	?	

* Rituals that were observed and recorded.

during the two weeks I visited Snake Bay in 1962. The date and place of burial is also given when known to me, in order that the ritual variations will become meaningful in the light of the discussion above. Those events that I witnessed are starred. Some of these have been described by Mountford (1958) who refers to the deceased by native name; these have been included in parentheses for the convenience of those who may wish to correlate and compare the published data.

Unless otherwise designated, all the deaths recorded in Table 17 were of adult individuals. The lack of poles for the *pukamani* for Black Joe's baby who died in 1954 was probably due to a combination of facts: another of Black Joe's babies had died the year before, and a grave had been made with a set of poles at Snake Bay; the new baby died in Darwin when only a few days old, and his ceremony was conducted at the grave of the other dead child using the same poles.

Mountford (1958:50-121) has described the burials of Sugarbag (Waniamperi) and Ruby One (Nulatini), as well as three preliminary dances for Sugarbag, one preliminary dance for Bob One's mother (Makapini), and one for Ruby One. He has also described the final ceremony at the graves of Sugarbag and Bob One's mother. Spencer (1914:228-39) and Harney (1957:82-98) have also published portions of the *pukamani* ceremony that they witnessed. The only justifiable lengthy descriptive introduction to an analysis of this ritual would be to follow one ceremony from beginning to end. This has not been done before, and it would graphically illustrate the complexities facing both the observer and analyst. But, if I describe one of the ceremonies, I should also describe the others, for although there is a basic outline for what should take place, and when and where, the "cast" and the "script" always vary according to who has died. Other parts of the "script" may vary with the performers.

The Tiwi regard the *pukamani* as the most important ceremony in a person's life in the world of the living, and even though the *mobuditi* has been released, the person's

existence in the living world is not finished until the completion of the ceremony. To the Tiwi the entire focus of the
ceremony is on the person now in the grave. This attitude
results in the consistent variations in cast and script. But we
cannot see the regularity of these variations unless we compare all the ceremonies available. When the predictable
variations have been isolated, there remain the unpredictable
ones that reflect the fact that some innovation by individual
participants is permitted and encouraged. There are still
other variations that have manifold causes and that can be
isolated only by viewing the entire ceremony in time and
place, after having determined what are the consistent elements and what are the expected variations.

The *pukamani* brings together people from every social
unit to which the deceased belonged or with which he was
affiliated. The Tiwi consider it necessary for all members of
these social units to participate in the rituals. It is the one
occasion, therefore (with the possible exception of warfare),
when all the different types and kinds of social units in Tiwi
society are represented. Obviously there must be some organization of the participants if they are all to gather for a
common purpose for several days and not have conflict or
chaos. The Tiwi realize this and provide a leader or a group
of leaders. They also prescribe certain rituals and kinds of
behavior for designated groups of individuals. The resulting
alignments of individuals, which disregard almost completely
the amount of day-to-day contact they have had with the
deceased, are striking. The consequent reinforcement of basic
social units and relationships is, to me, a most important
and illuminating aspect of the ceremony.

I intend to discuss, rather than describe, the *pukamani*
ceremony, emphasizing the separate elements of ritual and
behavior that are necessary to the conduct of the event. I will
also discuss standard and allowable variations, on the basis of
the relatively large number of *pukamani* rituals I observed
and recorded. Because this ceremony conceptually marks the

end of a Tiwi's existence in the world of the living, I believe
that it should symbolically indicate those elements in the life
of an individual Tiwi that are deemed "significant" by the
culture. And because this is the occasion for the organization
of social behavior on a large scale, it should also symbolically
indicate those elements in the organization of Tiwi society
that are deemed "significant" by the Tiwi.

I have arranged the discussion in a generalized chronological order, in that each element is discussed in the order in
which it becomes important, but with further reference to its
place throughout the entire sequence of ritual. Since I shall
continually refer to the entire sequence of the *pukamani*
ceremony, I feel that the reader should have the advantage of
knowing in advance the outline of the *pukamani*.

> Phase 1: The Burial
>> Discussion 1: *Pukamani* and Taboo
> Phase 2: Sending of Messengers and Selection of Workers
>> Discussion 2: *Pukamani* and Kinship
>>> a. Terminology
>>> b. Roles and Duties
> Phase 3: Preliminary Rites—The *Ilanea*
>> Discussion 3: *Pukamani* and Art
>>> a. Songs and Dances—the *yoi*
>>> b. Items of Manufacture
>>> c. *Pukamani* and Economy
> Phase 4: Final Ceremony at the Grave—The *Pukamani*

I have already described Phase 1, the burial (pp. 241-53),
and I will therefore turn to Discussion 1.

Discussion 1: *Pukamani* and Taboo

The people most immediately affected by the death of an
individual are those who are present when he dies. In ordinary circumstances, they are the people with whom he lived
and had regular and frequent contact. Immediately after

death and continuing until the conclusion of the entire ceremony, some of these people must impose upon themselves
rigid behavioral taboos; by doing so, they are considered by
others as "being *pukamani*." Who these people are, when the
taboos are imposed, and for how long they are kept depends
on several factors: (1) the degree of relationship to the
deceased modified by the actual amount of personal contact;
(2) relative age among those whose relationship to the
deceased is otherwise equal; and (3) absolute age.

1. Only the close consanguineal or affinal relatives who are
in the camp and have had regular and frequent personal
contact with the deceased are required to become *pukamani*
immediately after a person's death.

2. The relative age among those close kinsmen whose
relationship is otherwise equal determines which of them
shall be required to become *pukamani* at this early time.
The eldest among those in each degree of relationship will
assume the restrictions after the death and continue until the
end. The younger will be exempt until such time as final
preparations are begun, that is, the commissioning of the
workers.

3. Absolute age will provide certain exemptions to the
above. All very old people are exempt, as well as the young
girls not yet sleeping with their husbands, and young boys.
The taboos are considered too difficult physically for the old
and the young to undergo.

It must have happened in the past, as it did during the
period of April to December 1954, that two or more deaths
followed each other rapidly enough so that the resulting
periods of taboo and ritual overlapped. For some people the
overlapping is only in the ritual, but for others there is also
the problem of overlapping taboo. One cannot be *pukamani*
for two deceased relatives at the same time. A choice has to be
made, and this is based on the actual degree of kinship.
For instance, if a sister's sons's death is followed by that of a
member of one's sibling set, the mother's brother who as-

sumed the taboos for his sister's son will release himself from these taboos with an appropriate ritual and then reassume them when his close sibling is buried. Only those whose relationship to the second deceased is considered closer will do this.

Immediately after death, all the potential *pukamani* people paint themselves. This painting is hurried, and there is usually no attempt at design. They smear any convenient ochre, usually white clay, over their bodies, face, and hair. The surviving spouse has his or her hair cut very short, and a male has his beard plucked out or shaved off. One reason given for this practice is that "it makes the head and face easier to paint." Eventually every *pukamani* person will have his hair cut, probably for this reason. However, another reason was given for cutting the spouse's or *ambaru*'s hair, and that was because the deceased had but recently touched it. As we shall see, anything that has been recently in contact with the deceased is taboo. After the hair and beard are cut at the beginning of the taboo period, they are not cut again until the conclusion of the ceremony, at the ritual lifting of the taboos.

This initial painting is the first and major sign that one is *pukamani*. After the burial ceremony, those who are not obligated to continue with the restrictions until a later time wash the paint off. The others continue to wear it and may not wash their bodies until the entire ceremony is over. They renew the paint from day to day, and once the preliminary dances have begun, the painting is likely to be much more elaborate and in various designs.

Shortly after the burial, the *pukamani* women begin to braid and weave strips of pandanus into rings or bands called *yeariŋa*. These vary in width from one-half to two inches and are worn on both the upper arm and the forearm by both sexes. Eventually, as there is time to make them, both arms are entirely encased in these pandanus bands. Other arm-bands are specially made to be worn over the elbow by binding a flexible twig with pandanus and then attaching a small group of dangling bits of twine, hair rope, or colored wool with feathers on the ends. These elbow decorations are called *pamagini,* and they may also be held in the hand during the dances.

There is a rough correlation between the number of armbands worn and the closeness of the relationship to the deceased, but the number may vary according to who makes the *yeariŋa.* Women make these rings, and anyone who cannot provide himself with them must depend on someone else. As a result a man may have a smaller number of rings, although he should wear a complete set. These rings are painted over in the daily body painting, as they cannot be removed until the end of the ceremony. When a body design is made, it will appear on the rings as if they were, in fact, the bare skin of the arms.

They give two explanations for painting and putting on the *yeariŋa* and *pamagini:* "Because the culture hero, Purakapali, said so," and "So the *mobuditi* of the deceased will be unable to recognize them." I believe that both of the reasons are sufficient for the Tiwi, and that they should not be taken as contradictory. It is interesting, in the light of the second one, that a murderer is also required to paint himself immediately after the slaying in order to escape the wrath of his victim's *mobuditi.* In both instances the effect is the same: isolation and identification.

So identified, the *pukamani* people are under severe restrictions. They may not go near water, even salt water, because of the dangers represented by the rainbow spirit, *maritji.* It is probably for this reason that they cannot wash between paintings, and will not do so until they are finally released from the taboos. They cannot hunt for their own food nor may they touch what they eat with their hands. Someone must give them food and must also place it in their mouths; and if any food should drop on the ground during this process, no one may touch it. The *pukamani* person may not even carry his own food in a container. There are similar restrictions on carrying and drinking water. *Pukamani* persons may not touch the water container in any way; when they wish to drink, someone must raise the container to their lips. One rationalization I heard for these severe restrictions was, "They cannot go bush alone (because of the nature of the restrictions). Maybe they feel too sorry along that dead one. Maybe they kill themselves." This statement was surprising to me, not only because it was so reasonable but also because it was not the one that I had expected but never heard expressed—namely, if *pukamani* persons go into the bush alone, the spirit of the deceased might abduct and kill them.

There is a slight question in my mind as to whether the *pukamani* people are themselves taboo, for there is a restriction that young children may not eat food caught by a *pukamani* since it is considered dangerous for them. There is, however, no other evidence for such a feeling of taboo.

Pukamani people can hunt, but they must give their food away and eat none of it themselves. It may happen that two *pukamani* people are hunting companions, and in this case each will give his catch to the other and feed it to him. If it becomes absolutely necessary for the two *pukamani* to drink while out hunting together, they must lap the water from the water hole or billabong like dogs, for they may not use their hands.

And lastly, no sexual intercourse is allowed when one is under the *pukamani* taboos.

Usually a person is under these restrictions for a period of one to four months. But one man told me that he had once been *pukamani* for nine straight months. Under present-day conditions these restrictions may become an impossibility. For instance, a *pukamani* person who has a job in Darwin may know no one there who will undertake the feeding. If he trusts this role to a mainland native or even to a Tiwi whom he does not know well, "maybe they put poison in food."

When Ali worked for the army during World War II, a

close kinsman of his died and he became a *pukamani*. However, he was not allowed to wear his *yeariŋa* or *pamagini* so
he put them in a box that he kept near him. He carried water
for others, but could not drink the tea made from that water.
However, working with him was a friend who undertook to
feed him and otherwise look after his needs.

Sometimes "an old man" will tell a Darwin-bound *pukamani* that it is all right to wash himself and thus gain release
from the taboos. It is preferable to obtain permission (probably from the "boss" of the ceremony) but if necessary one
may release oneself without such permission. Bill Harney told
me that in the days when Malay luggers dropped anchor
offshore, women who had "love contracts" on board but who
were at that time *pukamani* would release themselves from
the taboo, sleep with their lovers, and after returning to shore
with their gifts would again put on their pandanus bands,
paint themselves, and carry on with the taboos.

To release himself from the taboos, either permanently
or temporarily, the *pukamani* individual washes the paint off
his body and removes the pandanus arm rings. This is usually
done during one of the preliminary dances if it is a temporary release, and, in such a case, when he returns to the
island or assumes the taboos for a subsequent death of a close
kin, he sleeps one night and then repaints and replaces the
pandanus rings.

The death of a Tiwi not only causes certain actions to
become taboo for a selected group of his kinsmen but also
makes certain objects and names taboo for everyone and certain places taboo to all but the most distantly related kin.

All material possessions owned and, in most cases, used by
the deceased are in themselves taboo. Items of little worth that
can be fairly easily replaced (this includes almost all traditional possessions) are taken to the grave along with the
body and left lying on top of the mound at the time of
burial. If anyone touches them, he will become ill. Occasionally some items may be held in reserve for someone who

is known to be unable to attend the main final *pukamani* ceremony. The absent one uses these as a "reminder" of the deceased in his "memorial" *pukamani*. During Ruby One's burial, her widower Jimmy was criticized for his behavior in dealing with Ruby's belongings, which he repeatedly removed from the grave in order to dance with them in his arms and then replaced. This was considered bad, "for it make him too sorry alonga that dead one." This was the reason most often given for the taboo placed on personal belongings. Inheritance of material objects is thus very simple. None of the close relatives want these items, for they will be reminded of the deceased.

There are some items, however, particularly today, which have an undeniable value, such as canoes, axes, and even permanent or semipermanent settlement houses. These are not destroyed or left on or near the grave but are eventually inherited by someone in the immediate family of the deceased. Both men and women can inherit. Who gets what is based on need. A man will get the canoe or perhaps a group of sibling-set brothers will assume ownership jointly. But before ownership can become a fact, these items must be made "clean." Cleaning is done by smoking, which drives the spirit of the deceased away, but it is usually not done until after the final ceremony. In 1962, however, the new and permanent house belonging to Jacky Navy was "smoked" within a week of his death. Spirits of the dead have been known to cut the mooring ropes of their canoes, setting them adrift so that they can be claimed by the salvager who may not be the rightful heir.

Any item that did not belong to the deceased but that had been used by him is also taboo. Anyone who reuses it will swell up and die. Should food be placed in a basket that had been touched by the deceased, it becomes highly taboo and is considered poisonous.

We would expect the body of the deceased to be considered taboo also, but there is little actual evidence of this reflected in behavior during the burial ceremony. In general those who handle the body are the people who are called "workers," who are considered to be the most distant relatives of the deceased resident in the country where his death occurred. At the same time we also find that there is much effort by the close relatives in the frenzy of grief to accompany the body into the grave. In the burial of Ruby One, it was a necessary part of the ritual that certain of the close relatives, including the widower, Jimmy, actually descend into the grave after the body had been lowered to say a final farewell. When Jimmy did this, a woman told me that in the old days, the *ambaru* used to copulate with the deceased in the grave; but on this occasion Jimmy only took a fire stick and burned his wife's pubic hair as well as his own.

It may well be that the body of the deceased is considered to be extremely taboo, but that part of the expression of grief—which is full of self-punishment and highly emotional behavior—is the deliberate disregard of this taboo. Certainly after the burial the entire grave area, for as much as a mile in circumference, is taboo to all except those who, as "workers," must prepare the area for the final ceremony. This taboo area is the personal hunting territory of the deceased until after the final ceremony. In contrast to this, the area in which the death occurred is not taboo but is often chosen to be the first ceremonial ground for the start of the preliminary *ilanea* rituals.

I have mentioned elsewhere the taboo on using the personal name of the deceased and the extension of the taboo to all personal names that the deceased may have bestowed on others, as well as to all words in use that resemble the name of the deceased. This taboo lasts long after the final rites are completed. In addition, there is a taboo on other personal names for the period of the *pukamani* itself. First, personal names of the *ambaru* must never be used, particularly by anyone working in the grave area. Moreover, his or her English nickname is also taboo. He or she is always addressed and referred to by the special *pukamani* kinship term, *ambaru,* similar to our use of the terms "widow" and "widower" in the same circumstances. There are other special *pukamani*-kinship terms that are used, both in reference and address, during the ceremonial period after the death of a kinsman other than one's spouse. As I observed their use, however, they did not seem to replace entirely the ordinary kinship terms but were used alternately with them, unlike the term *ambaru,* which was always used. The English names of surviving kin other than the *ambaru* were not apparently taboo, and their native names were only taboo in the grave area or if they had been given them by the deceased. I suspect that this may not always have been the case, and that in the past all the close kin would have been referred to and addressed by the special *pukamani*-kinship terms, as is the *ambaru* today. This would explain the existence of these terms. Indeed, it was only by chance that I learned they existed, and my information on them may not be complete.

Phase 2: Sending Messengers and Selecting Workers

Shortly after the burial and well before the start of the final preparations for the *pukamani* ceremony, messengers must be sent out to all areas where there are close relatives in order to announce the death and to give word when the final ceremony will take place. The messengers are chosen from the close relatives of the deceased but are not necessarily those under the *pukamani* taboos. It is impractical to send two messengers to the same locality, and no one under the taboos can travel alone for any great distance. These messengers paint themselves red and carry a single pointed hunting or "mangrove" spear (*murubuni*). Nowadays they have added the touch of message sticks, which Mountford mentions and illustrates (1958:98-107). These give the messenger added authority in his office. When the messenger draws near a camp he sits down at a visible distance, renews his paint, then slowly approaches the camp. Those in the camp have by now noticed his presence, and his close relatives come halfway to meet him. He tells them who has died, and the relatives fall on each others' shoulders and "have a cry."

It is the right and duty of a person's father, brothers, or sons to decide when the final ceremony is to be held. Should the eldest male member of the patrilineage of the deceased not be resident in the locality where the death occurred, one messenger goes first to him to announce the death and receive instructions to carry back to those who must make local arrangements.

In deciding when the final ceremony will be held, the first consideration is the time needed for everyone concerned to get the news and make arrangements to attend. The amount of time necessary for the home group to prepare must also be taken into account. The time between the burial and the final ceremony varies, therefore, but in general it is approximately three or four months.

Not until the messengers have returned, reporting their duty fulfilled and carrying orders, if called for, do final preparations begin. They take about two to four weeks, beginning with a preliminary series of *ilanea* dances and rituals and the selection of workers. During one of the first *ilanea* dances, workers are chosen from among the members of the kin group that is eligible to work. The workers must also be residents of the country where the grave is located. These workers receive a ritual commissioning. If more are needed at a later date, others belonging to this eligible group will be commissioned, but without ritual.

The patrilineal relative of the deceased who has assumed leadership of the local arrangements designates the workers by setting them aside during the *ilanea* upon nomination from other close kin of the deceased. Both men and women can nominate workers, and both men and women enter the preliminary discussion of how many poles should be cut and how big they should be. The workers themselves have a great deal of independence in their work, but these preliminary instructions are necessary as a guide to the close kin group's desires regarding the size of the final ceremony, reflecting both their sentiment and their ability to pay, as well as the status of their deceased kinsman.

The worker's tool is an ax. In the old days a stone ax was included in the gifts to workers, but today steel axes are loaned to them, and the leader calls for axes to be donated for loan. One of these axes is selected and the handle painted white. It is then set up in the center of the dance ground. The commissioned workers form a circle around the ax and give the "honey" call, followed by a round of songs and dances. Then the concluding calls are given for the *ilanea,* and the ritual is over.

Discussion 2: *Pukamani* and Kinship

A. TERMINOLOGY

I have previously discussed the basic concepts involved in Tiwi classification of kin into "close kin" and "long-way kin" (pp. 109-14). All close kin of the deceased must participate in the *pukamani* and certain long-way kin are expected to be there. The criteria for determining which long-way kin are expected are variously reckoned: (1) members of the matrilineal sib and, I believe, phratry of the deceased; (2) members of the land-holding group or limited patrilineage of the deceased; (3) coresidents of the area in which the deceased died or, if different, the area(s) in which he had lived throughout his life; and (4) individuals who are married to any close kin of the deceased, including himself, and, in the latter case, "one-granny" and "one-grandfather" siblings of the surviving spouse.

The special terminology that applies to kinsmen at the time of an individual's death group together these close kin and particular long-way kinsmen in less exclusive kin categories than is found in the ordinary kin classification system.

Each *pukamani* kin category has assigned duties and roles to perform in the ceremony. Long-way kin who are present will be classed with close kin who stand in the same ordinary kin terminological relationship to the deceased. Their roles and duties may, however, be different from the close kin so classified if as long-way relatives of the deceased they have married a close kin of the deceased. These "affinal" relatives may also be related to the deceased consanguineally and therefore have a conflict of roles and duties to perform. While each category of *pukamani* kinsmen has assigned duties to perform in relation to the deceased, all participants also have roles to perform according to their relationship to other participants. For example, it is obligatory in the rituals for spouses (actual and potential) as well as siblings to "help" each other in the performance of their duties. The greatest conflict appears to come when a close kinsman, married to a long-way kinsman commissioned as a worker, has to choose between two quite conflicting roles. I have recorded a number of cases where a close sibling chose to "help" her commissioned husband in preparing the funeral poles rather than perform her duties as a sibling of the deceased.

In Table 18, where the ordinary kinship terminology is correlated with the special *pukamani* terminology, the descriptive kin-type equivalents are given only for the close kin, for the sake of simplicity.

Although everyone in the first and third ascending and descending generations is called by the same term, *unandawi* (*unandaka*, female; *unandani*, male), I noticed distinctive behavioral assignments differentiating those I have included under the word "paternal" and those I have called "maternal."[1]

In the generation of the deceased and in the second ascending and second descending generations, there are four main terms, each denoting a definite behavioral distinction. How-

---

[1] In 1962 I checked again with my informants whether these kin were to be included under one or two *pukamani* terms and found my original data to be correct: there is but one term.

TABLE 18

SPECIAL PUKAMANI KINSHIP TERMINOLOGY AND CLASSIFICATION

Generations	*Unandawi*			
	Paternal		Maternal	
1st and 3rd ascending and descending	*iriŋani* (F, FB)	*imerani** (BS)	*iŋnari* (M, MZ)	*mariŋa** (ZD)
	intiŋaniŋa (FZ)	*imeraniŋa** (BD)	*ilimani* (MB)	*morti** (ZS)

	Pudawi			Yempi - 1 Yemawampi - 2	Ambarui
Generations: Ego's and 2nd ascending and descending	*imboka imbuŋa iŋgalaba* (Z)	*imaniŋa†* (MM)	*intamiliŋa†* (ZDD)	1- *amini* (FZS, MF)	*imbunei* (H,HB,WB)
			inim'uŋa† (BDD)	1- *ama* (FZD, FM)	*imbuneiŋa* (W, WZ,HZ)
	iwini iwuni iŋgalabini (B)	*amini†* (FF)	*intamiliti†* (ZDS)	2- *mawanini* (MBS)	
			inimini† (BDS)	2- *mawana* (MBD)	

* If these kinsmen are actual children of the deceased, they are referred to as *imiriwini* rather than the term *unandawi*.

† If these kinsmen are the actual grandparents or grandchildren of the deceased, they are called *kiakia* or *kirimika* rather than *pudawi*.

ever, I have included the *yempi* (FZS, FZD) and *yemawampi* (MBS, MBD) under one category because of observed similarity in behavior assignments. I shall refer to them by the shorter term, *yempi*. The group termed *ambarui* are closely related in fact to individual *yempi* and comprise the most restricted group, being formed of the surviving spouse(s) and their close "one-granny" or "one-grandfather" siblings. The *yempi* and the *ambarui* have special "helping" interrelationships in the rituals, although their duties to the deceased are quite distant.

The last division of kinsmen of the deceased are the *pudawi* (*pudaka,* female; *pudani,* male), who are close and long-way siblings of the deceased in his generation and those of his grandparents' and grandchildren's generations. A termino-

logical distinction is made between close and long-way grandparents and grandchildren that reflects the distinction found
in the ordinary kin-terminological system. Close grandparents
(FF, MM) and close grandchildren (ZDC, BDC) are called
kiakia or *kirimika*.[2] In spite of the distinction made here in
pukamani terminology, there is no observable difference of
behavioral assignment, other than exceptions granted for
absolute age of participants, and thus I have grouped these
terms under the single term *pudawi*.

It may be well to mention here that the "paternal" *unandawi*
and some of the *pudawi* will belong to the same limited
patrilineage. This is an important consideration for the
determination of ritual roles and duties. I should also mention that the "maternal" *unandawi* and the *pudawi* may, if
there has been a strict adherence to the preferential sib
exchange in marriage, all belong to one sib. But often they
are not in the same sib, and the sib appears to be ritually
significant only in determining who among the long-way and
nonresident matrilineal kinsmen are expected to be present
and to participate.

B. RITUAL ROLES AND DUTIES

In discussion I shall use the word "role" to refer to the type
of interaction among the performers in the ritual that is
determined by their kinship relationship to each other. The
word "duty" will be used for the basic division of labor among
the surviving relatives in organizing and carrying out the
necessary procedures in the ceremony that are their duty to
the deceased. This division of labor is dictated by their
kinship relation to the deceased.

The basic division of labor is between those kin who do
the physical labor of preparing for the burial and final *pukamani* ceremony, the "workers," and those who organize and
pay for the ceremony, the "employers."

---

[2] I suspect that these terms have sex denotations, but unfortunately my
data are incomplete on these terms.

The workers are the male *yempi* and their wives. The employers are the *unandawi, pudawi,* and *ambarui.* Some among this group of employers are the organizers and leaders, namely, those close kin who belong to the limited patrilineage of the deceased. In most instances the leaders will be all of the paternal *unandawi* and some of the *pudawi.*

The first duty of the *yempi,* the workers, is to prepare the grave for burial, which includes clearing the surrounding area for the dances. After the burial, certain of these *yempi,* who are all residents of the area in which the deceased is buried, are commissioned to cut the *pukamani* poles that will mark the grave for many years after the ceremonies are over. They must also prepare the dance grounds around the grave.[3]

Both commissioned and uncommissioned *yempi* have a definite role in the dance rituals. They must help their employers by joining them in the dances and songs, and when an employer is weary they take over and perform his role. The *yempi* mainly help the *ambarui* (surviving spouses), for this group will ordinarily be very small. The principal *ambaru* is obligated to be continually active, singing or dancing or both, but his role will at times be taken over by one or more of the *yempi.* The *yempi* also help the entire employer group to paint themselves for the final ritual. The workers rarely wear elaborate paint, because their first obligation is to their employers.

In return for these services, the employers must provide food for the workers during the period in which they are actually preparing the grave, cutting the poles, and clearing the dance ground near the grave; for their work prevents them from hunting for themselves, and their own close kin are usually working with them. In addition the workers receive tangible gifts of payment for the services at the burial, for smoking a settlement house, and for carving the funeral poles.

[3] The smoking of Jacky Navy's settlement house in 1962 was a service also performed by "workers."

The duties of the employers to the deceased are to organize and lead the prescribed rituals and to show their grief by following the special *pukamani* taboos and by performing special roles in the rituals. Generally speaking, all in the employer group are liable to the restrictions of the special *pukamani* taboos; but, as stated before, some are exempt until the preliminary dances *(ilanea)* begin, and others, at least today, never place themselves under the taboos. I do not feel that this was always so, but I have nothing but vague statements to the effect that "before everyone *pukamani.*" Regardless of this, all the employer group is restricted from going anywhere near the actual grave until the final *pukamani* rituals are held there. Even in 1954 detours were made around the grave area, even if the route would take the traveler a mile or more out of his way. The road between the Snake Bay Settlement and the expedition camp at Banjo Beach ran parallel to one of the main "graveyards" of the settlement. Many of the natives who were employed by the expedition were, at various times, restricted from using this road because of their *pukamani* status. At night, however, some of them considered it sufficient to cover their heads as they drew near and passed the area of the grave. This kind of problem did not exist in the past when there were no such things as permanent roads or graveyards, but only individual grave areas, many paths, and no normal need to travel at night.

One group of the employers provides the "bosses" *(alaura).* The bosses are the paternal *unandawi* and those *pudawi* who are in the patrilineage of the deceased. The men in the patrilineage will be the active bosses, but the females have a right to voice their opinions in any decision. The number-one boss will be the eldest male in the patrilineage, who may or may not be in the matri-sib of the deceased. Sometimes the eldest male will be only nominally the big boss; because of extreme age he may relegate the actual job of leadership to the next in line. There will always be a head boss of the residential group in which the death occurred, drawn from a local representative of the patrilineage of the deceased, regardless of whether this man is actually the eldest male of the patrilineage. The residential-group boss has to deal with the local ritual arrangements with the commissioned workers, who are *always* from the residential group in which the death occurred.

The boss of a *pukamani* calls his residential group together for the preliminary dances *(ilanea),* leading off in song and dance, and other ritual activities. If he is not the patrilineage big boss, he will wait until the messenger brings orders from the big boss before he starts the first *ilanea* and commissions the workers. It may be mentioned here that *ilanea* rituals are not confined to the residential group where the death occurred but are carried out by any residential group containing close kin of the deceased wherever they may be located—but only after the patrilineage big boss has set the time.

As an illustration of the principle of "boss ship," I list those who were actual bosses of the *pukamani* ceremonies witnessed in 1954.

Deceased	Boss of *pukamani (alaura)*
Black Joe's babies	Black Joe (F) = "big boss"
Sugarbag	(1) Toby (close B) = nominally "big boss" but aged
	(2) Ali (Toby's son) = "acting boss" of Snake Bay group
	(3) Ali's close brothers = general bosses
	(4) Katopi (true son of the deceased) = acting boss of the visiting mission group
Billy Pukamani's daughters	Billy Pukamani (F) = big boss
Patrick's baby	Bob One (FB) = "acting boss" for burial

Sizors . . . . Miki Two (B) and Paddy One
                            (B) = joint bosses for the
                            burial

I have purposely not included Ruby One's bosses in the
above list, for an interesting thing happened in this particular
pukamani. The acting boss for Ruby One was her husband
and principal *ambaru,* Jimmy. It is my strong impression
that this unusual situation grew out of "expedition interference." Jimmy and Ruby One were expedition employees,
and Ruby's death came shortly before the expected departure of all members of the expedition except myself. After
the burial of his wife, Jimmy was consulted by members of
the expedition for information regarding the time, place,
and events of the forthcoming *pukamani.* For reasons that I
believe were almost entirely dictated by Jimmy's intense
personal desire to please the expedition and gain recognition
from the whites, he undertook the leadership of his wife's
pukamani. He was better able to do this because there was
no big boss of his wife's patrilineage in the Snake Bay settlement at the time of her death. So Jimmy initially assumed
the role, and those in the settlement who would have
ordinarily taken over the leadership permitted Jimmy to
continue. But he encountered trouble from beginning to end.
He would call an *ilanea,* and no one would show up. Or he
would call an *ilanea* when some of his wife's patrilineal kin
were still in the bush hunting, and trouble would occur
when they returned to find that a ritual had gone on without
them. One of these patrilineal kin was a woman named
Ruby Two, who was a close father's sister of Jimmy's deceased wife (a paternal *unandawi*). She was the one who
caused Jimmy's fake suicide at the grave ceremonies, referred to earlier, and she was also the principal cause of his
threatened suicides in the previous months. The male members of Ruby One's patrilineage did their best to back Jimmy
up by adding their endowed authority to his assumed authority, and the result was enough to bring the "business" to

a close, but not without a great deal of confusion and ill will. One of the main problems in this arrangement was that Jimmy played two conflicting roles. He called the *ilanea,* but he did not lead them. The initiation of the songs and dances he rightfully left to the patrilineage while he played the *ambaru*'s role, and due to circumstances quite beyond his control, this same patrilineage was simultaneously involved in *pukamani* rituals for Billy Pukamani's daughters, and in these they were the leaders and the bosses.

The resulting ramifications of this highly complex situation were enough to drive both the Tiwi and the anthropologist to distraction, for no one could be in two places at once, and no one was quite sure which faction would win out and where the evening's ritual *(ilanea)* would be held or for whom. I remember one particularly exhausting Sunday. At ten o'clock an *ilanea* started for Billy Pukamani's daughters. Halfway through it a few dances were held for Ruby One, after which the *ilanea* continued with the main focus on Billy's daughters. Then just to confuse the observer, it seemed, the whole group went to another camp for a "memorial" *pukamani* for Sugarbag, held by a half-Iwaidja–half-Melville Island man. Here the dances were a mixture of Iwaidja and Tiwi style, with *didjeridoo*[4] playing thrown in for good measure. This was followed by a short *ilanea* for Ruby One held in the same place, in the middle of which was a "memorial cry" for Peter's father, who had died many years ago.

Although the *ambaru* is not considered a boss, his or her wishes are always taken into account. *Ambarui* are consulted when the major decisions are to be made, such as deciding how many poles should be ordered, but they do not have the final say. Their role throughout the entire sequence of ritual is quite distinct from that of the rest of the employer group of kin. The principal *ambaru* is always under the *pukamani* taboos from the time of the death to the conclusion of the *pukamani* ceremony at the grave. During the actual per-

[4] The *didjeridoo* is not traditional in Tiwi culture.

formance of songs and dances, the *ambarui* always act as a
group apart from any of the other groups of performing kin,
except that the *yempi* (workers) may join them. The
ambaru's songs are distinct in style from those of other
singers, and he often sings them on other occasions than the
organized rituals. His dance, which expresses his relationship
to the deceased, is with few exceptions the only dance form
he performs.

Except for the *ambarui* and the *yempi,* the remaining kin
have shifting roles in performing the actual rituals. The two
general rules are that brothers and sisters as well as husbands
and wives (actual and potential) must help each other.
Helping means to dance or sing with each other. Thus we may
find as individual dance partners the following: brothers and
sisters of the same matri-sib and patrilineage; brothers and
sisters of different sibs or patrilineages or both; and husbands and wives, who are always of different matri-sibs and
patrilineages. If my information is complete enough, we
rarely find all the members of one patrilineage or one matri-
sib exclusively helping each other in the individual dance
routines. It is kinship rather than social group that dictates
cooperative action in the *pukamani.*

We do, however, have a major division based on landholding groups at the final grave ceremonies. The present
settlement residential pattern makes it hard to find information on this division. Informants stated, however, that formerly each country *(tuŋarima)* "came in hard," that is,
separately, to the grave and formed its own ritual group with
its own selection of poles. Today, in every *pukamani* witnessed, there were only two ritual groups each with their
own dance ground and poles, and this situation was referred
to by my informants as "coming in soft."

Generally these two groups were referred to as the "Snake
Bay mob" and the "mission or Bathurst mob." It was noted,
however, that at any one funeral some of the residents of the
Snake Bay area would join the "mission mob" for the ma-

jority of the dances. It might be wise, without further information, to regard this division at the grave as based on countries, each group comprising one or more patrilineages or land-holding groups. Representatives of countries other than that with which the deceased was affiliated as a resident or land-holder, are there because they are members of the matrisib, or possibly the phratry, of the deceased.

The "home group," defined as the residential group in which the deceased died, forms one of the dancing groups at the grave. Members of that group may have married into it from another country and land-holding group. As spouses and residents, they must "help" in the "home-group" dances, but they are also obliged to "help" their siblings in the group from which they originally came and who represent members of their land-holding group. It was said that a man must come into the grave with his wife's people, that is, a man must also "help" his mother-in-law *(ambrinua)*. Thus we will find individuals shifting from dance group to dance group at the final ceremony, in performance of their ritual roles to other surviving kinsmen of the deceased.

One informant said that the reason for visiting groups to remain physically separated from each other and from the "home group" was because each distrusted the others. He added that sometimes they accused each other of causing the death. They kept apart to avoid any trouble during the actual ceremony. After the ceremony, it was every man for himself. One of the "memorial" services for Ruby One was conducted by a man named Zamat. He was a brother of Ruby's father and, as such, was expected and obligated to be present at the final *pukamani* ceremony. Zamat resided in the bush midway between the Snake Bay Settlement and the Bathurst Mission. He had been unofficially "banished" from both settlements, and at the time I believed that this was the reason for his not being present at the regular ceremony. However, Pilling informed me that Zamat and Jimmy's close brother, Charlie, had a long-standing feud unknown to me, and this seems to be a more logical reason for the complete separation not only in space but also in time for his performance of duty to Ruby One. When Zamat and his large domestic group did arrive, only the principal *ambaru* Jimmy joined them in their "memorial" *pukamani*.

To summarize the various roles during the *pukamani* rituals, we must view them through the individual. Every individual is affiliated either through assumed consanguineal ties or through affinal ties with two matrilineal groups—his own and his father's; several patrilineages—his own, his mother's and perhaps his spouse's; and perhaps several residential groups and one land-owning group. Throughout the ritual he is obligated as an individual to reinforce all these affiliations by interacting with all attending members of the above social groups with which he is affiliated or has been in close cooperative contact. Some of these obligations can be collectively carried out and the relationships reinforced at the same time and others cannot. And sometimes an individual will be joined by another who has a similar obligation. For this reason, we may perceive this reinforcement of relationships as if it were group action. It may be, but often it is actually carried out by each individual separately as a personal responsibility.

Phase 3: Preliminary Rituals—The *Ilanea*

An *ilanea*[5] is any preliminary dance ritual preceding the *pukamani*. An *ilanea* may also be defined as any funeral dance ritual that takes place outside the designated dancing grounds at the grave itself. As so defined, *ilanea* rituals form a part of the final thirty-six-hour graveside rites. Subsequent to painting the body, but before approaching the grave for the first time, each of the main groups of participants per-

---

[5] I have in my notes two names for these rituals, *natualiŋa* and *ilanea*. I have chosen to use the last one, for the Tiwi used it more frequently, and according to one informant it is the only "proper" term for this ritual.

forms an *ilanea* in the previously tabooed grave area, but outside the designated dance grounds.

In the old days, I was told, the "home group" held an *ilanea* each evening after the first *ilanea* in which the workers were commissioned. The visiting groups each held an *ilanea* in the evenings while "on the road" as they traveled to the country of burial. Once there, they also held *ilanea*s separate from those of the home group and other visiting groups while they waited for everyone to arrive and for the workers to announce that their work was finished. To some extent this is done today, except that there is only one visiting group from the mission. The *ilanea* is not necessarily an evening performance, but today, as well as in the past, it is more likely to be held in the early evening after the day's work or hunt and after the workers, who can work on their poles only during the daylight, have finished for the day.

The main events in both the *ilanea* and the final *pukamani* ceremony are songs and dances, but there are some features that are exclusive to one or the other. I propose to discuss the songs and dances separately.

Preparatory to the beginning of any *ilanea,* the close kin (the *unandawi, pudawi,* and *ambarui*) who are under *puka-mani* taboo repaint their body decorations. Those not under the taboos may also paint their bodies for this particular occasion. In connection with one particular *ilanea* rite, the fire-jumping (*wandiatapinda*), all men who have not completed their *kulama* initiation must paint parts of their bodies with black paint, "in imitation of *wakwakgini,* the crow." In the past, they were never supposed to let their father's sisters or their mothers watch this painting in black, for if those women watched, the men would become sick. Today this restriction is not enforced, and they paint in the camp.

The *ilanea* is first held in or near the camp where the death occurred. A clearing called the *milimika* is made for the dancing. A dance ground may be prepared later in a different place for other *ilaneas,* but there seems to be little consistency to this.

All *ilaneas* begin with two calls, the "honey" call and the "mosquito" call.[6] The origin of these calls is obscure. According to myth, the first *pukamani* ceremony was made by members of the honey sib. This appears to be a logical origin for this call; but a much more colorful explanation was given to me by one informant. The call, which is a low and moderately fast continuing chant of "oh, oh, oh, oh," followed by a series of "yip, yip, yip," was, so the informant said, their imitation of the chants of the British sailors as they hauled up the sails on the ships anchored off Fort Dundas in the early nineteenth century.

The mosquito call, which, I was told, marks the boss of the mosquitoes, *Rakama,* is something quite different. The origin of this call appears even more obscure. It is one long, continuous, high, vibrating note. One individual begins this high "yi" and before he loses breath other individuals take over so that the note is held without perceptible breaks for as long as five minutes. The emotional effect of this continuous, vibrating, high-pitched note, produced by many throats, is extraordinary. The Tiwi consider the mosquito call to be one of their unique cultural possessions. I was told that they often let loose this sound on unsuspecting mainland natives just to "scare them." Although I have absolutely no evidence, it might be that this call is a "war cry," and its use during these rites could be designed to scare the spirit of the deceased.

The *Wamuta:* The "Fight" Between Workers and Employers

If the workers have already been commissioned and have started to work on the poles in the grave area, the *ilanea* begins with their return to camp. The workers stop a short way from the *ilanea* dance ground and gather branches, dead

---

[6] Somehow I did not obtain the native terms for these two important ritual elements.

sticks, or stones, or they may already be carrying their proper throwing clubs *(muraguŋa)*. When they have collected enough ammunition, they give the honey call and then the mosquito call. Thereupon they rush the dance ground where the employers are waiting. A battle ensues, a mock fight to be sure, but the employers must be quite agile in dodging the missiles that the workers throw with some force and accuracy. When all missiles are thrown, the two opposing groups close in and wrestle.

Various reasons were given for this ritual fighting. Some explained that the workers were in "trouble" from having worked in the grave area, and that they came to the dance ground to fight those who had put them in this dangerous position. Others said that the fight was in reality a fight between the spirit of the deceased, whom the workers represented, and the close *pukamani* kin of the spirit. The wrestling, they said, transferred the workers' sweat, which "comes from the grave," and would make the close kin "good."

The *Wandiatapinda* and the *Irampumuni*

These two rites involved the men who, although they have begun the *kulama* initiation, have not completed it. One informant said it was a requirement held for the *wadjinati* grade. It is for these rites that the initiates are painted black in imitation of the crow. These activities, although related to initiation, are held during rituals for the *ilanea* and *pukamani*.

The *unandawi, pudawi,* and some of the workers gather at a distance from the dance ground upon the conclusion of the workers' fight. In the old days, the fire-jumping *(wandiatapinda)* always included tree-climbing *(irampumuni)*, but today the tree-climbing is often abbreviated to "tossing up" of the initiates, held as a separate rite from the fire-jumping. If tree-climbing is included, the group gathers at the base of a suitable tree. A fire is laid circling the base, and then all the initiates climb the tree, one after another, until they are arranged one above the other up the length of the tree trunk. The fire is then lit, and clouds of thick smoke arise. The fully initiated men call out "shark," or "alligator" country, which I was told referred to *pitapitui* localities (see pp. 138-43). While doing this they make appropriate imitative noises. A boy drops to the ground through the smoke, followed by another and another, until all have descended. I was unable to correlate the spirit-children locality shouted with that of the initiate in any way, but perhaps my data are incomplete.

Often today the tree-climbing is omitted. A small smoky fire is lit at some distance from the dance ground, and those who would have climbed the tree merely step over the fire and through the smoke. A short sequence of songs and dances may accompany this fire-jumping, with the jumpers circling the fire in dance before passing over it. The stated purpose of the fire-jumping is to clear the hair off the legs and thereby prevent sickness and broken bones. Although this ritual is obligatory for initiates only, the leader of the *puka-mani* may also join in.

After the fire-jumping, the leader leads the group back to the dance ground in a single file, singing a song. When they reach the cleared area the chain of men breaks into a dance. Then they retire to stand at the edge of the dance ground, and the *yoi* (dancing and singing) begin.

During the first *ilanea* for Sugarbag there was a rite that was not repeated in any of the other *ilaneas* witnessed in 1954. At the time I thought it might be a variation of the fire-jumping, for it involves tossing of initiates into the air, but there is no fire. This rite was called *yeripumani*. When I asked my informants in 1962 about this rite, they said it was a variation of the tree-climbing rite for initiates, to which they gave the name *irampumuni*. During the *ilanea* for Sugarbag, five young men were called individually into the center of the dance ring where they stood while the leader of the *puka-mani* sang and danced around each in turn. At the end of the song other fully initiated men joined the leader and helped him to toss the boy into the air. The boy then danced around the ring, ending with a downward sweep on his hand and a shout of *"Yoi!"* After this the leader sang another song, and he and the initiate danced together. Then the next young man stepped into the center of the ring, and the ritual was repeated. It may or may not be significant that the five initiates and the men tossing them into the air were all classified as *unandawi* in relationship to the funeral ceremony for Sugarbag.

The *Pumati:* The Mock Fight of Spouses (*Imbunei* and *Imbuneiŋa*)

Almost every *ilanea* contains a *pumati,* and this particular type of ritual fighting is also frequently included in the final *pukamani* ceremony at the grave. The *pumati* comes at some time during the sequences of songs and dances, and it often concludes the *ilanea.* An *ilanea* never begins with a *pumati,* however. Essentially it is a fight between all actual and potential spouses and is not limited to one's own husband and wife or wives. Both sexes gather ammunition in the form of branches, and a glorious and joyous free-for-all ensues. Brothers and sisters yell for help from their siblings when overpowered by a bevy of spouses and spouses' siblings. There is a great deal of shouting; and there are squeals of laughter, for tickling is also part of the game. Although no injuries ever seem to result from the flailing branches, the small children often wail in fright as they see their parents being attacked in what appears to be a real battle.

The *pumati* serves ritually to remove all restraint between those who are not actually married to each other. It will be remembered that persons who are potential spouses may actually form illicit love unions. Although the avoidance taboo between these potential spouses does not seem to be strongly enforced today, they naturally exhibit a certain amount of restraint in public. One of the favorite jokes my "sisters" used to play on me was to instruct me in shouting certain words and sayings to "our" potential husbands in full hearing of the entire camp or settlement. Fortunately or unfortunately, I could not translate what I was saying, and my "sisters" refused to do so. But whatever it was caused my "sisters" and "husbands" great amusement, partly, I believed, because I was breaking the avoidance taboos.

The *pumati* appears to be similar to the one-sided hitting of the adolescent girl during her *muriŋaleta* rituals by her husband and husband's brothers. The main difference is that in the *pumati* she can and does strike back. The *pumati* also serves to introduce individuals who may never actually have met but who fall into reciprocal spouse and sibling categories. It may be noted that this introduction allows "fighting" among spouses only; sexual license is not a part of the ritual.

Unlike the fire-jumping, tree-climbing, or tossing of initiates that occur during the *ilanea* rituals but that are related to the *kulama* initiation rites, the *pumati* continues to be an important part of the funeral ceremony today. This probably reflects the decreasing importance of the initiation rites in Tiwi culture. The importance of *pumati*, however, was apparent, for most of the "trouble" that occurred while I was present concerned the lack of people or of enthusiasm at an *ilanea* when the leader had decided that a *pumati* was to be included.

The *pumati* may be performed intermittently between groups of songs and dances, or it may be held all at one time. If more than one group of potential spouses is present, as is the case at the final grave ceremony and in the settlement today, one set of spouses sings, fights, and then retires to rest while the other set performs its *pumati*.

To conclude the *ilanea*, one man who is an *unandawi,* but not the leader, leads the others in the honey call and then the mosquito call. As he does so, he may face in the direction of the grave, for my informants stated, "He is telling the *mobuditi* that it won't be long now 'til we come."

Discussion 3: *Pukamani* and Art

The major part of the action in both the preliminaries and the final grave ceremonies are songs and dances. While other details of the *pukamani* were not difficult to record, for they occurred regularly enough and distinctly enough to give us plenty of time to gather almost all relevant information, the songs and dances were a different matter altogether. With these we had to record (1) the song and translation (none of us knew the Tiwi language) and its cultural context, if pertinent; (2) who sang the song and whether it was a new one or an old one; (3) who started the dancing and who joined him; (4) what they were marking in the dance, and whether the dance was a new one or an old one; (5) what the women were doing in the chorus; and (6) the relationships of all participants in the dance to each other and to the deceased. No single dance lasted more than a minute or two without a change in personnel, song, or dance step. In the preliminary rituals, it was a general rule that only one song followed by a specific dance was performed at any one time. But during the final grave ceremonies the participants divided into two spatially distinct groups, each with its own dance ground and dancers, and the recording problem was not only doubled but also complicated further because the dances and other rituals were simultaneous.

I have in my notes over five hundred recorded song and dance combinations, and this is probably no more than half of those I saw. As long as there were three of us recording (Mountford, Harney, and myself), the division of labor was sufficient to record almost all the above information on the songs and dances. Mountford dealt mainly with the photographic record, Harney with the songs and their translations, and I with the personnel record and the dance forms. After each rite or ceremony, the three sets of notes and impressions were integrated.

From September on, I was the only recorder, and a com-

plete record was virtually impossible. I feel strongly the lack
of a complete record as I begin my discussion of the songs
and their translations, and to the Tiwi the songs are perhaps
one of the most important elements.

A. SONGS AND DANCES—THE YOI[7]

The word *yoi* means "dance," but it is often used to describe
any part or all of the *pukamani* ceremony—the burial, the
ilanea, or the final grave rituals, all of which contain *yoi. Yoi*
are not limited to the *pukamani,* for they are also part of the
kulama ceremony. Therefore, I have chosen to restrict the
use of this word to the actual dances performed rather than
to call the entire ceremony a *yoi,* or dance. During the
pukamani the dances are accompanied by songs, whereas
during the *kulama,* the *yoi* (dances) were separate from the
kulama songs, and the men merely circled the *kulama* dance
ground in a slow walk while they sang their *kulama* songs.

Songs and dances are not the only forms of creative art
among the Tiwi, but they are perhaps the most important for
gaining prestige. It is expected that every male Tiwi will
become a composer of ceremonial songs, just as it is expected
that every male *unandawi,* whether he is a big boss or not, will
lead a song and dance when he is old enough and capable of
doing so.

It will be remembered that a major part of a male Tiwi's
initiation was the singing of his first *kulama* song in the third
year of initiation, and that one of the criteria for initiation
was that the boy must have a "good" voice. This was not,
however, a criterion for the female initiate. The Tiwi have
set styles or tunes for their song creations, and the words must
be made to fit the style. Special or "literary" words not used
in daily conversation, or sometimes even foreign words, will
be used if they "fit" the meter more readily. In the following

---

[7] C. H. Berndt (1950b) discusses and gives other examples of songs sung by
women during funeral ceremonies on Bathurst Island.

illustration the use of English words is easily detectable:

Purantiwali	*govermani*	*kerinbriknoma*	*tilianoma*
high man	government	plenty rich	plenty silver
padaimani	*krukari*	*terikra*	*workanmani*
payday	get gifts	?	working man
kaloai			
money?			

My informants often said that they could not translate certain of the songs because they did not know the meaning of some of the words. And the chorus of male singers might have trouble learning the verse being presented to them; if real difficulty was exhibited, the composer changed the wording to make it easier.[8]

The youngest composer on record during the 1954 *pukamani* season was a man of about twenty-five. He was the one who was "slated" for initiation capture, although his capture took place after my departure. He had completed his initiation by 1962 when I returned. This young man was the best song translator we found in 1954, as we had to choose our on-the-spot translators from those not continually involved in the singing and dancing. All the other composers on record were above the age of thirty-five, and most of them had gone through the *kulama* initiation.

The Tiwi have different names for their song styles, and each style has a restricted use. The *kulama* style is sung only by men, but may be "followed up" by the wives of the singer outside the ceremonial area. The *pukamani* style is also sung only by men. A number of other song styles are used during a *pukamani* ceremony, and these may be sung by either men or women. The *ambaru* (widow's) style is one of these. There is also a particular type of wailing song, the *umanunguni* or

---

[8] Hart (1930b:283-84) has called the language used in ritual singing a "secret" or sacred language. I disagree and consider it as a literary vocabulary only.

mamamiŋguni, which is sung by the *unandawi* but always on the sidelines and not as a featured song that is followed by a dance.

There were two other rarely heard song styles, the *aramari-geramor* and the *niŋawi.* The *aramarigeramor* is a style sung only at an *ilanea* by one man alone. No one helps him. The *niŋawi* style is a particularly nasal and "growly" chant, and is always accompanied by *niŋawi* dances, imitating the actions of these mythological inhabitants of the mangrove jungle. In performance, the *niŋawi* songs followed the pattern of the *pukamani* songs, the only difference being in the tune or style of the chant. They were sung only by their composer, a man who had lost his nose in a battle, and who appeared to be capitalizing on an unfortunate physical deformity.[9]

The pukamani *song style.* The *pukamani* songs, all of one style, conform to a general pattern in their performance. The words are composed by one man, either on the spot or carefully thought out beforehand. The composer begins by chanting one verse alone. The rest of the men, who stand in a semi-circle around the dance ground, pick up the beat of the song and accompany the singer by slapping their thighs or buttocks with their open hands. Gradually they also pick up the words of the song and begin to chant with the composer. When enough of the men have learned the words, the singer stops singing and begins to dance to the accompaniment of the chorus of men, who continue to chant and beat time. If the song has more than one verse, the composer will at the conclusion of the dance introduce the next verse in the same way. When he has finished his composition, another man may take up the same theme and give another verse, or he may introduce a new theme. In most cases the singer always dances to his own song, but occasionally the singer may have instructed a group of dancers to act out his song while he sings.

The culture hero, Purakapali, told the Tiwi "to sing the things around them," and so, like the *kulama* songs, the

---

[9] I owe to Pilling this suggestion of the correlation of style with deformity.

pukamani songs are about every subject imaginable to the Tiwi and are not traditional but individual compositions. The song belongs to the composer, and he may sing it again at another *pukamani,* unlike the restrictions against repeating a song during the *kulama.* Generally speaking, the anthropologist may class the subjects as (1) mythological, (2) historical, (3) current events, (4) fiction, and (5) natural history. One illustration of each is given below.[10]

Mythological (sung during the final graveside rituals for Billy Pukamani's daughters):

> Pukwi[11] sits down along the middle water at Ariŋgo.
> Pukwi pretends to make the cheeky, bitter yam.
> Muriupiaŋa and Uriupunala are sisters.
> An Old Woman digs the cheeky yams and makes a
>   fire and cooks them.
> Two sisters dig the cheeky yams.
> Muriupiaŋa said to Uriupunala, you carry the cooked yams.

(The next verse was about a broken leg, which was important for the accompanying dance style, as it indicated that the dancers were siblings of the deceased. The mythological theme then continued.)

> A big mob of Pukwi bosses.
> Muriupiaŋa and Uriupunala make a big place, a hole.
> Muriupiaŋa and Uriupunala make the fresh water.

Historical (sung at the final graveside rituals for Sugarbag): This song came directly after a series of verses telling of the mythological instructions given to the Tiwi for the performance of the *kulama* ceremony. See Mountford (1958:85)

---

[10] See Mountford (1958) for other examples.
[11] *Pukwi* is both the name of a mythological female creator and the word for matrilineal sib.

for a full description. The following was acknowledged to be a new song:

> They had a big fight at *kulama* time in the past.
> An old woman, Purpuraŋnimo (long dead), faced the
>   men and said:
> "Why did so many men jump on my husband?"

The song ended with the composer imitating the old woman's roars of anger. Most of the historical songs that we recorded concerned fights, feuds, or wars in the past.

Current Events (sung during an *ilanea* for Ruby One, just after the electric generator in the settlement was finally made to work for a twelve-hour period):

> Machines make engines.
> All the lights are like stars.
> Airplanes have electric lights.
> American mechanics make the lights.
> Strong men lift something heavy.
> The lights of the airplanes.
> Search lights on the clouds.

This song was not sung by one man but four. It seemed to be purely inspirational, one man's verse inspiring the next man's line.

Fiction: I have included this category because I am at a loss to decide where the movie-inspired songs should go. Unfortunately, I do not have the words for one of the most elaborate of these songs. When I asked for the translation, my informant looked at me with complete astonishment and said, "Why, it's Hopalong and the Indians, you should know that!"

Natural History: As these songs concern the natural environment of the Tiwi, it is not surprising that some of the subjects will correspond to the names of some of the matrilineal sibs. The following illustration concerns the flying foxes (fruit bats), a sib. These verses were sung during the burial and first three *ilanea* rituals for Ruby One. They were the compositions of half a dozen men. In between these verses other songs were interspersed:

> A big mob of flying foxes.
> You look, a big mob of flying foxes.
> The flying foxes are out in the late afternoon, eating
>   the blooms of the stringy-bark and woolly-bark trees.
> Cook the flying foxes and dry them in the sun.
> Hit them where they are thickest and break many wings
>   at once.
> We can't cross the river, because the crocodiles are in it.
> Look out! The crocodile is in the mangroves waiting to
>   catch us as we cross.
> The flying foxes call to each other, "Someone is hitting
>   us, we will go."
> She (the sea eagle, *irakati*) dives upon the flying foxes.
> She catches them in her claws and eats them, and the
>   rest fly away.
> No leaves in the trees; the foxes have flown away.

My initial thought concerning these songs was to regard them as "totemic" songs, but closer analysis showed that they were only at times concerned with a sib affiliation, and only in one particular way. In every individual funeral ceremony recorded in 1954, one sib and phratry was represented in a significant number of songs and dances. In every case, it was the matrilineal sib and phratry of the father of the deceased that was so emphasized. In the illustration given, the flying fox was Ruby's father's sib, and it was also her husband's sib. The leader of Ruby's *pukamani* was, improperly, her husband, but properly the leaders might well have belonged to the same sib. The question here is, whose sib affiliation dictates the choice for emphasis in songs? Do the leaders sing their own sib in the songs? Or is the father of the deceased the prime consideration? Or is the "dreaming" of the deceased the aspect so symbolized in song?

In answer to the first question, the principal singers are the *unandawi* who are in the patrilineage of the deceased. And by "marking" the dead man's father's sib in song they are also, theoretically, marking their own sib, as they are expected to be in the "father's" sib because of the preferential sib exchange in marriage contracts.

However, I do not believe that this is the real reason for their marking this particular sib. Throughout the *yoi* certain personal and place names are consistently chanted. The personal name is always that of the father of the deceased, and the place name that of the grave or country of the father. Furthermore, when asked why they should mark such a sib, our informants invariably answered, "They mark the dead one's 'dreaming.' " Calling the father's name and place of burial or country was "something they must always do." Today with the breakdown of the preferential sib intermarriages, the principal *unandawi* singers may well belong to several different sibs and phratries, yet they all sing and dance together to mark this particular sib affiliation of the deceased as his "dreaming."

In the flying fox song, several other animals were mentioned: the sea eagle *(irakati)* and the crocodile. Neither of these had anything to do with the matrilineal sibs of the deceased father, or her husband. Furthermore, these songs did not refer to any sib affiliation of the singers. It might be thought that they were included for the literary and dramatic effect they had in the story and dance of the flying foxes, and indeed they probably were, but the singers and dancers of these particular verses were in fact "marking" a particular animal because the associated dance was their *yoi,* their inherited dance form (see p. 302).

In other words, the subject of some of the verses in the song of the flying foxes dictated the singers' dance form. This is true of many songs that deal with natural objects. It is also true of many songs about objects and events of Western civilization, such as airplanes and boats, and of some of the storytelling songs. These songs may be traditional or new, and many of the dances, the *yoi,* are also traditional and belong to the singers. It is important to understand this relationship between some songs and the accompanying dances. Only when one considers the songs and dances of an entire *pukamani,* from burial to graveside conclusion, is it possible to decide why certain songs and dances are performed at any given time. Some are performed to mark the father of the deceased; others because the performers own the particular dance and perform it with their co-owners; and others are performed only to entertain. In this latter category fall all the new songs and dances, some of which may become traditional in the future. In the first case the song will dictate the dance form; in the second, the dance form will dictate the subject of the song or part of the song; and in the last case, since both song and dance form are new, no one but the composer knows which part he thought up first, the song or the dance.

As in the *kulama,* great prestige comes from being a good composer of *pukamani* songs, and, in addition, from being a good dancer. One can, however, become a good dancer before beginning to contribute many songs. The main singers and dancers of any *pukamani* are the *unandawi.* The paternal *unandawi* initiate the majority of the songs and dances; they are the leaders of the ceremony, and it is in the *yoi* that they exhibit most of their leadership. The maternal *unandawi* also initiate songs and dances, but not to the same extent. There was one exception to this general rule observed in 1954. In the *pukamani* for Bob One's mother, the maternal *unandawi* initiated and performed the majority of the songs, even though they were not considered to be the leaders. This was a ceremony for a woman who was not buried at Snake Bay. As far as I could tell, the reason for this exception was because the paternal *unandawi* were few in numbers in comparison to the maternal *unandawi;* normally these two groups should be roughly equal in numbers, so that the greater role of the paternal group stands out as significant.

The *pudawi*—the siblings, grandparents, and grandchildren—do not normally lead the songs and dances, although they may occasionally initiate a sequence. We must take into consideration that in this group we are likely to have individuals either too old or too young to take an active part. The siblings who may be the right age are those *pudawi* who, in most instances, initiate songs and dances. However, these are the same people who, as siblings, are also obligated to perform a certain type of dance that denotes their relationship to the deceased at least as frequently as they perform their traditional inherited *yoi.* The *unandawi* also have a "kinship" dance, but they do not perform this with anywhere near the same frequency required of the siblings. In some respects the siblings are like the surviving spouse *(ambaru);* their close relationship to the deceased is ritually expressed to a greater extent in their *pukamani* performance than is their relationship to the other performers.

The ambaru *song style.* This is quite different from the *pukamani* style. It is sung only by the *ambarui,* either male or female, but always as a solo. The *ambaru* song can be a featured song of the *yoi,* and as such is accompanied by a dance performed by the *ambaru* in the dance ground. In the dance the singer may be joined by other *ambarui* or workers who come in to help. The *ambaru* may also sing from the sidelines, sometimes concurrently with a *pukamani* song and dance in the dance ground. In this case the song is not followed by a dance. Often the principal *ambaru* can be heard chanting his wailing song throughout the camp or bush completely apart from any ceremony.

Workers not only help the *ambaru* in the dance but may also sing a song for him, using the *ambaru* style of chant. These people may also sing an *ambaru* song using the *kulama* style of chant. Generally these *kulama* style *ambaru* songs are sung on the sidelines or during the long vigil at the grave during the night when all are camped with the deceased for the last time during the final rituals. At this time most people are asleep, but the *ambaru* and his helpers, the workers, must keep up a fairly steady chanting of their *ambaru* songs.

The *ambaru* songs all deal with the personality of the deceased, or with the marital relationship of the *ambaru* to the deceased, or with the life history of the deceased. Here are a few samples:

> Don't make up yarns and trouble.
> He grew me up once since I was a little girl.
> He is my boss.

This song was sung by the *ambaru*, Jimmy, during his wife's final *pukamani*. In this case the "singer" of the song is the spirit of the deceased, who sings through the vehicle of its *ambaru*. Another of Jimmy's songs went: "When I copulate, you can see the knee tracks." When workers sing *ambaru* songs to help the surviving spouse, they sing as if they were in fact the *ambaru*: "I would just like to kiss Ruby." In one *ambaru* song, sung by a husband's sister of the deceased, the singer called the deceased to come and fight her because at one time the deceased would not listen to her advice about running after another boy. When the audience applauded this song, the singer ran to the poles surrounding the grave and repeated her challenge to the deceased.

The mamamiŋuni *song style and* aramarigeramor *song style*. Unfortunately I was unable to obtain the words that were sung to these two styles of chants. The *mamamiŋuni* style was heard a half-dozen times. It was sung by individual *unandawi*, not in a chorus, and was a wailing chant describing their personal relationships with the deceased. In this way this style is similar to the *ambaru* songs.

The *aramarigeramor* style I heard only once, and it was then sung by an *ambaru* during the last *ilanea* before approaching the grave for the first time.

The niŋawi *song style.* The words of the somewhat aberrant and individually owned *niŋawi* songs have been recorded by Mountford (1958:74-75). The composer described these spirit beings who live in the mangrove with their wives and children, and talk to each other in a particularly nasal voice. They call out to the living, occasionally luring them into their homes, from which no escape is possible. A peculiar "clacking" sound of the mangrove swamps is attributed to these spirits. In the dance that the composer performed, he imitated the peculiar "bent knee" walk of these spirits.

THE DANCE FORMS

The dances or *yoi* are as full of social implication as are the songs and are just as original and entertaining. I have in the preceding discussion of songs used the verb "to mark" in order to describe the symbolism of action or words referring to a particular subject. The Tiwi used this English word exclusively to describe what it was they were symbolizing in a song or dance, and I prefer to continue using this word (rather than "imitate" or "mimic") in order to emphasize the symbolic nature of these actions. What has been "marked" has been "emphasized," not merely imitated. Thus I consider the entire *pukamani* ceremony as marking the death of a fellow Tiwi, and the various parts of the ceremony as marking the sundry facets of Tiwi life.

Nowhere is this more evident than in the dance forms of the *yoi*. The anthropologist may classify these in a general way as (1) kinship dances, (2) traditional dances, (3) narrative dances, and (4) accompanying dances or women's chorus. I will discuss each type in turn.

The kinship dance forms. The kinship dances are special types of dance performed by individuals or groups of kin who have a particular relationship to the deceased. The *ambaru* (spouse's) dance is one of these. The topic that has been chosen to mark this particular degree of relationship is that of fighting off the spirit of the deceased, the *mobuditi*. When an *ambaru* dances, either alone or in company with a fellow *ambaru,* he or she carries a dance club or a set of throwing sticks. The *ambaru* waves these above his head and in the direction of the grave, and often hurls them into the bushes that hide the grave mound when the dance takes place by the grave itself. This dance is done with a distinctive high step. The *ambaru* also strikes his or her back with the clubs or throwing sticks. (It is interesting to note that if a Tiwi feels a muscle twitch in the shoulder, he regards it as a sign that some "spouse" is talking about him.)

The *ambaru* may also dance narrative dances to his special songs, or he may dance his traditional dance. But the majority of his dances are of the kinship variety.

The *pudawi,* or sibling dance, is another frequently performed dance of the kinship type. Again the Tiwi believe that a twitching muscle in a person's leg means that a sibling is talking about him; the sibling dance is focused around the subject of the leg, and is performed with a limp or with a completely useless and "broken" leg. Although both sisters and brothers of the deceased may perform this dance, it is more often observed as a brother's dance performed by men.

Iŋgalabini siblings (same father, but different matri-sib from the deceased) do not dance the brother's leg dance. In order to denote their special relationship they dance "toothache," covering their jaws or cheeks with their hands.

The maternal *unandawi* perform a kinship dance that is called *puladi* (breast or milk). This dance focuses on the breast, and although both men and women perform it, it is more frequently observed as a woman's dance. Again, if a person feels a muscle twitch in his breast, it is believed to be an indication that a mother, mother's brother, or sister's child is talking about him. This dance was not observed as frequently as either of the sibling types or the *ambaru* type, but more frequently than the type danced by the paternal *unandawi.*

Fathers, father's sisters, and brother's children, the paternal *unandawi,* have a kinship dance that was rarely observed. The "father's dance" appeared to have two forms. One marked the male sex organs and was performed only by males in this kin group. It may be noted here that the lack of female breast formation did not prevent male maternal *unandawi* from performing the *puladi.* The more common paternal *unandawi* (father's) dance was given the name *tuara* and was said to mark a fight with spears, an event often characterizing the first meeting between a father and his *pitapitui* during the dreaming of his children. The dancer always carries a spear in this kinship dance.

Kinship dances may be performed individually, but often two or more persons of the same degree of kinship to the deceased dance together. This type of dance often draws together two or more individuals from the separated dance groups at the final rituals at the grave.

The traditional dances. The traditional dances are perhaps the most important to the Tiwi. These dances are inherited by both men and women from their fathers. Each of these dances was originally invented by a man, and is considered to be his property. He may have given permission to one or more close brothers or another kinsman to dance it, and perhaps occasionally to pass the dance on to their children. Many of these traditional dances are very old, and thus the group that now owns them is in part formed by a patrilineage less exclusive than the land-owning group, the limited patri-lineage. The group of dance owners may be in fact a structural affiliation of a number of "patrilineages" if the originator permitted others to dance and pass on the dance to their children. Other than performing a particular dance together in a funeral ceremony, the traditional dance group has no significance or position in the society. However, as I mentioned earlier in connection with the dynamics of the matrilineal sibs, it is recorded that a dance group once declared itself to be a new matrilineal sib, and it continued to function as one (see p. 78).

Dances are still being invented. Some of the new dances seen in the 1954 series of funeral ceremonies may be popular enough to become traditional. Such is the hope of every inventor.

These dances are characterized by distinctive body posture and footwork, and usually illustrate the characteristics of the subject that serves as inspiration and is being marked in the dance. We have turtle dances, crocodile dances, shark dances, jabiru dances, pelican dances, buffalo dances, honey dances, flag dances, rain dances, frog dances, airplane dances, boat dances, canoe dances, various other kinds of bird dances, the *niŋawi* dances, and a telephone-radio dance that, I believe, was a new one in 1954. I am quite sure that there are many more traditional dances than those mentioned here. All these dances are really dance steps and may be performed individually or by a group of dancers. They may all dance the same step or a combination of traditional dance steps to illustrate a verse in a song with more than one character or subject. Mountford (1958:plates 29-30), illustrates a number of these.

Although these dances are owned by a limited number of people, their performance may include some who do not own the dance. Ownership involves the right of inheritance and the right to initiate the dance. A Tiwi may not perform a dance he does not own without the permission of one of the owners, but this is usually given during a ceremony when the owners are present and want to be helped.

To add to the complexity of analysis, some of these traditional dances belong to a group of people whose sib has the same name as the dance. But since the dance is inherited patrilineally, I cannot believe that this is anything other than pure coincidence rather than a significant structural factor. I do not believe that there are "totemic" dances any more than I believe that the songs are significantly totemic. However, as in the songs, we will find a significant number of dances that mark the matrilineal sib of the father of the deceased.

The narrative dances. The narrative dances are usually not traditional, but some, such as the canoe-building dance, have become traditional. Most often, however, they are a fairly long sequence of dances acting out in mime the words of a narrative sequence of verses concerning the mythological or historical past or events of the present. The best example of this type of dance is the one that Ali planned and presented at the grave of Sugarbag. Ali was acting boss of the home group, and weeks before the event took place, he told us to "watch out, for he had a proper good dance he was going to perform." The dance was performed when the workers were being paid for their work on the poles, which takes place during the morning of the final day of ceremony.

Ali inspected all the goods that were to be given to the workers, and then he began to sing:

"I stole money for these things and the police locked me up." To this song a brother, Malony, danced, and the women shuffled into the ring in a group with their hands locked in front of them as if they were in handcuffs. Then another brother, Tommy, ran away from the dancers; and, with Ali still singing the same verse, Malony ran after him, dragged him into the center of the ring, wrestled with him, and finally managed to "arrest" him.

Then Ali sang: "I am an officer and the telephone rings for payday." Four of Ali's brothers were now sitting by the grave mound away from the dance ring. As Ali sang they "received" the call, "wrote" out the message, "passed" it among themselves, and "read" it. The brothers then returned to the ring.

Ali now assumed a position of "authority," sitting on top of one of the *pukamani* poles. He called the name of one of the workers, who came forward.

Ali asked, "You worker?" and the worker nodded.

"You have wife? How many children?" Ali asked.

"You work for me, O.K. I pay you. Sign here." Ali concluded the dialogue.

The worker received his payment through the "store window," a hole carved as a design element in the center of the pole. The worker "signed" for his pay by placing his thumb print on the goods, and then passed the marked gift on to the other workers, who "inspected the signature" and "initialed" it with a "pencil." The marked gift was then passed back to the first worker, who, now satisfied, shook hands with his employer, Ali, and left, and the next worker was called to the "pay window."

In these narrative songs and dances new traditional dances may be born. In many respects we may consider these performances as similar to the opening night of a new musical review. The critics can make or break the composer, producer, or performers; and in the Tiwi *yoi* one person may hold all three positions. The kinship dances and the traditional dances may exhibit imagination and superior skill of performance, and if so they are acclaimed; but when they are just "run of the mill," they pass almost unnoticed. However, there is always criticism or acclaim when a new song sequence accompanied by original choreography is presented for review.

The women's accompanying dance form. The last dance form that I wish to discuss I have designated as "accompanying." I can find no better word for the chorus of women who as a group dance the typical woman's shuffling step in accompaniment to any other kind of dance form. Each dancer holds an *iruwala* or dance club over her head with one hand and presses the other hand against the small of her back. There is always a chorus of dancing women as a counterpart to the men's singing chorus. However, this does not mean that a woman may not at times be the featured dancer.

Women as well as young girls may perform traditional solo dances, or they may join their husbands or brothers in traditional dances, either because they may own the same dance with their brothers or because they must help their husbands. Women are often asked to play a role in the narrative dances; and, of course, they must dance their assigned kinship dance. About the only thing the women never do in the *yoi* is to sing the *pukamani*-style songs. They do, however, dance and sing the *ambaru* songs, and they may initiate these as well.

Because the dance step of the women's dancing chorus is relatively simple, we find small girls barely able to walk being encouraged to join the chorus line. The boys have a harder time. They may join the men's singing chorus as timpanists only, for the words are too hard and they have not yet learned to sing. The traditional steps usually require great skill to perform and are often physically exhausting. Before a boy can enter the dance ring, he must learn his traditional dance, and no toddler can do this. However, most boys of seven and up will dance at least once during a *pukamani* ceremony.

Summary. The *yoi* are the form and substance of the *ilanea,* and indeed of the entire *pukamani* ceremony. Through this medium Tiwi legends are kept alive, news is distributed, new theatrical productions are staged and reviewed, and prestige is gained or lost. Moreover, all kinship ties between the performers are strengthened through the intensified and prescribed interaction between siblings, spouses, and co-owners of traditional dances, many of whom may not be in daily contact. Similarly there is an increase in interaction between resident and nonresident members of various patrilineal and matrilineal groups. Since the purpose of the meeting is to "mark" the death of a common relative, the various roles the performers take is dictated by the degree of their relationship to the deceased, but often the action is quite without reference to him.

B. ITEMS OF MANUFACTURE

The *pukamani* ceremony provides opportunity for another expression of art and creativity. In order to mark the grave, a set of carved and painted poles are manufactured and set up around the grave mound. These poles are prepared by some members of the group of relatives who are classed as *yempi,* workers. In order to pay for this work the *unandawi, pudawi,* and *ambarui* also manufacture certain objects and collect others to give in return.

Objects said to be used as payment for the poles in precontact times were as follows: stone axes *(muŋwuŋa);* hair belts *(marowi);* cockatoo hair ornaments *(priplederi);* wooden spears—a two-sided barbed "girl" spear *(arawuni- giri),* and a one-sided barbed "man" spear *(taŋaliti);* water- carrying baskets *(tulika* and *tulini,* the former made from small palms, the latter from tall ones); bark baskets *(imulini);* white paint made into bricks *(tudiuŋini);* red paint *(yeriŋa);* yellow paint *(ariganuŋa);* "cooked" Imilu yellow ochre; an excellent red paint *(yeloŋtiŋa* or *imilu);* braided and woven pandanus armbands *(yeariŋa);* large arm rings with feathers attached *(pamagini);* goose down and feather pompons sus- pended on hair ropes *(tokwiiŋa);* and feather beards *(indian- diŋa* and *pakabino).*

In other words, almost every object manufactured by the Tiwi, with the exception of canoes and the *pukamani* poles themselves, is considered to be a proper gift to the workers in payment for the poles. The paint is used on the poles, and although some of it may be gathered by the workers, the employers are expected to provide the good varieties and to keep them in supply. The yellow ochre that comes from Imilu is of unique quality. The strength and purity of this ochre is far superior to that found in any other locality. As far as I could determine, although the deposit belongs to the owners of Imilu country and permission for mining is re- quired, no charge is made.

The ornaments, such as the cockatoo feathers, goose feather pompons, feather beards, and the like, are worn mainly by the employer group during any one *pukamani.* They are not destroyed, but are carefully kept for future use. Thus the employers must not only provide their own orna- ments if they are lacking, but must also supply the workers with these objects for their present and future use. The gift of stone axes may well be a prepayment, as is the gift of paint, for the worker must have this tool in order to shape the poles.

One item on this list that my informants gave me is puzzling. The gift of armbands to the workers appears odd, for only the employers who are under *pukamani* taboo restrictions wear these, and they are usually not kept for future use. At the conclusion of the *pukamani* the wearer rips them off and usually places them on the grave mound; this in part signifies the ending of the taboos.

Today objects of Western manufacture have almost completely replaced objects of native craft as proper payment. Tobacco, bolts of calico, ready-made clothing, steel axes and knives, mirrors, razors, pipes, and so forth, are given to the workers. At a rough estimate, in 1954 the value received for each pole was two to five dollars. Since ten to fourteen poles per grave was usual for an adult, the cost of these funerals was considerable. Although the material content of the payment has changed, the employers still provide much of the paint and lend axes. They also continue to manufacture the other objects, with the sole exception of the stone ax.

The bark baskets are not given to the workers but are left at the grave, usually turned upside down over the top of the poles. The elaborately barbed spears are often used in the dances, particularly in the "father" kinship dance, and are sometimes left standing beside the poles. The ceremonial ornaments, with the exception of the armbands, are taken home and used again.

Since Spencer (1914) and Mountford (1958) have both devoted long sections of their books to description and illustration of Tiwi native craftsmanship and art, I shall omit a similar discussion. I shall, however, mention that both the bark baskets and the beautifully barbed wooden spears are elaborately painted only when made for a *pukamani* ceremony. Women make the baskets and the men carve the spears. Both men and women may paint the baskets, and usually a man will paint his own spear. No two designs are ever alike nor is the carving on the spears the same from one to another. Each spear maker adds his own design in the area where the barbs meet the plain shaft, and a single carver will avoid repeating a design. A single, multibarbed, two-sided spear may take as long as a month to carve, even with steel knives; when the clam shell was the only small cutting tool, it took two to three times as long just to shape the spear.

In return for these gifts, the workers must make a set of poles for the grave. Elsewhere (Goodale and Koss 1967) I have discussed the cultural climate that the *pukamani* ceremony provides for the expression of artistic creativity among the Tiwi. I wish at this time to elaborate on some of the details of this work. I have already discussed the ritual commissioning of the workers and the general instructions given to them. I shall turn now to the actual carrying out of these instructions. One instruction that is understood but never stated is that poles must be cut from either ironwood or bloodwood trees. These are the two hardest woods on the island, and they best withstand the ravages of time, weather, and insects. If the workers were to cut a pole from a more easily carved wood, the employers would "growl." The Tiwi never care for a grave once the final ceremony is completed; but the presence of the grave, marked by its poles, is a sign of ownership of the district by the descendants of the person buried there. It takes many years for all traces of a grave to be obliterated, and once this has happened it is likely that the memory of the one whose grave it is has also been obliterated or diminished in the minds of the living. If no members of the original land-holding group have been subsequently buried in the same country, the land is "free," as there are no remaining marks of ownership.

To minimize transportation problems, the workers cut the poles from trees close to the grave. Since the individual poles are valued on the basis of over-all size, the workers must consider the combined wealth of the employers in deciding which trees to select. Some poles marking graves around Snake Bay measured approximately twenty feet tall, while others were a good three feet in diameter. Indeed, some were so big they could not be raised into position around the grave, but were left lying on the ground close by.

The workers may be given general instructions as to how many poles should be cut, but often they must determine this themselves. I was present at one such debate, and the questions asked were: "How many people do we expect to come from Bathurst? Is so-and-so expected to come from Darwin? Now we need eight poles for the home group, maybe we had better make six or seven for Bathurst, and if so-and-so is coming, we'll make another one." This group of workers had been commissioned as "a company" and were being collectively paid by the employers, so they were not counting the individuals who would pay but the combined wealth as well as the prestige of the employer group as a whole, for the employers would "growl" if there were not enough poles. The poles, as I have said before, symbolize the status and prestige of the deceased, as well as those of his surviving close kin. These symbols are necessary to facilitate the transfer of the deceased from the world of the living to the world of the *mobuditi* with the same relative status and prestige.

An individual employer may occasionally commission an individual worker to cut a pole for him. In this case the employer is himself liable to the worker for payment. Usually the selected worker is a man specially skilled in cutting poles. Although every Tiwi is at sometime in his life in the relationship of *yempi* to one who has died and will therefore be a pole cutter, some are better than others.

The actual amount of payment is not fixed in advance. The employers estimate how much it will cost them, and the workers estimate how much they can reasonably expect to get. The "payoff" takes place during the final hours of the *pukamani* ceremony at the grave. Prior to this the poles have been set up in the dance areas at a short distance from the grave in one or two straight lines (in each of the separate dance

Above: While singing *kulama* songs Joe and Ali circle the ring counterclockwise; Joe keeps time by beating two throwing sticks. *Below:* Two women and two young boys perform their inherited traditional dance, the shark dance.

Left: During a preliminary (*ilanea*) funeral ritual, young men perform the tree-climbing ritual which is related to initiation (*kulama*). A fire will be lit at the base of the tree, and the climbers will descend through the smoke. *Below:* The cooked *kulama* yams lie uncovered in the center of ring. Ali (second from right) rubs a yam on the head of his son while young Rosemary sits with her father, Jacky.

Above: Two men perform a portion of a new choreography depicting the capture of a "bank robber" by "the sheriff." *Below:* Two women dance during the *pukamani* rituals while the men beat time and sing.

Left: A widow dancing the *ambaru* dance. She strikes her shoulder with the woman's dance club. *Below:* A graveyard. In the center background are the recently carved and painted poles set up surrounding the grave of Ruby One, whose final *puka-mani* rituals have just been completed. The weathered poles in the right background surround old graves. Large bark baskets are placed over the tops of the poles at the conclusion of the funeral ritual.

grounds). If the workers are satisfied with the payment received, they move the poles to the grave mound, where they
are set in a circle around the mound. If a worker is not
satisfied, he can refuse to set up his pole in the new location,
and, until things are straightened out, the pole will remain
set in the dance ground, sometimes forever. Although the
workers may work as a "company," they are paid by the
group in whose dance area their pole is placed, and their
individual share of the payment is in proportion to the size
and number of poles they have produced, alone or with aid.

Generally the production of a *pukamani* pole is carried out
by one man from the first felling of the tree to the last stroke of
the paint "brush." However, when the group is working as a
"company," advice is freely asked for and given; and actual
help is given when it is needed to finish the work in time.

Pole cutting is usually men's work, but the workers' wives
may help with the painting. Theoretically, women can also
cut the poles, but they rarely do so because of the physical
strength needed in handling the huge logs. One day, my good
friend Dolly came to me and said that her husband had been
commissioned to cut a pole for Ruby's *pukamani,* but he was
unable to do so because he had to go to Darwin. The employers had asked her to cut the pole. Would I like to come
and help her? And so I also was commissioned as a worker,
although I did not fully realize this until the payoff, when I
received a pound of tobacco and a pipe as payment. This
payment came as a complete surprise, for I had already made
a "deal" with the employers, that in return for my work I
would like all those personal ornaments that are usually
thrown away after the ceremony. I received the ornaments,
but I was also forced to accept the payment, otherwise Dolly's
and my pole could not have been moved to the grave.

The working men suggested that Dolly and I should make a
very small pole, and that it should be very simple in carved
design. Since this was the first pole for either of us, we took
their suggestion. When it came to the painting, the men left

us alone, and the result was perhaps the most unique pole of all. Dolly and I would discuss each row of design, and when agreed we would proceed to paint in opposite directions around the pole; by the time we met on the other side each of us had added our own variations. While I was doing my best to paint in Tiwi style, the working men kept exclaiming in apparent admiration at my "true American Indian" design.

To the Tiwi the pole is an abstract creation, even though they give names to certain elements of design, such as "windows," the hollowed out portions of the pole; "ears" or "masts," the projections left on the top; "breasts," the little nobs found around the circumference of the pole; and so on.

Once the pole is carved and "cooked" over a smoking fire to dry the surface and blacken the background, it is rubbed with a fixative—sticky orchid juice, honey, or, best of all, turtle egg. Then the artist takes up his chewed twig brush and contemplates the pole again, fixing the design in his head before he begins. The painted designs, like the carving, contain elements that are common to all Tiwi artistic creations. With one naturalistic exception painted in 1954, all the designs are abstract, made up of lines, bars, circles, and dots in every conceivable combination. Individual styles are evident, and they may become localized to some extent.

However much the individual creator follows his developing style, his completed poles are not copies of each other. In order to get a representative series of poles to bring back to the University Museum, I commissioned individual workers to "copy" poles that they had recently completed for a *pukamani*. I selected the workers by choosing poles that contained the variety of elements I wished to show, but it was just not in the Tiwi artist to copy; they included the elements I wanted, but added variations, since the poles had to be unique. For more detail in regard to the art of the *pukamani* poles, see Mountford (1958:107-18).

The poles described by Spencer in 1914 were much less

elaborately carved than those being produced in 1954, but the steel ax was just being introduced in Spencer's time. With a stone ax the Tiwi could cut fairly large poles, but they confined the carving to simple forms. We saw a few stone-cut poles which were still standing in 1954. The main artistic effort before the steel ax was in the painted designs, whereas today the carving has become equally as important as the decoration.

Although the *yempi*'s main work is the poles, they must also prepare the dance grounds, clearing away all stones and roots that might injure the barefooted dancers. They also cover the grave mound with branches so that the employers cannot see it when they come to this area for the first time since the burial.

C. THE ECONOMIC ASPECTS

The economic aspects of the *pukamani* are quite interesting. In ordinary day-to-day economic cooperation, any gift or service is not immediately repaid, but there is an obligation to return the payment eventually. This obligation is in many cases an individual obligation. A parent must "help" a child until the child is old enough to return the "help"; siblings and sib-mates have obligations to "help" each other. One usually acquires such obligations only from those with whom he is in fairly constant contact. The economic obligations between a son-in-law and his mother-in-law are definitely restricted to two individuals.

Pukamani employer and employee obligations are also dictated by kinship, but the obligations acquired during a *pukamani* end immediately thereafter. The payment for services received is immediate, and once it is accepted all obligation ceases. Those workers who buried the body are paid directly afterward. Payment for the smoking (cleansing) of Jacky Navy's house was the concluding act of the ritual. Those workers who perform services before the final ritual may or may not be commissioned to carve the poles. There is

no continuing obligation on either side. *Pukamani* obligations are between groups of kin who do not have any cause to
be obligated to each other in the ordinary day-to-day events.
Furthermore, individual employees do not feel obligated to
hire their previous employers when circumstances dictate a
change in duties. But because the role of receiver or payer
is entirely dictated by kinship and not by wealth, prestige, or
skill, every man and woman will be in one role or the other
approximately an equal number of times during his normal
life. The result for the individual is a continual widening of
his economic relationships, and for the society a continual
redistribution of island wealth. There is no organized trade on
Melville Island. The *pukamani* ceremony, however, could be
regarded as ritualized trade.

Phase 4: The *Pukamani* Ceremony, the Final Rituals

In order to put some flesh on the dry bones of the preceding pages, I shall present the *pukamani* rites in narrative
form. The main elements of the final ritual have been included
in the preceding discussion, but I have made little attempt to
show the actual relationship between these elements. I have
chosen to describe the final rites for Ruby One for several
reasons. First, they represent the ritual for a woman, and I
wish to return to my emphasis on the Tiwi woman. Second,
the rites for her presented more unexpected variations than
did the others observed, and they are, therefore, more interesting. May it be understood, however, that in all major
respects the *pukamani* for Ruby One was no different from all
the adult *pukamani*s observed, with the exception of the
confusion in leadership. It makes no difference to the conduct
of the ceremony whether the deceased is male or female,
except for the sex of the principal *ambaru*. What does make a
difference is whether or not the deceased is a young child,
and the numerical strength of her close kin, for these two

considerations are taken into account in determining the number of poles and the number of participants.

I will also describe Zamat's "memorial" *pukamani* for Ruby One because I was able to obtain a song and dance record. In the main *pukamani* I was unable to cover these aspects adequately, being the sole recorder at these events.

Sunday, October 10, was chosen for the start of the final rites in the *pukamani* for Ruby One. The principal *ambaru,* Jimmy, called for an *ilanea* before the beginning of personal painting. Albert and Yamyam, both *unandawi,* and Albert's wife Agnes waited with Jimmy at the site of the previous *ilanea* for others to come. Finally two old men, Wanganui and Big Tom, and their wives appeared. These men were also *unandawi.* Big Tom, helped by one of his wives, danced his traditional dance of the *djirowa* bird, stamping his feet in the dust and flapping his flexed arms like wings. No one else showed up. The others had already moved down to a large field about an eighth of a mile from the grave and had begun to think about the painting. Also, Billy Pukamani had chosen this very day to commission his workers and send them out to cut the poles for his daughters' forthcoming ceremony. Jimmy and the others gave up their idea of a preliminary *ilanea* after the single dance by Big Tom and walked down the hill to join the others.

After a great deal of talk and casual visiting, the crowd began to paint about noon. The painting of the body before the final rites is an art form in itself. Every part of the body, except that covered today with a skirt or loin cloth *(naga),* is painted, usually in intricate multicolored designs. First black charcoal is rubbed on the body to make the dark skin even darker. Then the colored ochres are carefully painted over the black base, using the same abstract elements of design that are found on the poles, baskets, and spears. Even the hair and beard are often colored in designs; and, most importantly, the face is completely painted, excluding only the eyeballs. Husbands paint their wives and are in turn

painted by them, and the workers help where generally
needed. The children come last, but by this time they may
have splattered enough paint on themselves to require no
further work. Others are elaborately painted by one or both
of their parents. Cockatoo feathers fastened on a hairpin of
polished and pointed wallaby bone are placed in the hair.
Around the neck or wrists they tie feather balls and place
feather beards over the men's natural beards and the women's
bare chins. Belts of hair and colored wool are placed around
either the head or the waist. About five in the evening the
painting was completed. The disguise of most was perfect,
for the natural features of the faces were almost completely
obliterated by the lines of design. Again the designs are in-

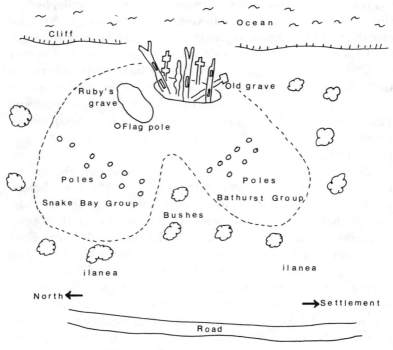

Fig. 15 *Pukamani* ceremonial ground

dividual, no two alike; however, certain people have developed a design that they repeat from *pukamani* to *pukamani*.

Jimmy, the *ambaru*, and Wanganui, Yamyam, and their wives, as well as Jumbo and his wife, Ruby Two, all *unandawi*, had brought with them and laid out for display the goods they had collected to pay the workers. I estimated the value of the cloth and other items contributed by these people alone at thirty-five dollars.

When everyone was ready, they started down the road toward the grave of Ruby One (see Fig. 15). Big Tom and Ali led the procession, carrying with them the items for payment, as well as two large *pukamani* baskets and a number of elaborately barbed spears. As they approached the spot where they were to leave the road on their way to the grave, the group split in two. The home group included people from the area of the Snake Bay Settlement and the country around the Garden Point half-caste mission. The other group included the Bathurst visitors and those of the Snake Bay Settlement who were originally from Bathurst Island.

The home group, led by Jimmy, held a small *ilanea* just off the road, beginning with a honey and mosquito call. A smoking fire was lit, and through and around the smoke the *unandawi* sang and danced:

> "A man speared a man a long time ago."
> "A big fat *niŋawi* waddles as he walks."
> "A big warship has a big engine."

As Yamyam, Big Tom, Miki Geranium, and Deaf Tommy danced to these songs, they held the large baskets and the spears in their hands and passed through the smoke of the leaf-fed fire.

Meanwhile the Bathurst group had moved on, rushing toward the brush-covered grave mound wailing as they ran, and then retired to the dance area with its row of eight poles that the workers had designated as being for them. The home group then ran through the bush and out into their dance clearing and, without stopping, ran through their line of ten poles toward the grave mound. Three men carried Jimmy aloft as they made the headlong assault. A "flag" pole had been placed just in front of the grave; and in the rush Yamyam deliberately headed for it, struck it with his head, split the pole in two, and knocked himself flat on his back, momentarily out of commission. Just short of the grave they all stopped and began to wail and beat themselves on their backs with sticks and clubs and to cut their heads with large knives. Jimmy and several old women continued on and threw themselves on the bushes covering the grave, wailing loudly. Finally, after the mourning had gone on for several minutes, the home group retired to its own dance ground.

Before anyone could begin a *yoi* (song and dance), Ruby Two, a paternal *unandawi* (FZ) from the Bathurst group, ran over to the home group and started a big row. "All the poles in the Bathurst area are small. We demand that the big one of Henry's be moved over to our area." The working boys, in whose hands rested the entire decision as to the placement of the poles, countered by saying, "It should be Ruby Two who should shift, for she properly belongs with the home group." This Ruby would not do, for reasons unknown. Bob One, a worker, moved one of the bigger poles and exchanged it for a smaller one. But still Ruby Two was unsatisfied, for the big pole was not the one carved by Henry. Suddenly Jimmy broke away from the group and rushed toward the grave. When he was opposite the broken "flag" pole, he threw himself high in the air, landed flat on his back, and lay motionless. The working men rushed to his side and carried him back to the dance ground, where he lay in their arms without a sign of life. Both the schoolteacher and I were convinced that Jimmy was "shamming" his unconsciousness, but the Tiwi were taken in, and mouthfuls of water were sprayed over his face and he slowly revived.

His close brother, Charlie, was beside himself with rage. When Jimmy revived, Charlie grabbed his hand and said, "Come, we go to the mission." Jimmy replied, "No. This is our business, and we must finish it. But if there is any more row, I shall kill myself properly. I will cut my throat."

The cause of all his trouble, Ruby Two, came up to him wailing loudly and beating her chest with her hands. In front of him she cut her head with a large knife until the blood ran down her back.

Both groups then retired to their respective dance areas and the *yoi* began. Big Jack (MB), his forehead painted solid black, half of his lower face yellow and the other half red, danced *puladi* to the accompanying chorus of women. Then Jumbo and a brother danced the woman's shuffling chorus step, and they were followed by the women *ambarui*, carrying dance clubs over their heads as they circled through the poles wailing separate *ambaru* songs. By now it was quite dark, and fires were lit along the sidelines, casting their flickering light upon the colorful dancers and poles.

Suddenly a huge burning branch came out of the darkness and landed in the middle of the dancers in the home group's dance ground. The dancing stopped. Don, a young man from the Bathurst dance group but a resident of Snake Bay, calmly said, "I threw the fire because there are not enough people to dance in our group." There were many harsh words and promises that in the light of the morning they would have a proper big fight. The atmosphere was like a tinderbox, and the women who had flung me out of harm's way whispered a warning not to ask any questions of anyone until it was all over.

After an hour's cooling-off period, one of the paternal *unandawi* from the home group went over to the Bathurst group and initiated a song and dance. He then invited them over to his dance grounds to continue dancing with the home group, which they did.

Ali began with a cowboy-and-Indian theme, the one which

I "should have recognized." Big Tom had a major part when he was chosen to "stick up the bank." It was a jovial theme to choose, and soon both groups entered into the spirit of the dance with laughter and good will. But that ended the evening's dancing, and all retired to their family campfires on the edge of the clearing to sleep.

During the long night, Jimmy kept vigil and chanted *ambaru* songs softly as he walked back and forth between the poles and the grave. At the conclusion of each song, a woman's wail would be heard from one or another of the camps. Bob One, a worker, spelled Jimmy from time to time and, using the *kulama* style for his songs, punctuated his words with the beating of two throwing sticks.

At first light the next morning, the area came to life. Cooking fires were lit and billys put on to boil for the morning tea provided by the superintendent. All seemed peaceful, then suddenly the Bathurst group started another row. This time it was because they felt they had not received their proper share of sugar. There was no mention of the previous evening's trouble.

It was eight o'clock before the *yoi* began again. Nym started in the home group with a song of rain falling, and he danced in the ring with his hands aloft and his fingers pointing toward the ground, marking falling rain. Then two female *unandawi* joined Nym in the ring, holding branches in their cradled arms as if they were holding babies (the mother's dance). Nym then sang another song, "A baby is born," and joined by two other fathers danced the shark dance. The loose dust of the dance ground rose in choking clouds, almost obscuring the dancers.

Then another *unandawi* sang a verse continuing Nym's theme, "When a baby is born a big group of people come to look at the pretty baby." To this all the "fathers" entered the ring, and their wives entered from the opposite side and danced with them.

Joe, a worker, and two *pudawi* men then danced the

"brother's" dance. They first circled the ring dragging one leg behind them, then held their "broken" leg in the air while they hopped about the ring. They ended up by sitting on the ground with their hands beneath them and thumping their injured legs hard on the ground in time to the clapping of the male chorus.

Old Wanganui then sang a song of Pukwi, the sun. He sang of how cold he was and asked the Old Woman to bring up a fire stick. He sat in the center of the ring shivering and pretending to try to light a fire. Finally, a brother danced in and handed him an actual fire stick, and the dance was over.

Billy Two and a brother of his then ran into the ring from opposite sides and tore around the circle five or six times at terrific speed. Then they faced each other and danced their traditional shark dance. They held the left arm rigidly upward and to the side, the face turned in profile and pointing toward the raised left arm; the right arm they held straight down and back and moved it in jerky stiff movements. They alternately raised their feet high with knees turned outward, then stamped into the dust, raising the foot again with a flick of the ankles, kicking the loose dust into the air. The tempo of the men's beating of their hands against their thighs increased, and the dust rose in clouds until the dancers suddenly brought their hands together down between their legs and cried "Poop" to finish the dance. The shark dance is perhaps the most difficult of all the traditional dances and certainly one of the most exhausting. Every muscle of the body is brought into play.

The next two dancers also danced the shark dance, followed by two others dancing as birds. Then Billy Two and Jimmy's brother danced toward the grave with fighting clubs in their hands. As they approached the grave they held one of the clubs high in the air and shook them at the grave as their feet stamped in the dust; the fighting *ambaru* dance. As a finish to their dance they hurled the clubs into the bushes that covered the grave with a cry of the fight, "Brr, brr."

Big Jack entered the ring and with both his arms held rigidly upward he marked *tuŋgrinuŋki,* the eagle, as he chased a brother "shark" around the ring.

In the Bathurst group four small girls had joined the women's chorus of dancers and were being carefully instructed in the shuffling step and the correct holding of the dance clubs. The youngest did such a good job that she was sent into the ring alone and received a tremendous ovation when she finished. She was only two years old.

The gifts to the workers were now laid out on top of each individual pole or on the ground close by. Jimmy, taking over the *unandawi*'s role, conducted the payoff in the home group, but he did so while singing and dancing *ambaru* as he called each worker up and handed the payment over. In this he was helped by two other male *ambarui* and one male *unandawi*. As the gifts were received, the workers danced their traditional dances to signify that they were satisfied. When it came my turn, I chose the easy way out and danced the woman's chorus dance, for it was impressed upon me that dance I must or commit a grave social error by not accepting my rightful payment and thus permitting my pole to be moved at this time.

As each pole was paid for, the worker carried it to the grave accompanied by the nonworkers, who wailed as it was being repositioned by the grave. The Bathurst group paid their workers separately, and in this group the *unandawi* did the paying.

When the workers had finished repositioning the poles and had removed the bushes hiding the grave, each group again rushed the grave. The Bathurst group went first, and when the first rush and wailing were over, the *ambarui* in that group started to dance around the grave. Then the home group rushed and wailed, and a few danced the shark, bird, and buffalo dances after the rush. The wailing continued and increased in intensity, the grievers leaning on the poles and burying their heads in their arms. Knives were passed from hand to hand, and the grief-stricken people were alternately restrained from cutting their heads and given knives to do so. Several mourners rushed at the poles, leapt high in the air, placed their feet against the pole, and fell backward, caught by other ever-watchful kinsmen or workers.

During the latter part of the final wailing, all the *pukamani* people who had been under taboos took containers of water and washed off what paint was left on their bodies. Then they removed their arm bands and other ornaments and placed them on the grave, and the men among them shaved their beards for the first time since Ruby's death.

The groups reformed. Each gave the long honey call and followed it with the high shrill mosquito call. Then they slowly melted away into the bush, calling out *"nimbaŋi"* (goodby) to the *mobuditi* as they left.

One week later Zamat and his large domestic group arrived and, accompanied by Jimmy, set off for Ruby's grave. Zamat was a brother of Ruby's father and was the *unandawi* who led the group. While still on the road, the group stopped and held a short *ilanea* beginning and ending with the honey and mosquito calls.

Moving on, they stopped just at the edge of the Bathurst group's dance ground, and Zamat sang a song of murder. Then with a piercing mosquito call he led his small group rushing to the grave, where they fell on the poles and wept. One woman flung herself through the poles and cast her body over the mound itself.

Retiring to the dance ground with his group, Zamat began his series of songs:

"The beach stones are white."

"Sometimes birds sit on them."

*"I don't live in Bathurst anymore, now I live in this place,
    This is my home."*

Zamat was singing the words of his dead daughter; he was not referring to his own residence. A son of Zamat sang, "I have lost one leg," and first striking his leg against a pole, he danced around the ring holding the injured leg high in the air. Then came a song referring to a sib in Ruby's father's phratry: "There is a lot of pandanus in this country." This was followed by, "The baby drinks from the breast," and two men danced with the shark-dance step, but held their breasts as though cupped in their hands. "The baby cries for milk." Again the two men danced the *puladi*. "She was born in Bathurst a long way away," and again the *puladi* dance. "At Bathurst she stayed two weeks in the hospital," and the two men danced a final *puladi*.

The whole group danced to the next series of songs, which dealt with a speed boat and its engine and propeller. This was followed by "Our sister slapped us on the face," and two women came into the ring holding their cheeks, the *iŋgala-bini* sibling dance. A singer then sang: "A lot of birds walk on the beach," and he danced marking a bird, after which he sang again: "A man runs in the sand."

Zamat shouted, "Turumuta," the name of his deceased brother. Then he sang: "Turumuta was a great fighter, / He killed all the enemy," and he entered the ring and danced an angry shark dance, calling "brr, brr, brr," the noise a shark makes as he swishes his tail through the water in anger. Zamat continued:

> Turumuta fought with a fighting spear.
> He kills lots of people.
> No one can catch him, he is too good.

The next two songs were of sharks, leading Jimmy into his traditional shark dance.

> *"A big shark kills a sting ray."*
> *"Where there is a big sand bank there is a big mob of sharks."*

The final song was about a boat. Then they gave the mosquito call and rushed the grave for the final time, wailing, beating, and cutting heads for some fifteen minutes.

Just before the group said the final *nimbaŋi* and departed, its duty to Ruby One completed, some of its members went over to wail at Sizors' grave. He had been buried only two days before, close to the grave of Ruby One, and his *pukamani* ceremony would begin in a few months' time.

CHAPTER TEN

Tiwi World View
and Values

I believe that one of the primary goals of anyone involved in ethnographic field research is to learn how to behave and think as a guest of the host culture and society. Participant observation demands this, so that the observer does not become the observed to an extent that precludes the gathering of relevant data. The guest-observer strives to predict with reasonable success her hosts' behavior and sequence of cultural events based on what she has learned of the rules and values of the host culture and her knowledge of the personalities and goals of her individual hosts, teachers, and informants.

I remember vividly a moment in 1954 when I felt I had reached a significant point in my education as a guest of the Tiwi. With my hosts I was sleeping at the grave during a final thirty-six-hour *pukamani* ritual. I awoke and heard the *ambaru* singing as he kept vigil and circled between the poles and the grave. Around me most were asleep except a few women who wailed softly as the singer concluded each verse. A feeling came over me that "All was right with the world," and I lay content in an aura of peace. Then I remembered who I was, and contentment was replaced with anxiety as I asked myself why I should feel such "rightness" while participating in a Tiwi funeral; had I lost my objectivity? I began to review in my mind what I had really learned about Tiwi concepts and values.

Throughout the many months I had as much as possible shared Tiwi life, I could remember no time when my values seemed in conflict with those of my hosts. What they did, in most instances, was quite foreign to me, but why they did it— their explanations and rationalizations—were for the most part completely familiar and understandable to me. In 1969, after having been a guest in another culture that has had appreciably less contact with Western culture than had the Tiwi, I realize that perhaps some of the reason I experienced little conflict of values as a guest of the Tiwi was because of their prior knowledge of, and perhaps compromise with, my own culture. But I do not believe this alone can account for the similarities in the two value systems. Perhaps had I been privileged to visit Melville Island a century before, greater contrasts might have been apparent.

When I began analysis of my field data, the question of Tiwi values that I posed to myself that night at the funeral ceremony continued to interest me. It was the reason for my choosing to present my data in the framework of the individual life cycle and ritual. For I believe that as the individual member of the host culture learns his cultural concepts and values, so may the guest observer and the reader.

I have mentioned previously that my choice of a female ego was originally made (1) because I had concentrated in the field on using female informants, (2) because I myself was a female observer, and (3) because I thought it might be an

interesting variation in presentation of data. I did not conceive that the data themselves might be significantly different
from a male-oriented study, especially as the amount of female
participation in the total culture was found to be remarkably
great. Having now completed the analysis and compared it
with those made by male observer-guests using primarily male
informants, I have two unanswered questions: (1) Do Tiwi
males and females acquire similar values? and (2) Do male
and female Tiwi hold similar concepts of the world in which
they live?

The basic concept of the three worlds of the Tiwi—the
world of the unborn, the world of the living, and the world of
the dead, and the belief that one can pass through each of these
worlds but once—appears to be held by all Tiwi, regardless
of sex. However, some aspects of these worlds appear differently to males and females. Unfortunately, as I did not
realize this while I was in the field, I can only discuss this in a
general way, giving a few specific examples that have emerged
from the analysis.

In all three worlds the emphasis is on interpersonal relationships rather than on relationships between human and
nonhuman forms in the environment. The physical world
and the nonhuman life, once having been created, is conceived as a fixed environment in which the Tiwi in all three
worlds live, hunt, love, fight, and die as members of a relevant
society. The bases upon which the three societies are formed
are conceived as being slightly different in their totality but
related to each other.

The society of the unborn, that of the *pitapitui* appears to
be made up of localized groups formed on the basis of common
matrilineal sib affiliation. Communication of living sib members with *pitapitui* of the same sib is strangely lacking.
Women, through whom a sib member passes from one to the
other of these two worlds, exhibit little interest in the life
and concept of the *pitapitui*. When pressed by the anthropologist, they said the *pitapitui* looked like small indis-

tinguishable birds, but I strongly doubt that women ever see or think about their unborn children to any significant degree. In contrast, the concept of this world of the spirit children is a most important element in the Tiwi male's life and philosophy. The *pitapitui* take a human form when men see them playing on the sandbanks, and when they appear to their fathers in dreams. They not only look human, they act human, hunting and fighting as well as playing. The *pitapitui* are symbolically emphasized in male ritual roles: the paternal *unandawi*'s (father's) kinship dance in the funeral ceremony, the spear dance *(tuara),* commemorates the common aspect of a spirit child when seen by its father in dreams. I believe, too, that the sequence of *kakaritjui imuŋka* songs in the *kulama* ceremony may also be symbolic of the male emphasis of this world of the unborn.

The single goal or value held by a *pitapitui,* it seems, is to be born into the world of the living. This they can only do by interacting with their fathers. Although fathers are usually said to find their children, in almost every case given to me children found their fathers (this in spite of the fathers often being far removed from their children's localities, particularly in the settlement pattern of residence today). There does appear to be a belief that individuals in the world of the unborn can communicate with those in the world of the dead. It was said that a man's dead father would help his son to find a spirit child if necessary. Here again, the emphasis is male oriented: females do not interact with the world of the unborn. They are no more than a necessary vehicle in the important male act of transferring individuals between two worlds.

An individual who has successfully transferred to the world of the living retains his matrilineal affiliation and gains a "dreaming" affiliation through the act of transference. He has been born through the actions of a male member of a different matrilineal sib. This sib, his father's matrilineal sib, becomes the newborn's "dreaming." Thus every individual in the world of the living has a dual matrilineal sib affiliation that distinguishes him as having become a member of the new society. I have said very little about the Tiwi's relationship to members of the sib that is his "dreaming," except to indicate its importance in marriage exchanges. However, it is interesting and significant that it is this affiliation of the deceased, the "dreaming," that is symbolically emphasized above all others in the rites of transference of an individual from the world of the living to that of the dead. A significant number of songs and dances performed in all *pukamani* that I observed were said to "mark" the "dreaming" of the deceased, which in all cases coincided with his father's matrilineal sib.

In the few glimpses into the world of the dead, the world of the *mobuditi,* that my living informants related to me, it was obvious that the social relationships of the *mobuditi* were those they had formed while members of the world of the living. A mother was seen with her children. A man and all his wives welcomed a brother stolen from the world of the living. Some of my informants maintained that *mobuditi* could also form new relationships, marrying other *mobuditi* and finding children, and certainly new members of their local groups, as they welcome anyone buried in their territory. Because of this latter concept, it appeared to me that the society of the dead was basically organized on a local basis, and that matrilineal affiliation was not an important concept of unity. Throughout the entire funeral ceremony, the matrilineal ties of the deceased were entirely overshadowed by those of local unity and patrilineality.

In the world of the dead, individuals maintain all achieved skills and prestige that they had acquired in the world of the living. Unlike the *pitapitui,* who have an expectation of transferring to another world, the *mobuditi* live in a world where there is no hope of change. Nothing they do will affect their social identity, and this concept is in distinct contrast to that held by individuals in the world of the living.

In the world of the living, as in the two bracketing worlds,

Tiwi are conceived as unique beings first, and only secondarily as members of social units. The first ritual act focused on them is the giving of a unique name, one of many they will acquire throughout life. With the possible exception of the yam ceremony, all Tiwi ritual is ego-oriented, a rite of passage. If the *kulama*-yam ceremony is traditionally or primarily an initiation ceremony, then we find no exception. There are no rituals belonging to one kind or type of social unit, or to a specific unit to the exclusion of any other. How the social units are conceived of by the Tiwi has been dealt with in detail in Chapter 4. Here I wish to emphasize only those that I believe are paramount in Tiwi view of the social life of the living.

The different character of the male-female world may be apparent in the differential emphasis given the two types of sibling sets—the "one-granny" sets emphasized by my female informants and the "one-grandfather" sets emphasized by the presumably male informants of other observers. It is possible that as a result of recent changes in Tiwi life, the importance of the paternal sibling set has given way to the present-day emphasis on the maternal sibling set, but I do not believe that this explanation should be assumed until the possibility of fundamental male-female differences in world view are explored more fully than I have been able to do here.

Throughout the funeral ceremony sibling ties are emphasized almost to the same extent as the affinal ties to the deceased. The sibling kinship dance is performed significantly more frequently than any other kinship dance, save for that of the surviving spouse.

Both male and female Tiwi view their culture's rules governing choice of mates as providing them with considerable freedom and variety throughout their life. Men achieve variety through acquisition of multiple wives, while females can anticipate a succession of husbands; and both sexes manage a limited amount of sexual variety outside of marriage. The preferred exchange of wives between matrilineal groups and within a land-holding group is not considered as a restriction on individual males or females. I believe this is primarily due to the preferred exchange contracts in which it is not the husband-wife relationship that is primary but rather that of the son-in-law and mother-in-law. Since a woman's husband normally has little to say about preferred exchange patterns set up by his mother-in-law's father for his children, any effect a marriage has on group exchange patterns is delayed for two generations. Thus a woman's successive husbands may come from a variety of matrilineal groups and land-holding units without affecting the preferred marriage exchange pattern of her daughters. So each Tiwi conceives his or her own marriages as being comparatively free of the preferred pattern, while the contracts leading to a son-in-law–mother-in-law relationship are thought of as being quite restrictive.

The social unit formed through marriage is, I believe, conceived of differently by males and females. To begin with the institution of marriage is considered a privilege and an achievement by males, while for females it is a fact of life, as much a part of one's living existence as growing older, learning to talk, or having a child. Sexual intercourse for a female is prerequisite to her reaching physical maturity; not so for the male, for whom it is an achievement and a mark of individuality. The domestic group that a female joins upon taking up residence with her husband is dominated by her husband and his previously acquired wives. Her own mother is quite likely to be a member of the residential group of which her domestic group is a part. The domestic group from a female view is, however, an unstable unit with periods of minor fluctuation as children are born and sons-in-law become members, alternating and contrasting with times of major change when she and some of her co-wives become members of another male's domestic group. For a male, the domestic group that he forms upon marriage is a far more stable unit, increasing only in size as he is successful in acquisition of wives, and changing in personnel only through birth, death, and addition—all minor and constant changes, but with the exception of those caused by death, ones that he views as achievements.

Personal achievement appears to be the dominant value for which Tiwi males and females strive during their existence in the world of the living. Economic independence and achievement is encouraged at an early age for both. Children are taught that only when they are very young or when they become old may they expect someone else to feed them. Cooperation in providing and sharing of food are dependent activities. Correct behavior in relation to the natural environment is also taught early, for the individual alone is responsible for his or her success in obtaining the necessities of life. It is significant, I believe, that Tiwi women not only provide the majority of the daily food supplies but also the daily protein. Males residing in a group of which they are not the dominant member (as when they are resident in their mother-in-law's group) are expected to contribute fairly frequently to the larder. Of course, by the time a male achieves the position of dominant member of a large domestic group, he is usually in the elderly category and may expect to be fed by the younger members of his group, his wives, and the unmarried children. But the Tiwi consider food provision to be a woman's work, with only the exotic foods of the deep sea and the air to be in the male domain, and women can gain considerable renown by excelling in food supply, particularly in those aspects requiring knowledge and skill in hunting small game.

Ritual participation is also encouraged of all living Tiwi at a very early age. It is considered to be an individual obligation that will assure success and health for the participant, and an individual may also express himself through such activity. Opportunities for males to express their individual qualities, and thereby gain prestige, appear to be more obvious and variable than those granted to females. Rituals provide the

male with opportunity to express intellectual ability in the
composition of poetry, dramatic ability in the dance and
choreography, and creative skill in painting and carving.
Outside of ritual a male may excel in leadership and skill in
fights and battles or in political manipulation in the marriage-
contract game. These variable avenues to male success require
somewhat different qualities of personality; some men
achieve in many or all of these fields, others in only one or two,
and some either do not desire or lack the ability to excel in
any of these activities. But the values of Tiwi culture do require that all males must be given the opportunity and be
encouraged to try for expression as individual and outstanding personalities in the world of the living.

Beyond the fact that all females are considered as unique
individuals during their life, opportunities for self-expression
are less variable and less obvious. Women are not expected to
be innovators or creators—they do not even create "life"!
They have the opportunity and are encouraged to participate
in the rituals to a great extent, but they are not expected to
innovate new forms of participation. Women do, however,
compose songs to their lovers and deceased husbands, but
these do not gain their composers much prestige, although
some of these songs have become famous and long remembered. Older women can gain a certain amount of prestige
politically by expressing a dominating and forceful personality. Within a domestic group such women can control the
lives of their sons-in-law, and to some extent those of their
husbands through extramarital affairs.

Although the opportunities for prestige and self-expression
do not appear to be as great for the female as for the male
Tiwi, the basic equality of the two sexes as unique individual
members of the society is stressed in the culture. The fact that
both males and females are initiated into the adult world in
the same ritual and at the same time is an unusual aspect of
Tiwi culture. The dominant role that is given the female in
the affinal *ambrinua* relationship is another expression of the

Tiwi value of the individual quality and equality of women in the world of the living.

The Tiwi "way of life" appears to be directed more toward survival of the members of the society than survival of the "way" as a separate concept. The universe of the Tiwi is a linear one, composed of three stages through which individuals pass only once. The major aspect of the "way" is the ritual progression of the individual through the stages. While status and personality of each individual is fixed in the first and third stage, in the middle stage he or she may experiment and innovate, and by so doing affect significantly his or her special identity not only in the world of the living but in the final world as well.

Since the beginning of the twentieth century, opportunities and inspiration for experimentation and innovation and for finding success in new mediums have been pyramided. There has been almost no resistance to the changing content of life among the Tiwi. There have also been some remarkable successes in collective and individual adaptation to new ways of life. The teaching of new skills leading to new occupations has been greeted as a welcome opportunity for gaining individual success and prestige in this world and the next. Traditional ways are disappearing with little apparent anxiety, because, I believe, it was never the means that were of value, but the opportunities available. Some of the elders expressed to me their anxiety that the younger Tiwi would not be able to achieve equal prestige with "whites" when engaged in similar activities, but they felt that this was only a matter of gaining equal education, training, and opportunity to achieve, and to them this was the value of life.

Glossary

Alaguni	Special digging stick used in *kulama* (yam) ceremony.
Alaura	Leader(s) of a funeral ceremony.
Alintini	Water rat.
Aliŋa	Young (pre-puberty) girl.
Ama	Kin term—father's father's sister.
Ambarui (pl.); ambaru (s.)	Term of address for surviving spouse (widow), in use during period of mourning.
Ambrinua	Term of reference of mother-in-law and son-in-law.
Amini	Kin term—father's father/mother's father.
Aminiyati	Group of descendants from a common father's father.
Andului (Andulina, Anduliŋa)	Matrilineal sib, "fresh water."
Anera	Placenta.
Aŋamani	Kin term—mother's mother's brother.
Aŋintumurila	Term for a boy's chief initiation director.

341

Apa	Type of song sung during *kulama* (yam) ceremony.
Apakulitupa	An initiate.
Aplimeti	Name of tree which is marked during girl's puberty ceremony.
Arakulani	Age grade term: a "big" man in the prime of life.
Aramarigeramor	A song style.
Aramipi	Group of affiliated matrilineal sibs; a phratry.
Arau	Oyster.
Arawunigiri	Wooden spear carved with double row of barbs, a "girl" spear.
Ariganuŋa	Yellow paint (ochre).
Arikortorrui	Matrineal sib, "woolly-butt tree flower."
Arikuwila	Matrilineal sib, "stones."
Awri-apa	"Father of a son."
Awri-awri	Woman who has given birth to a boy—"mother of a son."
Badamoriŋa	Barren woman.
Binyama	Wild apple.
Bulubuŋa	Ceremonial belt made of human hair.
Daniŋgini	Fruit bat, "flying fox" (cf. *muraŋimbila*).
Diamini	Dingo (wild dog).
Didjeridoo	Drone pipe (a mainland Aboriginal musical instrument).
Dioni	Wild yam variety.
Djirowa	A bird.
Ibobu	Bandicoot (marsupial rodent).
Ikwani	Fire (cf. *uriubila, kudalui*).
Ilanea (alt. *natualiŋa*)	Preliminary mortuary dance rituals.
Ilangini	Ceremonial neck ornament worn by initiates.
Ilimani	Kin term—mother's brother.
Iliŋa	Carpet snake.
Imaniŋa	Kin term—mother's mother.
Imbalinapa	"Father of a daughter."
Imbini	Ring of braided grass made for and used in *kulama* ceremony.

Imboka	Kin term—younger sister.
Imbunei	Affinal term—husband.
Imbuneiŋa	Affinal term—wife.
Imbuŋa	Kin term—older sister.
Imerani	Kin term—brother's son.
Imeraniŋa	Kin term—brother's daughter.
Imilu	Type of yellow paint (ochre); type of red paint.
Imiriwini	Reference term used for actual children of deceased father during period of mourning.
Imulini	Bark basket.
Imunka	Soul (of spirit or man).
Indiandiŋa	Artificial feather beards worn ceremonially.
Inimini	Kin term—brother's daughter's son.
Inimuŋa	Kin term—brother's daughter's daughter.
Intamiliŋa	Kin term—sister's daughter's daughter.
Intamiliti	Kin term—sister's daughter's son.
Intiŋaniŋa	Kin term—father's sister.
Intula.	Age grade term—an elderly woman.
Iŋala	Cycad variety.
Iŋgalaba	Kin term for a sibling who has the same father but whose matrilineal sib differs from that of ego.
Iŋgalabini	*Iŋgalaba* younger brother.
Iŋgalaboka	*Iŋgálaba* younger sister.
Iŋgalabuni	*Iŋgalaba* older brother.
Iŋgalabuŋa	*Iŋgalaba* older sister.
Iŋnari	Kin term—mother.
Iŋnerti	Name of yam oven, a part of *kulama* (yam) ceremony.
Iŋwati	Honey.
Irakati	Sea eagle.
Irampumuni	Ritual act—"tossing of initiates in the air."
Irikupe	Crocodile.
Iriŋani	Kin term—father.
Iriti	*Jabiru* (a bird).

Irula	Age grade term—an elderly man.
Iruwala	Dance club.
Irwili	Mangrove worm.
Itamuŋa	White-tailed rat.
Iwaidja	Mainland Aboriginal tribe.
Iwini	Kin term—younger brother.
Iwuni	Kin term—older brother.
Jidjini	Bird (yellow honey-eater) (cf. Tokombui).
Kakaritjui	Children.
Kiakia (alt. *Kirimika*)	Term of reference for actual grandparents and grandchildren of deceased person.
Kitjini	Age grade term—a small boy.
Kitjiŋa	Age grade term—a small girl.
Koraka	Bird's egg.
Korka	Cycad nut variety.
Krutui	Matrilineal sib, "red ochre."
Kudalui (Kudalini, Kudaliŋa)	Matrilineal sib, "fire."
Kuduka	Turtle egg.
Kulama	Variety of wild yam; name of yam ritual; name of initiation ritual; an initiated person.
Kulaminatiŋa	Female second-grade initiate.
Kulpaniati	Male second-grade initiate.
Kuperani	Blanket lizard.
Kurawi (Kurani, Kuraka)	Matrilineal sib, "bloodwood."
Kutaguni (alt. Murtaŋapila)	Matrilineal sib, "ironwood."
Malikanini (s.); *malikaniui* (pl.)	Age grade term—a youth (male).
Mamamiŋguni	Cf. *umanunguni*.
Mandipalawi (alt. Mandubowi)	Matrilineal sib, "house fly."
Manduiŋini	Dugong.
Maputi	Fish (generic term).
Marakamani	Male first-grade initiate.
Marakumariŋa	Female first-grade initiate.

Mariŋa	Kin term—sister's daughter.
Maritji	Spirit being.
Marowi	Ceremonial hair belts.
Mawana	Kin term—female cross-cousin.
Mawanini	Kin term—male cross-cousin.
Miatui (Miati, Miatiŋa)	Matrilineal sib, "pandanus."
Mikiateramuŋa	Female sixth-grade initiate.
Mikiaterima	Male sixth-grade initiate.
Mikidara	Male fifth-grade initiate.
Mikidariŋa	Female fifth-grade initiate.
Mikigula	Fully initiated male; last grade of initiation.
Mikiguliŋa	Fully initiated female; last grade of initiation.
Mikijeruma	Initiation term recorded by Spencer.
Mikinatiŋa	Female fourth-grade initiate.
Mikinatriŋa	Male fourth-grade initiate.
Mikinyertiŋa	Initiation term recorded by Spencer.
Milimika	Cleared ceremonial dance ground.
Miliŋani	Throwing sticks.
Milipuwila (Milipunila, Milipukala)	Matrilineal sib, "white cockatoo."
Mipari	Fan palm.
Mobuditi	Ghost (male).
Mobudriŋa	Ghost (female).
Morti	Kin term—sister's son.
Moruŋa	Wild yam variety.
Muani	Type of iguana.
Mudaŋanila (Mudaŋala)	Matrilineal sib, "crocodile."
Muludaga	Variety of shellfish; "cockle" or clam.
Muŋwuŋa	Stone ax.
Muraguŋa	Fighting club.
Muramiramili	Ritual area, the "lying-down" place, during the *kulama* (yam) ceremony.
Muraŋimbila (Muranila, Muraŋgala)	Matrilineal sib, "flying fox" or "bamboo."
Muriŋaleta	Age trade term; a girl who has recently reached puberty.

Muripiaŋganila	Name of a female mythological being.
Murtaŋapila	See Kutaguni.
Murubuni	Type of unbarbed spear; a "mangrove" spear.
Murukubara	Age grade term—young woman who is sexually mature but who has not become pregnant yet.
Naga	Piece of cloth used as clothing by both males and females in the post-mission period.
Natualiŋa	Cf. *ilanea*.
Nia Yirt'amini	Cf. *aminiyati*.
Nimbaŋi	"Good-by."
Niŋawi	Spirits who inhabit mangrove swamps.
Niŋyka	"Chosen follower"; a type of wife.
Pagini	Urine.
Pakabino	False beard worn ceremonially.
Palinari	Period of mythological time; "dream-time."
Pamagini	Ceremonial ornament worn on elbow.
Paramanui	Small mischievous spirits of the woods.
Parimariŋa	Age grade term—a woman who has reached menopause.
Paruliaŋapila	Matrilineal sib, "salt water mud."
Patiŋa	Water snake.
Permajigabruŋa	Ritual act; the "standing up of the basket" during the *kulama* (yam) ceremony.
Pernamberdi	Status term—"mother of a girl."
Pira	"Go on," "continue."
Piruŋa	Type of snail.
Pitapitui (*pitapitini, pitapituŋa*)	Children who have not yet been born; "spirit children."
Poperiŋanta	Woman who is pregnant.
Priplederi	Ceremonial ornament made of cockatoo feathers worn in the hair.
Pudawi (*pudaka, pudani*)	Term of reference for a sibling of the deceased during period of mourning.

Pukamani	Mortuary ceremony, objects connected with mortuary ceremonies, persons under mortuary taboos, mortuary taboos.
Pukwi	Mythological spirit being; the sun; type of matrilineal descent groups called here "sib."
Puladi	Woman's breasts; type of kinship dance performed by matrilineal *unandawi* during mortuary rituals; the "mother's dance."
Puliarliŋa	Mangrove snake.
Pumati	Ritual "fight" between spouses during mortuary rituals.
Puŋaluŋwila	Matrilineal sib, "red stones."
Purakagini	Owl.
Purakapali	Name of an important mythological being.
Purilawila (Puril-aunila, Purilaka)	Matrilineal sib, "mullet fish."
Puruti	Kind of fish; a mythological being.
Rakama	"Boss" of the mosquitoes; a spirit.
Tabuda	Camping place; a small geographical division.
Tajinati	Age grade term—a young boy.
Taŋaliti	Carved wooden spear with barbs on one side only; a "boy" spear.
Tapaliŋa	Stars.
Tapitabui (Tapitabini, Tapitabuŋa)	Matrilineal sib, "march fly."
Taraka	Wallaby.
Tarakalani	Turtle (generic name).
Taramaguti	Status term—the "first or oldest" wife; the "head" wife.
Tarni	Kind of sickness.
Tarula	"Riflemen"; the name by which the Tiwi referred to the Iwaidja tribesmen.
Timandiŋa	Affinal term—husband's mother.
Tjapara	The moon; a mythological being.

Tjilarui	Jabiru (a bird).
Tjilati	Brolga (a bird).
Tjiruwa	A bird.
Tokombini	Name of a mythological being.
Tokombui (Tokom-bini, Tokombuŋa)	Matrilineal sib, "yellow honey-eater," a bird.
Tokwiiŋa	Ceremonial ornament; a feather ball.
Tuara	Kinship dance performed by paternal *unandawi* during mortuary rituals; "father's dance."
Tudianini	White clay used as paint.
Tudiuŋini	White clay in bricks.
Tugula	Sweet tasting root.
Tulika	Small water basket made from *tulini* palm.
Tulini	Cabbage palm; a water carrying basket made from cabbage palm leaves.
Tumaripa	Center of the ceremonial dance ground for *kulama* (yam) ceremony—the "navel."
Tunuŋa	Blue-tongued lizard.
Tuŋarima	Large geographical division; a "country."
Tuŋgrinuŋki	Eagle.
Turinduri	Whistle duck.
Ubona	Variety of wild yam.
Uluŋga	Crab.
Umanunguni (alt. *mamamiŋguni*)	Song style, sung during mortuary rituals; a wailing song.
Unandawi (unandani, unandaka)	Term of reference for kinsmen of the deceased in the first and third ascending and descending generations, used during mourning period.
Ununduŋa	Vine used in hafting stone ax.
Ununga	Opossum.
Uriubila	Matrilineal sib, "fire."
Uriupianila	Name of a mythological woman.
Urukiliki	Geese.
Uruŋara	Variety of wild yam.
Ururatuka	Tree rat.

Uteriman	Variety of snail.
Utuŋa	Red ochre.
Wadjineti	Male third-grade initiate.
Wadjinetiŋa	Female third-grade initiate.
Wakitapa	Variety of mangrove worm.
Wakwakgini	Crow.
Wamuta	Ritual "fight" between workers and employers during preparations for mortuary rituals.
Wandiatapinda	Ritual act, "fire jumping," that occurs during mortuary rituals.
Waniyati	Cf. *wadjinati*.
Waŋgini	Armbands worn during *kulama* (initiation) ceremony.
Waŋini	Mongrel dog (domestic variety).
Weari	"Wake up."
Wilintuwila (Wilintunila, Wilitiŋala)	Matrilineal sib, "parrot fish."
Yauamini	Kin term reported by Spencer. Cf. *amini*.
Yeariŋa	Woven pandanus armbands worn during mourning period.
Yeloŋtiŋa	Red ochre paint.
Yempi (alt. *yemawampi*)	Term of reference for cross-cousins, cross-grandparents, and cross-grandchildren of deceased during mourning period; the "workers" during preparation for mortuary ceremony.
Yeriŋa	Red paint.
Yeripumani	Cf. *irampumuni*.
Yoi	Dance (n. and v.).
Yurantawi	Stingray (a fish).

Bibliography

1955 *Ancient Seed Plants: The Cycads.* Missouri Botanical Garden Bulletin, 43, no. 3.

Ashley-Montagu, M. F.

1940 "Ignorance of Physiological Paternity in Secular Knowledge and Orthodox Belief among the Australian Aborigines," *Oceania,* 11, no. 1:110-13.

Barrau, Jacques

1965 "Witness of the Past: Notes on Some Food Plants of Oceania," *Ethnology,* 4, no. 3: 282-94.

Basedow, Herbert

1913 "Notes on the Natives of Bathurst Island," *Journal of the Royal Anthropological Institute,* 43:291-324.

1925 *The Australian Aboriginal.* Adelaide. F. W. Preece and Sons.

Berndt, Catherine H.

1950a *Women's Changing Ceremonies in Northern Australia.* Paris. L'homme, Tome 1, Cahiers D'Ethnologie de Geographie et de Linguistique.

1950b "Expressions of Grief Among Aboriginal Women," *Oceania,* 20, no. 4:286-332.

Berndt, Ronald M.
  1955   " 'Murngin' Social Organization," *American Anthropologist*, 57:84-106.
  1957   "In Reply to Radcliffe-Brown on Australian Local Organization," *American Anthropologist*, 59:346-51.
  1958   "The Mountford Volume on Arnhem Land Art, Myth and Symbolism: A Critical Review," *Mankind*, 5, no. 6: 249-61.
  1960   Review: C. W. M. Hart and A. R. Pilling, *The Tiwi of North Australia*, in *Oceania*, 31, no. 2:153-55.
  1964   *Australian Aboriginal Art*. Sydney. Ure Smith.

Berndt, Ronald M. and Catherine H.
  1954   *Arnhem Land, Its History and Its People*. Melbourne. F. W. Cheshire.
  1964   *The World of the First Australians*. Chicago. University of Chicago Press.

Capell, A.
  1942   "Languages of Arnhem Land, North Australia," *Oceania*, 13:24-50.
  1956   *A New Approach to Australian Linguistics*. Oceania Linguistic Monographs, no. 1, ed. A. Capell and S. Wurm. Sydney. University of Sydney.

Davidson, D. S.
  1926   "The Basis of Social Organization in Australia," *American Anthropologist*, 28:529-48.
  1928   *The Chronological Aspects of Certain Australian Social Institutions*. Philadelphia.
  1937   "The Geographical Distribution Theory and Australian Social Culture," *American Anthropologist*, 39:171-74.

Elkin, A. P.
  1933   "Marriage and Descent in Arnhem Land," *Oceania*, 3:412-16.
  1937   "Beliefs and Practices Connected with Death in Northeastern and Western South Australia," *Oceania*, 7:289-91.
  1938   *The Australian Aborigines*. Sydney. Angus and Robertson.

1944   *Aboriginal Men of High Degree*. Sydney. Austra-
         lasian Publishing Company.
1950   "The Complexity of Social Organization in Arnhem
         Land," *Southwestern Journal of Anthropology*,
         6:1-20.
1951   "Research in Arnhem Land, A Preliminary Report,"
         Oceania, 22:290-98.
1953   "Murngin Kinship, Re-examined and Remarks on
         Some Generalizations," *American Anthropologist*,
         55:412-19.
1955   "Arnhem Land Music," *Oceania*, 26:127-52.

———, R. M. Berndt, and C. H. Berndt
1950   "Social Organization of Arnhem Land," *Oceania*,
         21:252-301.

Frey, H. K.
1949   "A Bathurst Island Mourning Rite," *Mankind*,
         4:79-80.
1950   "A Bathurst Island Initiation Rite," *Mankind*,
         4:167-68.

Goodale, Jane C.
1957   "Alonga Bush," *University Museum Bulletin*, Uni-
         versity of Pennsylvania, 21, no. 3:3-35.
1959a   "The Tiwi Women of Melville Island, Australia."
         Ph.D. dissertation, University of Pennsylvania,
         Philadelphia.
1959b   "The Tiwi Dance for the Dead," *Expedition*, Bulle-
         tin of the University Museum of the University of
         Pennsylvania, 2, no. 1:3-13.
1960a   "Sketches of Tiwi Children," *Expedition*, Bulletin
         of the University Museum of the University of
         Pennsylvania, 2, no. 4:4-13.
1960b   "Tiwi of North Australia," in R. W. Habenstein
         and W. M. Lamers, *Funeral Customs the World
         Over*. Milwaukee. Bulfin Printers.
1962   "Marriage Contracts among the Tiwi," *Ethnology*,
         1, no. 4:452-66.
1963   "Qualifications for Adulthood," *Natural History*,
         72, no. 4:11-16.

1970   "An Example of Ritual Change among the Tiwi of Melville Island," in A. R. Pilling and R. A. Waterman (eds.), *Diprotodon to Detribalization: Studies of Change among Australian Aborigines.* East Lansing. Michigan State University Press.

————, and Joan D. Koss

1967   "The Cultural Context of Creativity among Tiwi," in June Helm (ed.), *Essays on the Verbal and Visual Arts: Proceedings of the 1966 Annual Spring Meeting of the American Ethnological Society.* Seattle. University of Washington Press.

Harney, W. E.

1957   *Life Among the Aborigines.* London. Robert Hale, Ltd.

————, and A. P. Elkin

1943   "Melville and Bathurst Islands, A Short Description," *Oceania,* 13:228-34.

Hart, C. W. M.

1930a   "The Tiwi of Melville and Bathurst Islands," *Oceania,* 1:167-80.

1930b   "Personal Names among the Tiwi," *Oceania,* 1:280-90.

1954   "The Sons of Turimpi," *American Anthropologist,* 56:242-61.

————, and A. R. Pilling

1960   *The Tiwi of North Australia.* New York. Holt, Rinehart and Winston.

Hiatt, L. R.

1962   "Local Organization among the Australian Aborigines," *Oceania,* 32, no. 4:267-86.

1965   *Kinship and Conflict: A Study of an Aboriginal Community in Northern Arnhem Land.* Canberra. Australian National University Press.

1967   "Authority and Reciprocity in Australian Aboriginal Marriage Arrangements," *Mankind,* 6:468-75.

Jones, F. Lancaster

1963   *A Demographic Survey of the Aboriginal Population of the Northern Territory, with Special Refer-*

ence to Bathurst Island Mission. Occasional Papers in Aboriginal Studies, no. 1. Canberra. Australian Institute of Aboriginal Studies.

Jones, Trevor A.

1956   "Arnhem Land Music: Part II, A Musical Survey," *Oceania,* 26, no. 4:252-339.

Kaberry, P. M.

1935   "Death and Deferred Mourning Ceremonies in the Forest River Tribes, North-West Australia," *Oceania,* 6, no. 1: 33-47.

1939   *Aboriginal Woman, Sacred and Profane.* London. George Rutledge and Sons.

King, Philip Parker

1827   *The Survey of the Coasts of Australia.* London, John Murray. 2 vols.

Kooptzoff, Olga, and R. J. Walsh

1957   "The Blood Groups of a Further Series of Australian Aborigines," *Oceania,* 27, no. 3:210-13.

Lawrence, W. E., and G. P. Murdock

1949   "Murngin Social Organization," *American Anthropologist,* 51:58-65.

McCarthy, F. D.

1957   *Australia's Aborigines, Their Life and Culture.* Melbourne. Colorgravure Publications.

McConnel, Ursula H.

1937   "Mourning Ritual among the Tribes of Cape York Peninsula," *Oceania,* 7:346-71.

Meggitt, M. J.

1962   *Desert People.* Sydney. Angus and Robertson.

Mountford, Charles P.

1956   "Expedition to the Land of the Tiwi," *National Geographic Magazine,* 59, no. 3:417-40.

1958   *The Tiwi, Their Art, Myth and Ceremony.* London. Phoenix House.

————, and A. Harvey

1941   "Women of the Adnjamatana Tribe of the Northern Flinders Ranges, South Australia," *Oceania,* 12, no. 2:155-62.

Murdock, George P.
  1949   *Social Structure.* New York. Macmillan.
Needham, R.
  1962   "Genealogy and Category in Wikmunkan Society,"
            Ethnology, 1, no. 2:223-64.
Pilling, Arnold R.
  1957   "Law and Feud in an Aboriginal Society of North
            Australia." Ph.D. dissertation, University of Califor-
            nia, Berkeley.
  1962   "A Historical versus Non-Historical Approach to
            Social Change and Continuity among the Tiwi,"
            Oceania, 32, no. 4:321-26.
Radcliffe-Brown, A. R.
  1930a   "The Social Organization of Australian Tribes,
            Part II," *Oceania,* 1, no. 3:333-34.
  1930b   Review: *Davidson's Chronological Aspects of Aus-
            tralian Social Organization, Oceania,* 1:366-70.
  1951   "Murngin Social Organization," *American Anthro-
            pologist,* 53:37-55.
  1954   "Australian Local Organization," *American An-
            thropologist,* 56:105-6.
  1956   "On Australian Local Organization," *American
            Anthropologist,* 58:363-67.
Roheim, G.
  1933   "Women and Their Life in Central Australia,"
            Journal of the Royal Anthropological Institute,
            63:207-65.
Rose, F. G. G.
  1960   *Classification of Kin, Age Structure and Marriage
            Amongst the Groote Eylandt Aborigines.* Berlin.
            Akademie Verlag.
Shapiro, Warren
  1968   "The Exchange of Sister's Daughter's Daughters in
            Northeast Arnhem Land," *Southwestern Journal of
            Anthropology,* 24, no. 4:346-53.
  1969   "Miwuyt Marriage, Social Structural Aspects of the
            Bestowal of Females in Northeast Arnhem Land."
            Ph.D. dissertation, Australian National University,
            Canberra.

Sharp, Lauriston
 1952   "Steel Axes for Stone Age Australians," in E. H. Spicer (ed.), *Human Problems in Technical Change.* New York. Russell Sage Foundation.
Simpson, Colin
 1953   *Adam in Ochre.* New York. Praeger.
Spencer, Baldwin
 1914   *Native Tribes of the Northern Territory of Australia.* London. Macmillan.
Stanner, W. E. H.
 1956   "The Dreaming," in A. A. G. Hungerford (ed.), *Australian Signpost: An Anthology.* London. Angus and Robertson.
 1959   *On Aboriginal Religion.* Oceania Monographs, no. 11. Sydney. University of Sydney.
 1965   "Aboriginal Territorial Organization: Estate, Range, Domain, and Regime," *Oceania,* 36, no. 1:1-26.
Warner, W. L.
 1937   *A Black Civilization: A Social Study of an Australian Tribe.* New York. Harper.

Index

Abortion, 145
Acculturation: in burial practices, 251, 252-53; as subject of song, 294; effects of, 339
Adoption: of non-Tiwi, 120; between siblings, 124; case, 149-50
Affiliation: of sibs, 78-80, 81, 82-84, 94; of phratries, 81; of moieties, 81; in conflict, 88; of matrilineal units, 98; of patrilineal units, 98; in settlement residence, 98; of landholding groups, 102
Affinal kin: terminology for, 114; funeral attendance of, 271. *See also* Kinship
Age: as social category, 22; estimation of, 59; and marriage, 53, 59-66 *passim*, 125; and kinship terminology, 113; and food distribution, 172; and initiation, 206-7; among co-wives, 227; and death taboos, 262
Age grades: terms for, 31
Airplanes: as dance form, 297, 303
Ambaru: defined, 241; songs of, 241, 243-44, 298-99, 323, 331; dances of, 241, 245, 246, 298, 300-1, 323, 335; ritual roles of, 247, 253, 268, 278-79, 280, 318, 324; as special kinship term, 263, 269; mentioned, 298
Ambrinua relationship: taboos, 52; obligations of, 52-53, 117-18, 281; in secondary contracts, 55; in domestic unit, 73-76; and residence, 101, 117; importance of, 126; in song, 187, 194; symbolism of in ritual, 195; dominance of /oman in, 227, 336, 338

American Indians: in song, 294
Aminiyati. *See* Patrilineal sibling set
Antbed: used in *kulama* fire, 194-95
Apple: distribution of, 5
Armbands: in ritual, 307
Art: study of, xxii; mentioned, xxiv; at funeral rituals, 261, 289-317; visual forms of, 306. *See also* Painting
Assault: law concerning, 231
Ax: used in hunting, 38, 154-56, 158, 162, 169; hafting of, 156; inheritance of, 267; as worker's tool, 271; as ritual payment, 307; stone, 316-17

Bandicoot: distribution of, 5; hunting of, 152, 154, 161, 167-68
Baptism, 252
Barrenness: and woman's status, 149
Basedow, Herbert, 10
Baskets: bark, 156-57, 190, 308-9; fight over yam, 201; water, 239; as ritual payment, 307; on grave, 308
Bathurst Island Mission: mentioned, xvi, 53; established, 10; school, 12; residence at, 13-14, 98, 104; and country affiliation, 16-18, 85; sib distribution at, 19-21, 85, 86; and marriage, 54, 57, 90-94 *passim*, 126; and polygamy, 57, 59, 60; burials at, 255; residents as funeral visitors, 321
Berndt, Ronald and Catherine: on Tiwi, xix; on moieties, 80, 87; on phratries, 82-84, 85, 87; on sibs, 82-84, 88, 94; on descent groups, 108
Birds: collection of, xvi; varieties of,

358

Goodenough, W. H., xviii

Grave: importance of, 95, 97, 99; and ghosts, 100, 237, 238, 249; and land rights, 102; settlement area, 243; described, 244, 247; jumping over, 245, 248; groups of, 246; rushing of, 248; Christian, 253; tabooed, 255, 268, 276, 283; preparation of, 275; dance grounds at, 282; camp at, 299; not cared for, 309; positioning of poles, 310, 315

Grief: expressions of, 247, 248, 249, 321-22, 326-27, 328

Grimster, F. H., xvi, xvii

Growth: customs associated with, 28

Gsell, Father M. S. C., 10, 11

Hair: cut as death taboo, 263

Hallowell, A. I., xxi

Harney, W. H.: mentioned as guide, xvi, xvii, xviii, 12; and Elkin on sibs and phratries, 82-84

Hart, C. W. M.: on Tiwi, xix; on the name, 14n; on personal names, 29, 32; on marriage, 53, 67; on sibs, 82-84; on phratries, 82-84, 85; on patrilineal descent group, 95, 96; on local organization, 103. See also Hart and Pilling

Hart, C. W. M., and Pilling, A. R.: on names, 32n; on marriage, 53, 55, 56, 61n, 67, 118; on matrilineal clans, 76n; on land rights, 96; on patrilineal sibling set, 97

Health: and the kulama ceremony, 198, 216-17, 220; and toxic foods, 223

Home group: defined, 281; ilanea, 283

Honey: collected, 5, 152, 168; taboo for initiate, 209; as dance form, 303

Honey call, 245, 271, 285, 288, 321, 327; discussed, 284

Housing: described, 25; inheritance of, 267

Hunting: use of dogs, 6; of buffaloes, 10; use of fire, 13; recent decrease in, 13; by new mother, 28; instruction in, 35, 38, 44; of crocodiles, 36; equipment used for, 38, 159; taboos, 48, 50, 264; division

of labor in, 151-54; role of women in, 169; luck in, 174, 204, 230; influence of spirits in, 174-76; during rainy season, 176; burning of grass, 176-77; rights in, 177; by mobuditi, 239, 268; by employers, 275; mentioned, 233

Husband: role in conception, 137

Iguanas, 168

Ilanea: before funeral, 178, 321, 327; place held, 268; selection of workers, 270-71; leadership of, 277; description of, 279, 288, 319; discussed, 282-88; mentioned, 261

Illness: due to taboo violation, 48, 49, 266; related to cycad nut, 179; related to wild cashew, 179; from nonperformance in kulama, 221; ritual treatment of, 235-36; caused by mobuduti, 238-39, 240

Incest: and the sib, 77; and matrilineal descent, 86; and moieties, 91; defined, 111; taboos, 113, 131

Infancy: death during, 242-46

Initiates: director of, 207; hiding of, 215-19 passim, 222; role in kulama ceremony, 217; "killing" of, 218, 222

Initiation: of men, xxii; of women, xxii; grades of, 31, 205; and kulama ceremony, 183, 220, 335; discussed, 204-14; rituals, 283; tossing in air, 286-87; importance in singing, 290; capture for, 291; mentioned, 191. See also Kulama ceremony

Insects: varieties of, 5

Ironwood: distribution of, 4; used for poles, 309

Islands: naming of, 7

Iwaidja: as buffalo shooters, 10; contact with Tiwi, 11; expulsion of, 11; and sorcery introduction, 224; dances of, 279

Japanese, 11, 12 202n

Joy, George, xvi

Kapok: distribution of, 5

King, Philip Parker, 7

Kinship: and residential group, 26; and marriage, 67, 68, 97, 109, 110-11; importance of mother's mother, 71; importance of father's father,

95; and residence, 101; close kin defined, 109; long-way kin defined, 109; categories of, 113; and food distribution, 171-72; and initiation, 207; and attendance at *pukamani*, 257, 261, 264, 271, 318; and ritual behavior, 260, 272; and death taboos, 262, 263; marked in dance, 300, 301, 333; mentioned, 72

Kinship terminology: collection of, xxii-xxiii; mother, 28; special *pukamani*, 31, 269; use of, 31; father, 32; siblings, 34, 71, 72, 75, 76; for spouse, 44, 116; for mother's mother, 71; for father's father, 95-96; criteria, 109, 110; and modifications by age, 113; affinal, 114

Kinsman: maternal, 110; paternal, 111

Knife: used in mourning, 244; used in bloodletting, 249

Kulama ceremony: women's roles in, xxii; and food taboos, 172; ceremonial ring, 192; change in, 213; participation of initiates in, 213-19, 335; significance of, 219-25; symbolism of, 220; as preventive medicine, 236; mentioned, 255, 293, 294

Kulama initiation, xxiii, 11, 283; and food taboos, 172; rituals held during *ilanea*, 285-87. *See also* Initiation; *Kulama* ceremony

Kulama songs, 290, 292; style used by *ambaru*, 298-99, 324

Kulama yam: toxicity, 181, 182; importance of, 181-82; described, 191; cooking of, 197; personification of, 197; and health, 198, 199

Land: rights for use, 95, 96, 99; defense of, 96, 97, 103; and residence, 97, 100, 101, 102; rights to resources of, 176. *See also* Countries

Landholding groups: membership in, 13, 99, 100; types of, 70; and descent groups, 95, 98; and endogamy, 101; and marriage exchange, 101, 102, 105; and residence, 102; affiliations of, 102; geographic boundaries of, 102; distribution in settlements, 106; importance of, 108; and kinship, 109, 110; and

funerals, 271, 280; and grave of ancestor, 309. *See also* Land ownership

Land ownership: rights to, 13, 95, 99, 102, 179; and patrilineal groups, 97, 100; and burial, 97, 99, 102, 256, 309

Language, xviii, 31, 188

Law: concerning extramarital sex, 131, 132; the "growl," 132

Leadership: of sib, 91; of country, 176, 177-79; in funeral rituals, 249-50, 260, 276, 277, 295, 318, 327

Lizards, 5, 152

Local group: discussion of, xxi, xxiii; and endogamy, 86, 98; and patrilineage, 98; influence of settlements on, 99; and dreamings, 142; of *mobuditi*, 237, 334. *See also* Countries; Residential groups

Long-way kin, 111

MacCaffery, R. K., xvii

Magic: introduction of, 195, 224, 234; and *kulama* ritual, 223; as cause of death, 225, 233-34, 246

Malaria, 5

Malay, 6-7, 8, 11, 158, 266

Mangrove worms, 168

Marriage: absence of reported classes, xxi; with Iwaidja, 11; and country organization, 18, 98; before puberty, 43; rituals of, 47, 50-52, 96; secondary, 51, 55, 60, 61, 62, 64, 118, 336; polygyny, 57, 58, 59, 62; monogamy, 62; primary, 62, 64; and relative age, 59, 63, 66-68; and kinship, 67, 68, 97, 111, 113, 114; and matrilineal units, 77, 79; and residence, 101; and prestige, 114; and generation, 116; preferential, 118; choice in, 120, 125, 335-36; and initiation, 206; and sex, 227; relationship in song, 299; mentioned, 251

Marriage contracts: relation to women's puberty ceremony, xxiii, 48, 50, 54, 55; for *aliŋa*, 43; between *ambrinua*, 52, 53, 336; types of, 54-57; in settlements, 54; secondary, 55-57, 101, 119; father's rights in, 56; voiding of, 56, 122; elopement,